DEVIL INCARNATE

Wayne Thallon is an ex-civil servant and criminology graduate. He is also the author of *Cut-Throat: The Vicious World of Rod McLean – Mercenary, Gun-Runner and International Drug Baron.*

DEVIL INCARNATE

A DEPRAVED MERCENARY'S LIFELONG SWATHE OF DESTRUCTION

WAYNE THALLON

MAINSTREAM
PUBLISHING

EDINBURGH AND LONDON

First published in Great Britain in 2007 by
MAINSTREAM PUBLISHING COMPANY
(EDINBURGH) LTD
7 Albany Street
Edinburgh EH1 3UG

ISBN 9781845962067

This book is a work of non-fiction based on the life, experiences
and recollections of Athol Visser as perceived by him. It is not
intended to be an authoritative factual account of the incidents
described. In some cases names and details of people and places
have been changed to protect identities and privacy

Map on page 6 © Gilles d'Amecourt. Map on page 8
© Gilles d'Amecourt and Chris Tarpy. Picture section
images 3, 4, 6, 7, 8, 9, 12, 13 © Rhodiechat.com. None
of the soldiers pictured appear in the text of the book

A catalogue record for this book is available
from the British Library

Typeset in Sabon and Frutiger

Printed in Great Britain by
William Clowes Ltd, Beccles, Suffolk

To Djibouti

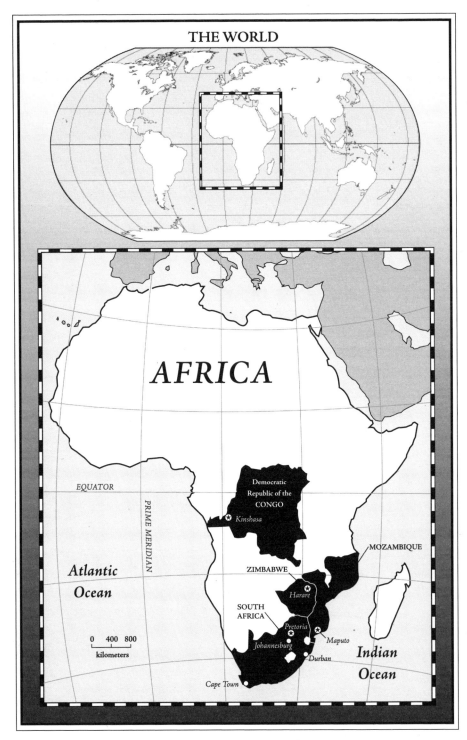

Africa today

I am the snake that devoureth the spirit of man with the lust of light. I am the sightless storm in the night that wrappeth · the world about with desolation. Chaos is my name, and thick darkness. Know thou that the darkness of the earth is ruddy, and the darkness of the air is grey, but the darkness of the soul is utter blackness.

Aleister Crowley, *The Vision and the Voice (Liber 418)*

The Congo, 1964

CONTENTS

FOREWORD

I pressed stop and put down my pen. I said thanks but he was already sleeping. So I just stared. Trying to understand him was like shaping sand in your hands: it was what it was until the moment you let go. And while many before had mistaken his lifeless gaze for a soulless self, I now saw that an empty shop window could sometimes lead to an Aladdin's cave. You just needed permission to enter. And I'd been granted it, because I was Rod McLean's nephew and had got to know him better during the writing of my previous book, *Cut-Throat*.

Meeting Athol Visser in former times had always been frightening: he was cold, he never laughed and when he caught your eye he looked right through you. He could so easily have been a Hitler, a Pol Pot or a Stalin – but as I sat in Satan's lair amongst the flies and stifling heat of an African summer, I found that simply to label him as evil was inadequate, while to justify his actions, even to a believer, was insulting at best and derisory at worst. Besides, he'd done neither himself until he knew what this word and these actions meant.

His living space, once a palace, was now in squalor, while his body, now ravaged by Aids, decomposed before me. The stench was noxious, so much so it could almost be seen, and every evening, as we finished, it combined with the setting sun from a blood-red sky to form an eerie hue. And now alone, as he'd lived, Visser would suffer and no doubt die. I had been with him for nine days solid.

My journey with him had taken me across the world and spanned the decades, yet I never left his bedside. In that time I felt it all: fear, grief, anxiety and, on a few occasions, a guilty admiration, if only for his spirit, rather than his actions. But I soon found that these feelings paled into insignificance as I found my role rapidly shifting from author to witness. He was a bad man for a long time and nobody had sought to stop him. He was a murderer, an arms dealer and a drug trafficker. He was a mercenary, a war criminal and an apartheid assassin. In fact Visser had committed the worst but, for a man who could never grasp remorse, each day remained an inescapable hell as he wrestled with the only thing that had ever bothered him: his own thoughts from his own mind. Appeasing these, it became obvious, was his driving force.

'You sometimes forget that you exist,' he said to me one morning. 'Each day's a battle to take the edge off yourself, which makes life very simple, like an addict, almost – consumed with very few goals other than getting by. It's easy to forget who you are. It's a spiral; it's a spiral and I can't ever stop. And when it's bad, and the tunnel closes in, I go to work. I create a storm and sit in the eye. That's where I find my peace.'

The price of his peace, though, was all too often other people's suffering.

Athol Visser, or Ivan, after Ivan the Terrible – a name that stuck from his mercenary days in what is now the Democratic Republic of the Congo (referred to by Visser as simply the

Congo throughout) – had moved from Edinburgh as an infant to a new life in Southern Rhodesia (now called Zimbabwe) after his father was killed in the Normandy landings. Like much of Africa, Rhodesia was a frontier country with a frontier lifestyle, where risk and reward shared bed space with bedlam.

Leaving the shadow of a Nazi-shattered Europe, his mother's remarriage to a white Rhodesian spelled a promise that most would have jumped at. And she did, as initially it was everything she'd hoped for and more. That was until the wind changed. An evening of unparalleled barbarity survivable by only a few triggered a hellish rebirth in Visser, who went on to pursue his very own lifestyle of fiendish deliverance.

Joining the British Army after a hasty exodus from Southern Rhodesia in his late teenage years, he did his hard yards in Kenya, before becoming a mercenary in the Congo. Both were ideal breeding grounds for his eventual gravitation towards apartheid, in the last days of white-ruled South Africa, and its very clandestine dirty war. This journey twisted and turned right into the heart of NATO's best-kept secret: Operation Gladio.

Visser's actions are indeed disturbing, and his thoughts even worse – so much so that his story might have been better left untold, were it not for this secret soldier's very public influence. In amongst the many unfolding tragedies he has plotted and planned, he has served both himself and his apartheid government in equally chilling measures, culminating in an attempt to bomb hundreds at an anti-apartheid rally in Glasgow and his self-professed role in the merciless slaying of Olof Palme, the much-loved Swedish prime minister, in Stockholm in 1986.

It is important to appreciate that the following story is Athol Visser's perception of events and individuals rather than an indisputable factual account. His perceptions perhaps testify to his disturbed state of mind following the traumatic events of his childhood. The account is verbatim. It is penned as spoken, straight from the mouth of a man with only one thing in mind: not sorrow, but revenge. For what and why will eventually become clear, but it is for that and that alone that Visser is finally breaking his silence. This is not, then, the typical rogue redemption story. It pulls no punches, nor makes any attempt to do so. It is the undiluted story of a man who goes from victim to antagonist, while fighting every inch of the way for money and country against what he sees as the devilish threats of communism and black-majority rule and for his very own sense of self – perhaps his biggest struggle of all.

Wayne Thallon

I

THE DEMON SATED

My sleep was light like a veil and could be torn if I wanted.
As if from another world, another life, the sounds of reality
came filtering into my dreams: the scraping of chairs, the
movement of furniture, the muffled tones of labour. To my
eight-year-old mind it was Christmas back in Scotland and
my parents were moving about the house, placing my well-
hidden presents under a freshly cut tree. But my dad was
dead. I had moved with my mother to a strange new land
with a stranger new father.

The moon was full in a cloudless sky and reflected on
the whitewashed walls around me, while the noise of the
crickets, as numerous as the stars, drifted in through my
half-open window, carrying with it the hypnotic calm of
an African night. Soon my veil would become a mask, and
I'd wear it forever.

I was the last one he took. It made sense, of course. I
posed no threat. I thought he'd pulled my arm from its
socket, the way he'd yanked me out of bed, as if he was
hauling a body out of the water. And then, locked in his
vice-like grip, with his smell a black-man's acrylic stench

that made me gag in between screams, he marched past the opened bedroom doors to the top of the landing and the burst-open security gate – a cage-like structure, fascinating to a young boy but, to a household in Africa, an essential but now inadequate security measure.

Saying nothing, but full of intent, he lifted me up and carefully negotiated the darkened staircase, which cut back on itself before breaking out into an auspicious hallway, stuffed so full of animal trophies, paintings and ghoulish trinkets that it kept a child awake at night, when it seemed like a true passage to hell. And that night hell began there, just beyond the heavyset door at the end, which was slightly ajar and emanating light. This strange light was coupled with an eerie silence. I struggled. I think I kept on screaming, but fear so acute is paralysing – I know that now. He gently shouldered open the door, and my Christmas was revealed: no tree, but instead my mother, stepfather, stepsister and her husband to be, bound, gagged and individually strapped into chairs that he'd sourced and manoeuvred from the breakfast room, three rooms along.

They screamed behind their gags – socks, I guess, stuffed in and taped over. But their eyes, all of them, made more noise than a thousand voices, while my stepsister, a girl I'd only known some weeks, seemed the worst affected, as she steadily turned blue, the result of a blocked nose and the onset of panic.

I thudded down onto the solid wooden floor, then felt his knee in the fold of my back, hard, until he'd taped my wrists, my ankles and then my mouth. I felt his hand press down on my neck as he leaned in, like he was going to say something, but an inch away from my face he stopped short and bizarrely seemed to be inhaling me. Through my tears and my anxiety I saw him smile, then, without a word, he hopped up and, with a knife that seemed to materialise from nowhere, he slashed my stepsister's gag, nicking her flesh and producing a bloody scream. Still without a word he held the knife to her throat, while gesturing for her to be silent. Through her sobs she complied. He disappeared.

Strange, I thought, he'd rearranged the furniture. Gone was a solid glass coffee table, usually home to two full-size ivory tusks, one ornately carved, the other shiny and polished. The sofa set, one three-seater and two twos, had been shoved against the walls and now, upon the boxing-ring-like Persian rug, my family sat bound, each one taking a corner facing in – towards an unoccupied seat. It wasn't for me.

I struggled with my restraints, but the more I fought, the more they tightened. I saw my stepfather fighting – thrashing back and forth like a convict trying to escape the chair. He was a tough-looking man, bulky and rugged – a hunter type and a pioneer. But now, with as much power as me, he sat useless. His son-in-law to be, a rich tobacco farmer in his early 20s and the heir of vast plantations north-west of Bulawayo, had been presented that night by my stepsister as a trophy. And he was – my stepfather couldn't have been happier, having spent the money already. Now he was someone else's trophy. From the ground I looked up at my mother. She looked at me. Her half-shut lids and long stare of disbelief are what keep me awake at night.

The minutes seemed like hours, but within five of them he reappeared and, brandishing a pistol, he sat on the chair in the middle stroking it against his black, scarred face and surveyed his work. Now, to all logical adults, our fate is determined by prior experience, the lessons we've learned from past outcomes, and what we do can directly affect it. But to a child it's simpler. The world exists just as far as you can reach, while ignorance is truly comforting. But within that moment, that frozen pocket of intention, we sat together. This was his world, and by force we were his guests. And so, as he fidgeted and gestured, our own fears would be realised.

There are few times in life when you actually aspire to be robbed. But stuff can be replaced, and the upset of it rationalised. So, as we sat there, all of us who could prayed to be robbed. But big 'A'luta', as I would later name him, our uninvited host, seemed in no hurry for riches.

Jumping up, and with a viciousness he'd not yet revealed, he grabbed hold of my mother's hair and pulled her by it, kicking her as she went, through the double doors and into the adjacent dining room. Seconds later he re-emerged and slapped my stepsister's face with such force that the blood from her cut splattered her boyfriend's face. Then he taped her mouth shut again and, with a smile and another gesture of silence, went back through to the dining room. We heard the muffled screams of my mother's rape.

After ten minutes he brought her back, a subdued and broken woman who couldn't look up, and whose self-imposed sense of shame was as obvious as her swollen face, where A'luta, the beast, had thrashed her. He stuck her back on her seat as she bled down her legs, before stretching himself like a satisfied lover and lighting a cigarette from a packet he'd found on the wall-length bookshelf behind me.

By now the tension was so thick that my stepfather openly sobbed from behind his gag and was no longer that great white hunter but a broken man reduced to suffering, as even his frenzied attempts at breaking free had stopped. And while my stepsister shook with shock, her tobacco-cultivating boyfriend alternated between rage and sheer panic – and now, more panic than rage. Yet while we boiled, A'luta chilled. He seemed to be in his element, playing us for his amusement like the conductor of an orchestra. I watched him. His face, hands, chest and stomach, which I could see through his open shirt, were badly scarred, like he'd been thrashed with a cowhide bullwhip.

With his last drag he stood up, pushed my stepsister back onto the floor, ripped off her blouse and stubbed his cigarette out on her breasts. As the embers danced and fell, and the pain engulfed her, he grabbed her hair and threw her onto the couch against the wall. Again with a frenzied viciousness that appeared to materialise at will, he pulled up her skirt, ripped off her pants and, while the rest of us cried, more in lament than fear, he sodomised her hard, measuring each raping thrust with a hating grunt. He was punishing her – all of us.

I suppose he was done – well, he stopped, breathed deeply, bent forward and zipped himself up. Then, by pushing her face hard into the sofa, he levered himself up and gazed angrily at my stepfather, before gathering himself, lighting another smoke and, with complete derision, grabbing my stepsister to throw her back onto her chair. We were now an hour into the fiendish episode – well, I was. I could only guess at how long the others had suffered before that, as he'd drugged and dragged them to their fateful positions.

I knew the house staff would come early. They lived in two cottages at the bottom of the oversized garden, which left the beast with a time limit, a cut-off, if you like – but then that was a double-edged sword. I was too young to ponder it, but for sure the rest did. At that moment we were desperately searching for signs – signs to A'luta's intentions. With all the hatred on his face, which he made no attempt to hide, murder seemed the logical progression. I glanced at the clock – not yet three.

He disappeared again, but this time the banging of pots and pans were the sounds that came back. He was in the kitchen, eating something; that was confirmed when he rejoined us clumsily stuffing the remnants of a sausage down his disgusting, slob-like mouth. He belched, then lit another smoke and made to say something but again stopped short. His vow of silence made little sense. If he did have a voice, he'd decided to keep quiet, remaining like an animal and acting like a beast. Within a moment he stood up and began browsing the books behind me. He grabbed an *Encyclopaedia Britannica* and flicked some pages, before arrogantly belching and throwing it just past my head. Then he opened the cupboards below, to reveal a well-stocked drinks cabinet. He stood there scratching his head. He seemed disinterested, but his eyes then caught on another pack of Madison Reds, as yet unopened, which he ripped apart like a Cambodian with a food parcel.

He disappeared again, but only to the toilet, before returning to take his chair and move it to in front of Tobacco Man, my stepsister's boyfriend. Placing its back towards him, he sat the wrong way round and, leaning against it, began staring. He kept this up for some minutes before, like two striking snakes, his hands leapt around his neck and squeezed. Tobacco Man began choking, his eyes began to bulge and, after the red gave way to purple, he began to lose consciousness. At that moment, and only then, the beast let go, leaving Tobacco Man sucking in air from his overworked nostrils. A'luta laughed for the first time and, like an overgrown child, laughed long and hard while looking around, as if to see others laughing along with him.

Looking back, I'm now disappointed. I wanted the beast to be so much more, to be something of a technician, a creator, of sorts, but instead he stumbled through on impulse and did what he did because he had to. Without warning he did it again, then again, and again. Each time, like a bemused monkey, he laughed, as each time Tobacco Man had the life squeezed out of him only to be slapped back to life, for all our amusement.

Bored with that game he stood up and, from nowhere,

began punching my stepfather, over and over again, in the face, the head. Then he pulled him up by a handful of flesh from the right cheek of his face, shoved him face down on the couch, took a knife to his pants and began raping him too. The more he struggled, the more A'luta dug the knife's handle into him, thrusting it into his spine, his neck, his head. Then worse still – as he became frenzied, he attempted to slash his neck, only missing by an inch and nicking his left shoulder. When he was done, the beast yanked my stepfather onto his feet and began pointing at his groin – I later figured my stepfather had an erection. Like a dumb kid with his pants pulled down at the pool, my stepfather stood there, accepting the ridicule. A'luta had consumed him, had broken him, and by my stepfather's very compliance the beast had won. Laughing, he threw him back down, turned around and kicked me so hard in the stomach that I couldn't breathe. As I lay winded, I watched him beat them all. From slaps to punches, he used them like a punchbag until they were out or dazed. Only then did he make his preparations.

From beside the front door where my stepfather had kept his shooting sticks and umbrellas, A'luta found a kitbag, which he emptied and refilled with whatever limited spoils he wanted. On seeing his feet in front of me for the last time, I did think I'd die. Childhood usually brings with it immortality – the idea that death only happens to others and that old people are born that way. But, when I was only eight, A'luta stood before me blade in hand, my willing executioner, unable to hear my pleas or screams, and my immortality was lost. Instead he turned around and took the knife to my stepfather's throat – but instead of cutting he shook his own head and carved a cross on his forehead like he was marking livestock, then did the same to my mother, stepsister and boyfriend. He spared me the cross – I don't know why. All done, he left – and left us bound and gagged for the staff to find. In all he could have left with thousands. Instead he would leave with hundreds, but a million's worth of memories. That was his prize. My prize was life.

A'luta in Portuguese, a language I'd later learn, means 'the struggle'.

II

FROM BAD TO WORSE

What Henrietta thought when she let herself in is beyond me. She spent the day crying. It took my stepfather an hour to get up from his seat and he only did so to insist that the police weren't called. Then he set about burning the furniture and cleaning his guns in an attempt to regain his manhood. My mother made herself busy with meaningless chores and it was halfway through the day when she succeeded in having a doctor come. My stepfather's determination that no one found out was stronger than his care for our well-being. Tobacco Man tried to console my inconsolable stepsister but, like the others, she'd just been shagged by a coon: what could he say? I wondered why he'd spared Tobacco, until I saw his seat. Whether from fear or near death he'd soiled himself and the furniture around him. It seemed that even A'luta wasn't up for a shitty arse.

So I sat where it happened. And, left alone to watch the clean-up, I saw them withdraw so far inside themselves that they acted like strangers in an elevator. I now see that the young mind has a way of distancing trauma – or at least holding it off to be cashed in later. So, within that pocket,

I dreamt and, while I did, my eyes surveyed the shelves, the broken glass, the blood and stains, the cigarette ends and the encyclopaedia, still open on the floor and untouched from where he'd left it. I stood up and cautiously made my way over to it. No one was watching so I picked it up and slowly manoeuvred into a corner, where some of the smoke from my stepfather's cleansing bonfire was drifting through a window.

It was open on L, and on a word I could only just make out: 'Lycanthropy'. I was about to read it when my attention was caught by a voice. It drifted in with the smoke. It was the doctor, a nice old woman who was the caricature of an old maid but sharp as you like and nobody's fool.

'Please, I understand – I really do,' she said calmingly. 'There's no other crime like it. When a shop's robbed and a man gives up the money rather than his life, we applaud. But when a woman is raped, we find it easier to judge the victim. You can't be blamed for this – it's not your fault.' Then silence. She must be talking to my mother, I figured. 'That's why people don't report it. For fear of being blamed. It's a double standard that leads to acceptance of shame – you know, that this was an intended robbery that somehow went wrong, and so your wife and daughter made it into something else. That's like saying a bank deserves to be robbed simply because it has money in it.' She was talking to my stepfather! Trying to convince him to go to the police – to take action. It might have been 1950s Rhodesia but it wasn't the Stone Age. Why would he need persuading?

His answer was clear. A moment later he entered with Solomon the gardener and, within a few angry grapples, the Persian rug, a priceless artefact from Persia, joined the charcoal. No sooner had I got back to my encyclopaedia than the kind doctor gave me a special sweet for 'good little boys' – it probably seemed easier to knock me out than deal with me.

The next morning I woke up to shouts and screams, which made my blood run cold. Bolting down the stairs and out into the garden, I found my stepfather 10 ft away from Solomon, who was holding a sack and beating it like his life depended on it. He dropped the sack and, to my horror, out crawled a virtually newborn puppy. My stepfather laughed. 'That's a Kaffir-hater for life. Now, where's the next one?' And with that he disappeared into the garage and emerged holding, by the scruff of the neck, two of the cutest big-eyed puppies you could imagine. Without a thought he gave them to Solomon, who then thrashed them to within an inch of their lives. I looked at him. 'Yes – the first face they see after that beating's a black one! It's what we used to do in the old days,' he explained, hiding behind a forced laugh. 'These are Rhodesian Ridgebacks and I've got three of them – the best security you can have. They're bred for hunting lions, you know. Big lungs for stamina but with fat necks, big paws and bloody sharp teeth for the rest!'

I made for the dogs, as, stunned and traumatised, they struggled to find their feet. 'Hey!' he shouted. 'Stop there, you little bastard. Don't you touch those fucking dogs! Being left alone makes them angrier!' I stopped and stared hard. I hated him, though in later life I'd know what he meant.

Lunch was difficult. Dinner was impossible. No one spoke and the silence was deafening. Like the anointed they sat, their scarred foreheads a mirrored reminder of the secret they kept. They ached. There was no escape and they knew it, while I, the lucky one, sat alone but not in isolation. Tobacco Man stayed for two days, when even two minutes was a struggle, but, after citing a tobacco reason, he 'tobaccoed' off, leaving my stepsister to fold. He'd never see us again, though I'd sure see him.

Three days later my mother stopped getting dressed in the morning. She stopped brushing her hair or applying her make-up and, instead, gave up. She drank tea; she smoked cigarettes; she took pills. Her eyes swelled up and her face puffed out. Then, three days after that, she moved into the spare bedroom: a sparse, clinical space with bare walls and a hard wooden floor. She even cried in her sleep. My stepfather said he called the doctor but, more than likely, she pitched up herself. In any case Mother began revealing the thoughts that she'd kept from us. 'I keep telling myself that it was just like bad sex,' I heard her say with my ear to the door, 'that it could have been worse.' She paused. 'That he could have kissed me.' Then another silence. My breathing seemed loud. 'I felt embarrassed by my pale, hairy legs, seeing myself through his eyes and wondering for an instant what I must look like to him. But then, in that moment, the utter shame at myself for having, even for a second, wanted to be attractive to him.' The doctor tried to edge in but stopped short. 'During it I tried to be someplace else. I could still feel it when he hurt me and I knew I was bleeding but I just waited for it to be over. But it wasn't. It will never be over – and that was his fee for my life. I'd often wondered what I'd do if I was raped. Would I fight or just lie back and take it? Would it really be that bad? I'd always told myself that I'd put up a fight. But it was impossible. What could I do? What? Tell me, what was I to do? I feel so terrible, like I betrayed my husband by not fighting more, like I've cheated, been with another man, a black man, a black man in white Africa. Oh, Christ!'

'Listen, dear,' tried the doctor, before being interrupted again.

'And my husband – he can't even look us in the eyes after, you know, what happened to him. You do know, don't you? I mean, did he tell you?'

'It's all right, dear. I thought as much.' She began to whisper, so I held my breath to hear. 'Rape – I mean, what happened – was the sexual expression of aggression, not the aggressive expression of sex. And sex it wasn't. It's not even about the sex or the need for it; it's about control. And that's why it was what it was: it was coercion, not consent.' She continued, but I couldn't. Footsteps on the stairs sent me scurrying to my room.

The world doesn't stop turning, but people do. And so, as time went by, my family stayed firmly in the power of A'luta, our god or devil – no difference. He'd made us and now he owned us, and, like trauma victims who develop nervous tics, they carried his physical mark and were prisoners, self-imposed, within his compound. My stepsister had gone from beauty to beast, my mother maintained her numbness and my stepfather developed his lifelong obsessions. He'd killed A'luta more times than possible in fantasy but, weak and defeated, not even the necessary once in reality. Our staff kept us going – as silent and functional as the furniture – while at school I was useless, loud and fundamentally indignant. For that I was beaten.

I can't put my finger on it exactly but there came a point when my stepfather stopped seeing me as his son and more like a lodger. It started with him removing any suggestion that I existed from the ground floor: my school picture, my coat that hung by the door, my sports shoes and wellies. Then his stuff – seemingly trivial, unthreatening objects – became landmines should I ask for or go near them. My room was no longer my room but a guest room in which I slept, my possessions being stored in a closet, my boyish trappings removed by the staff. Then his problem was me. We had never been close but now we were even further apart. He spoke to me only to give me rules. I couldn't lie along the sofa or laze about; I had to be doing something constructive and doing it quietly, something that suggested I wasn't taking liberties with his sweat or toil. He never beat me – well, not that much – but perhaps what he did was worse. He engaged my head, adult versus child, a mind against a brain, reason against reaction. Instead of walking on eggshells I lived in one of his making. He justified it all to my mother, of course, as discipline. My mother – too weak to care – rationalised it all till it made sense. At dinner I'd eat with a wooden plank rammed down my collar for posture and a book under each arm, 'to shoot down the chicken' – a reference to my splaying elbows while cutting. And so it went: me the voluntary participant, as all this madness must have made sense. I mean it had to, otherwise why would an adult, even one so despised, be doing this? It could only be because he was right. I was bad and so had to be corrected. Of all my stepfather's actions his one true legacy was the gift of guilt – a guilt for being – and I could never change that.

Soon, as the black-and-white certainties of childhood became the shadowy greyness of early adolescence, the roles that had always defined and separated us, or in all honesty my stepfather from A'luta, disappeared. My world became a simple one: like a prisoner I learned to avoid, innovate and, most importantly, disassociate. The real world became a performance to be watched during school hours; the rest was down to me. My mother and stepsister gathered cobwebs, using the overgrown hedgerow like organic burkhas, shielding them from the gaze of the outside world. My stepfather, who I now referred to as Hugh, ruled like an uncompromising mullah whose laws were enforced with an unnecessary sadism. His instructions for me went from stiff to downright cruel, as an action was encouraged one day yet banned the next. But even then I wanted to please him. The slightest bit of praise from the tyrant shattered my certainty of his evil, wrong-footing me and making me doubt myself. He was clever at that – it was manipulation at its finest. That was until the day the wind changed.

Above the African heat the storm clouds would gather and for three minutes lash the earth till the gutters became rapids. Then, as quickly as they had come, they were gone, the rain evaporating as rapidly as it had fallen. I loved it: the violence of the storm followed by a pocket of calm – and the smell, the smell of heat and moisture coupled with lush vegetation, like a hothouse in a botanic garden that stretched forever. I'd always stand outside in the rain, showering and steaming like the ground beneath me. My mother and Hugh never paid much attention, and the school soon treated it like a 'special need' for a 'special child'. And so, on this day, as I'd done so many times before, I walked the two miles home from school – wet but happy.

Our gates were large, cast iron and white. Later they'd be electric openers but, for the moment, a rattle of a heavy chain that snaked between them was enough to summon a gardener. Today, though, the response was unusually slow. Then, when Solomon arrived, the usually placid man refused to look me in the eyes. So I froze, afraid to enter, overcome by a boyish dread.

'Sir – please!' he beckoned, but I wouldn't budge. Two days beforehand I'd cut my finger, nicked off the tip while playing with a penknife. My mother, who'd been in bed for a week with some mystery illness, had taken an unusual interest in me, sitting there and staring, just me and her, looking at me in a way I'd long since forgotten. She'd smiled. She'd kissed me. We'd even laughed as she briefly stood up to reveal her nightdress was back to front. Then, as I'd felt a warmth inside for the first time in a long time, the footsteps on the stairs had made me scarper, knowing that I'd be punished for this affection. Now, standing at these fucking gates, I was convinced I was about to pay.

A voice from the house broke our stand-off. It was Hugh, but his tone seemed unthreatening, so, like a coaxed animal, I entered. It took exactly 48 steps to get from the gates to the front door. On step 30 Henrietta came out. On step 37 she walked past me with a tear in her eye. On step 49 my wretched life, for what it was worth, changed forever.

The air was heavy and I thought it smelled. Hugh stood at the foot of the stairs, his usual expressionless face as macabre as the stuffed trophies around him. Through the ajar door, so poignant on A'luta night, I saw my stepsister sobbing, head hung in her lap. I made for her but a shovel-like hand stopped me and instead pushed me up the stairs. Hugh guided me the whole way up, staying close behind me like a fly-on-the-wall film crew. And then I knew. I turned the corner and she was dead. My mother, my mum, my last hold on reality, was lying, unclaimed and unloved, in a hovel not of her making. So I stood there and, in my isolation, felt truly alone.

Had it been moments or hours, I wouldn't have known, but the bumps and sounds of laboured breathing signalled its arrival. Solomon and another gardener, Brown, like two amateur removal men, were negotiating a large, undignified box just bigger than a coffin through the tight turns of our upper floor. Then, like two capos from Auschwitz, who each day narrowly avoided the gas chamber themselves, they timidly manhandled my mother into place and waited for the signal. But it never came. Instead I lost it. At the base of the bed sat a tea chest, and on top a leather-bound writing pad sporting a collection of porcupine quills where the pens might be displayed. Screaming like a devil I leaned forward, took a handful and rammed them into Hugh's face. With the strength of a madman, I thrashed, time and time again, without looking, until they'd snapped off, half in my hand, half in his flesh. As the blood poured from his face, and with Brown wrapped around me like a constrictor, he punched me to a pulp, to where, like a ball of tangled rags, I lay slumped, dripping my blood into my mother's open casket.

'You bastard!' he belched through his perforated mouth, before I felt his boot, hard, into my side, which knocked me flat. 'You bite the hand that feeds you? You ungrateful cunt! After all I've done for you! You know what? You miss her, eh? You miss her? Well fucking be with her!' And with that he tipped me over and into the coffin, before slamming the lid shut, pressing me face down onto her cold and rigid body. Through the wood and my panic I heard Solomon plead, but then silence. I yelled and screamed, each time taking in mouthfuls of her hair, but nothing. Soon I heard the bedroom door slam and then the rusty lock turn. I was alone and he'd left me to die. Closed in so tight that I couldn't move my hand behind forward, or my hand above down, I could only listen to myself suffer. Like a cub caught in a trap I gargled pain as I slipped in and out of what reality I had. If I didn't know what claustrophobia was before then, I certainly did now. In shock my body trembled and my stomach retched, but in the darkness, pressed in, I lay. This was ultra terror, a place where I learned to envy the dead. And there, face to face with it, I did.

III

SCREAMING RABBITS

It will seem obvious that I lived. But every day I need to convince myself that I didn't die and land in hell. I don't remember being let out, who did it, or for how long I was in – only that the sky was dark again. And as for surviving without air? I can only thank Africa for that. Between the loosely fitting hinges and the termite holes I was able to breathe – not that Hugh was to know that when he shoved me in. At any rate, hell on earth is where I live now and if that's where I'm heading after, to another hell after earth, then I challenge it to be worse.

I never saw my mother's grave. I don't even know if she has one. I know that, around that time, Hugh ripped out the dozen banana trees we had at the bottom of the garden and replaced them with a tennis court. I never did see him play tennis. I never asked how she died, and when the doctor who'd made it her business to always drop by suddenly dropped out, I did the same. Without school, friends or allies, every waking moment hurt, while every sleeping one was excruciating. Nothing was worth anything and there was no way of escape. Hugh kept up his torments, energised every time he saw his scars in the mirror, but that was the norm and so I lived it. Even when I realised he was sharing a bed with my stepsister, I couldn't have cared less.

When we first arrived in Southern Rhodesia, we would laugh at Solomon. First of all he thought he was a prophet, a real all-singing, all-dancing mouthpiece of God, and secondly not only did he not know his own age, on us asking about his four kids, he'd indicate their heights with his hands. Now, some time after my mother's death, I found myself doing the same thing. I knew I was 6 ft, so I figured I must have been about 15.

My mind then was usually shades of the same grey but on one day I was having an especially bad time of it. My lower back hurt, I couldn't stop sweating and, as my heart raced without respite, my bowels gushed like a storm drain. After trip ten to the toilet I hobbled onto the patio, which commanded a view of the garden. The garden sprawled forever, sweeping downhill to staff cottages and the compound's housed mechanics amongst a treeline at the far end. Like an urban junkie I hobbled down there, my drooping shit-caked joggers threatening to fall down past my emaciated hips, my already filth-ridden socks getting almost no protection from the mud by my half-on, half-off slippers.

The momentum of the hill pulled me down, though I winced as I thought about the effort it would take to turn around and walk back up. Soon I was near the tennis court. I stood there and stared. I hadn't been here in all that time. Instead, I'd viewed this area from the top, as if looking at a postcard, and filled out the rest in my head. The court was barren except for a corner – the one farthest away. There an assortment of weeds sprouted like an organic oasis in the man-made gravel. I was about to dwell on why but my eyes were drawn to a run-down red-brick cottage, which on a closer look was a small barn, no bigger than three sheds stuck together. The grass there was wild, where the garden had reclaimed the space from an otherwise over-maintained property, the spoils of cheap Rhodesian labour. I wandered over, stopping short to retch, but with nothing in me I soon had my hand on the brickwork. On rounding the building I saw that the blind side had an open front and inside sat a sequence of cages starting at chest height, probably to avoid the dogs, which by this time were so dangerous that they had to be locked in the garage until night.

It took a moment but then, one after the other, sniffing, with their buck teeth showing, out came the rabbits: five, then ten, then twenty – a whole load of them. I'd never even known they were there. I figured they were Hugh's. I don't know where he'd got them from: Britain probably – I mean I'd never heard of an African rabbit – but anyway, there they were. Another bout of the shits sent me scurrying to the corner but, as ever, it was short-lived. Like a fish out of water I stood there gasping and staring. There they were, just sitting there, doing their thing – being fucking rabbits. In the middle, cut into the wire mesh, was a flap fastened with a makeshift peg. Unhooking it, I watched myself reach in and grab the biggest one, and by the scruff of the neck manoeuvre it out, to where I held it, in my weakness, some inches away from my face. But then it happened: it laughed at me! That's right: it laughed! Cunt!

Like a heavy calling in a debt I thrust it up against the cage, both hands around its throat, squeezing and snarling at a rabbit – yes, a fucking rabbit! And then, then it screamed. The once passive ball was now screaming, a wretched, high-pitched shriek. For the first time in its own mindless life it knew something beyond needs. Then it flopped. I felt the last beat of its heart and saw the lights go out in its eyes. And so we stood, me no more of an excuse for a human than this lump for a rabbit, me breathing heavily, panting almost, it draining piss, which ran down my arms and mixed with the blood from my scratched up wrists. But by Christ, I felt calm. For the first time I could remember, a true calm overcame me. This was different from any sort of calm I'd ever felt, like the difference between a cigarette and a joint, or a shot and some methadone. It was a calm with a buzz, less of an awakening and more of a homecoming – and I recognised it; it felt right. I had created the storm but within it, in the eye, I had sat in the vacuum.

I dropped the dead bunny and instantly, like a hound with a scent, wrenched the mesh, and this time two-handedly pulled another one out, dropped to one knee and squeezed again. I suppose I spent an hour doing it, perhaps more, but I only stopped when I'd arsed the lot. And then I was angry – not for what I'd done, but because I'd run out of rabbits. Their panicking scream was my new music, like a mantra of terror that I'd spend hours replaying in my head, over and over like a catchy pop melody.

That evening I thought of nothing else. Like a teenager who'd experienced lust for the first time I replayed the scene, each time working myself up, getting more and more aroused, having to beat myself off. I'm telling you it was fucked up, but there you have it. The next morning I woke up and, as early as I could, I ran – where the day before I'd hobbled – down to the bottom. But they had gone and I was gutted.

I figured Solomon had cleared them. He'd witnessed some terrible shit in his life, so a scattering of rabbits was unlikely to spook the old prophet. As for Hugh, I didn't even think about him. I was now a junkie and I needed a fix to take the edge off the morning. I looked around: I needed a kill. I saw a bird pecking the ground just a few feet away and, like a right arse, I launched myself at it – missing more by days than by feet. With a face full of dirt I patted myself down and, more on impulse than anything else, I made for the garage. But from a good ten yards away I could hear the growling. Then, after taking one look inside and thinking about being on the wrong side of these three horrible bastards, I passed. Besides, I'd always had an affinity with the dogs. They were just as fucked up as I was. The bad in them had been made worse, while any good that remained had long been starved out.

It's funny: until that point I'd spent a lifetime thinking about choices but at every turn I'd seen a brick wall – and then beyond that a whole load of nothing. As a kid I was choice-less. As I got older, the world around me got smaller when it should have grown, and the choices that should have come seemed the same as before – only this time covered in salt, or, at best, pepper. That day I felt hollow, making me miss something I'd never even had. If a sane man is able to go crazy, then surely a madman can go sane? Right then I felt sane – and sanity hurts.

There was nothing to kill that day. I could have harvested the plant beds for a bug or two but that wouldn't have been nearly enough. Instead I headed straight back to the house, where no one was about, or so I thought. I could feel myself getting tense again and within a moment my mind was in a bad place. I hated the fact that I seemed to have no choices, that there was so little I was able or allowed to do. The difference between a caged animal and a caged human – as I'd later fully explore – is that the human knows he's caged. That was me.

In the distance I could hear banging. It came from the road or a house on the other side of it. In any case it came from over the wall and sounded like works. It had started early but I'd somehow forgotten about it, even though it was loud – like a sewage worker in the shite house getting used to the smell, I imagine. Anyway, it was twelve or one and as I made my way up the stairs I felt a gush of wind brush past me, suggesting that the main door had opened. Now I knew that was odd, because all the staff except

Henrietta had to enter through the kitchen, and Hugh and my stepsister were away for the day. Then I heard a click as it shut, so I froze. It should have taken a few seconds for whoever it was to pass me, but nothing. At that I made the few extra steps to the bend, where the stairs doubled back up on themselves, and I took a knee. From my perch I imagined the very sight that a second later I saw: some spade bastard shuffling past, carrying the replacement carry bag that sat by the door, next to Hugh's shooting sticks and trinkets. Well fuck me, it was a thief! My heart almost stopped. He made his way into the living room. I heard the opening of drawers, then a fumbling of something metallic – silverware, perhaps – and then the cabinet, the one A'luta had shown such interest in.

They say be careful what you wish for. I'd spent a boyhood wishing to be alone. Now, at that moment, at that precise fucking moment, when being alone was the duff option, fate had once again shat in my face. I thought about my next move, I think, but I suppose in reality I just acted, and so, creeping like an escapee under the searchlight, I made my way to Hugh's room – a place I'd refused to enter since my mother's death. I knew he had guns. I used to know where they were, but when I got there the cupboard was bare, Hugh having hidden them a long time before, fearing a 9-mm wake-up from his far from prodigal son. Then I heard another clatter from below, reminding me of another time, and at that I searched in the corner to find it. It looked like a stick with a heavy chunk of metal on the end – which it was. But, for those who want to know, it was used by hammer throwers at the Highland Games for practising. So I grabbed it and crept down the stairs, with hands so sweaty that it looked like snails had slithered down the banister, checking my step every time my house guest fumbled his swag. I knew exactly where he was, so I got to the edge of the door and, crouching to half my height, saw him bent over in the far corner, stuffing a silver cigarette lighter into his bulging Santa Claus sack. Within a heartbeat I was across the floor, and crash! I fucking belted it right into his skull! I raised it again, shocked that he wasn't out cold, as instead, in a note for the scrapbook of weirdness, he got the spaghetti legs, wobbled one way, then the next, then turned round with a look of confusion and tried to shake my hand. So I stood there and watched him, before, for reasons unknown to me at the time, I grabbed an Indian-style basket chair from the corner and shoved him down.

Now I'd be lying if I said he was a big man, but he was an adult, and I was still a boy. He was a road worker, his badge-less company overalls a giveaway. But as I stood there, trying to figure it all out, I suddenly felt alive, alive in a way I'd not yet known, as for the first time I had choices. He had none. I could have called the police, but one of their favourite responses was 'Emergency? Sure. Can you come and get us?' I could have shouted for the staff, now on their one-meal-a-day break. And, of course, I could have coshed him again, even though he was now a man with two heads, the lump growing rapidly by the second. But instead I now saw that I owned him. He was now my possession, my rabbit. Why should I want to give him away? I thought quickly, then moved quicker. I bolted through to the ironing room next to the kitchen, which doubled as a storage place, and, like a friend eager to please, I took a roll of gaffer tape. I was so excited! Back in front of him I removed my own socks and stuffed them tight down his throat, before taping his mouth shut in a manner that clearly overdid it. I knew I had an hour, maybe one and a half, but no more, and I'd have to be quick. I grabbed hold of him and he willingly followed. I'll never forget that: walking hand in hand like an overgrown toddler.

Out on the decking I scanned the length of the garden, with my mind as well as my eyes. I decided that the best play area was probably round the side of the house: it was isolated and was where we used to have barbecues before A'luta came. So I took him round there and sat him down on a wooden seat, half-eaten, half-weathered. But then I stopped. I was so intent on getting somewhere safe that I hadn't figured out what to do. Now, all dressed up with nowhere to go, I felt lost. 'All right – eh, what do you want to do?' I said, standing over him, my heart beating so fast I felt sick. I played for time and, while giving myself an added moment to think about it, I taped his hands down, just like A'luta had done. 'Right!' I said, trying to exude confidence. 'Let's – God, I don't know,' and with that I leaned in and bit on his ear, hard. God, it hurt him! Like a scavenger dog I shook my head ferociously until I had it clean off. 'You like that?' I said to him, leaning back and spitting it out. 'Do you? Right, let's try something else, let's . . .' I looked down to see a blunt chisel and rusty hammer sitting next to the cobwebbed woodpile. I placed the chisel on his kneecap and, with as much strength as I could muster, whacked it down hard, making him wail out like Christ on the cross. God, that felt good. But then I figured the chisel unnecessary, so I changed position, almost sitting on his lap to keep his feet down, and crash! I smacked the hammer onto his good knee, shattering it with a crushing blow that even the birds could hear. The hammer was fun. I hit him frantically all up and down his legs – I found his shins gave him the most discomfort. I smashed them up so bad that even his open fractures fractured, splinters – no, more shards of bone – flying off and landing some feet away. 'Are you having fun?' I asked him. 'Are you? I'm so happy you came round. I mean, if two people can figure out how to have sex without lessons, then I think this should be no problem.' But he didn't reply. He'd lost consciousness and that annoyed me. I tried to wake him, as if he was a friend who'd had too much to drink. 'C'mon, c'mon,' I said, slapping him on the face. But he wasn't for moving. I took a step back and scratched my head. What the fuck was I going to do? He was alive – I mean, breathing means alive, right? Fuck I was pissed off. I looked at my watch. I had half an hour to go!

Now I'd have to get rid of him before the staff got back. I bolted round to the garage but halfway there detoured to the shed at the base of the swimming pool where the pump mechanics were situated. I'd always seen a load of tins sitting about, so I figured there'd be petrol there and I'd burn him. Instead I found paint, methylated spirits and some other fucking thing that was clearly not for the job. So I took the spirits and a bunch of rags that had been soaked in something stinking and marched back to the site.

He was still out. Gathering an assortment of wood and combustible objects, I fashioned the most amateur pyre imaginable. Then, like Guy Fawkes on a council estate bonfire, I pulled my friend, now gurgling again, into the middle and doused the lot in spirits. But I'd forgotten to get a lighter. Cunt! So in I went again, found matches and, with more excitement than I could bear, lit the whole box and from a safe distance chucked it and waited on the whoosh! Whoosh? Bastard! Not even a 'wish'. Instead of being burnt to a cinder, he was lightly roasted: medium fucking rare. I was trying to dispose of a body, not to cook a side. So I tried to get in close, but what flames there were beat me back. I ran to the pool and took the pole used for cleaning. On my return he was moaning. It seemed the heat had jolted him, but the socks stayed firm. I shoved him hard with the pole, tipping him backwards into the smouldering logs and then, using it like a pinch bar, I levered him again through the smoke and cinders until he rolled right out, no different to a burnt-up log. I ran around to grab him. His overalls were burnt clean off, as was his hair, but on taking a hold I dropped him. Fuck he was hot! A few feet away, next to the woodpile, sat a wheelbarrow. So I pulled it over, removed my own T-shirt and, using it like an oven glove, manoeuvred him onto the tipped barrow, before, with more effort than I'd ever exerted, I righted it.

By now the sweat was pouring off me. If I hadn't understood the value of fitness before, I did then. I looked at my watch and saw I had about ten minutes. What the fuck was I going to do? Hugh would kill me, or worse, and of the few people capable of achieving that fate he was certainly one. I took the handles and, wearing nothing but joggers, I legged it halfway down the garden, before realising that, if I was going to bury him, I'd need a shovel and a safe and seldom-visited place. Almost sick with fatigue I spent the next ten minutes in a real-life wheelbarrow race, touring the acreage for a secluded spot, which I was unable to find. Finally exhausted, and with my toasted friend now squirming in agony, making barrow balance impossible, I collapsed in a heap no further from where I'd started.

Then it came to me: the dogs. Now you've got to remember my age and my obvious inexperience but, to me at that time, faced with discovery and as tired as I was, the dogs seemed like a gift from heaven. So I steadily climbed the garden gradient and then, after ensuring our privacy, wheeled ourselves to the side door and poked my head in. They were there and fuck they were hungry. Now to me this heap of dehumanised shit smelled bad, and I mean real bad – burnt hair and skin is enough to turn anyone's stomach – but to a near-starved dog this was nothing short of a Christmas turkey done to perfection, and, being black, he was corn fed. Taking the handles and using the barrow to prise open the door, I edged in slowly before bursting it open. I tipped him and ran, slamming the door behind me and leaving the barrow inside. The noise was inspiring!

Just as Eskimos have a thousand words for snow, I was gathering a mental library of the sounds of pain. Shredding by dogs has a tune of its own and it's beautiful. It was their power. It was so overwhelming that I knelt, my ear hard against the door, just listening to their music. Like a storm that strikes from nowhere, the frenzy of growling, screaming, gnashing and ripping was soon followed by a calm that deafened. And that's when the real eating began.

I could have sat there all day but the sound of shouting in the garden snapped me back. Scrambling to my feet, I tore back to the fireside, knowing the staff wouldn't touch the garage. I tried desperately to make some order out of the bomb site I'd created. I pushed the logs and charred remnants into the centre and fanned the remaining flames. I took the hammer and chisel and chucked them into the hedge. Then, looking down at my legs, I saw the splattering of blood, sinew and bones from where I'd pulped his. There was nothing for it: off with the joggers! Now in nothing but my pants – a classic set of brown Ys – I tossed the joggers and mopped and swept up. Finally, in a slight panic, I pranced about the garden, returning everything from spirit drums to pool poles, before ending up standing – pale, soaked and by Christ stinking – only feet away from the garage door, where a bemused house staff, battle hardened from years of service, stood saying nothing but thinking everything. I squinted. They left.

And so there I was. Dressed in my pants, pressed hard against the door and with a heart rate that was unsustainable, I steadily entered the arena. But, by God, what had I done? I suppose I'd expected to see a forearm or two being gnawed down for bone marrow. But instead I saw a house of fucking horrors, as blood, bile and sinew coated the garage as thick as the stench was real. I was sick. For the first time my physiology had beaten my tolerance. In the corner the dogs, their snouts red with globules, sat in amongst a dismembered carcass more intact than not, while the head was still just about attached, hanging down from a raised torso by a collection of veins that loosened with every bite and tear from the canine demons. I loved it. If this was the animal world, then it was unforgiving. If this was a life without subjectivity, then a heart was redundant. But more so: if this was anything other than what I was witnessing, then I couldn't see it. And it was for that fact that I was home.

I knew I'd have to clean up. I knew it would be a cunt of a job. In fact I knew all the things you'd have to know to get away with it. And that knowledge of course was worrying in itself. But instead of all that what did I do? I only realised when I was doing it. On all fours I jostled for position and now, smeared in as much blood as them, I ate.

He could never have known it but, within those few hours, the unlucky thief had given me more lessons than a lifetime at school. And, of them all, two had stuck out. The first only became obvious as life went on, while the second, well, the second is what both made and saved me. Of all the wars I've fought in, most of them have been incognito and on the wrong side of the lines. Either for flags or money I've made my business in total anonymity. Without rank or insignia, tags or ID, I've murdered and maimed from pillar to post while my enemies, safe in the knowledge of their unaccountability, have enjoyed their privilege that no quarter is given. Surrender was never an option. We were the terrorists, while they were the regulars. They had artillery, tanks and air cover. We had nothing. Across the line you had no friends to help you and no place to go to in a hurry. Across the line the enemy rode in trucks, walked the bush trails and slept in bunkers. Across the line was a lonely place and most who crossed it never came back, as the would-be robber's bewildered mates on the road, the ones who'd pushed him over the fence and hoped for the spoils, discovered. There was a line and that day he had crossed it!

By modern standards the garage had more evidence than a stabbing in court. But between a soapy hose down and a hessian sack – once used for dog beating, now for bone crushing – I made light work of what was a right bloody mess. The next morning, though, I woke up to Hugh going mad, shouting and swearing at everything in sight. But I just didn't care. I wasn't cured but for the first time I had a means of taking the edge off, and I could now see that my days as a punchbag were numbered. So I dressed myself, this time properly, and in what few clothes I had I headed towards the noise.

'You bastards!' he shouted. 'You absolute fucking bastards! I'm going to kill you!'

I took two steps onto the veranda, which overlooked the garden, and found him standing, rhino-hide whip in hand, staring straight into the garage. 'Fuck!' I thought. 'I'm done.' But as soon as I thought it I relaxed, as at that moment I found a peace in the inevitability. So what if I was dead or thereabouts? I imagined he'd found a hand in the rafters or something. But on walking over to stick my head in the block, he lashed out and struck one of the dogs, Jimmy, with such a force that it near sliced him in half.

I ran over; the dogs were now my brothers! 'What the fuck?' I shouted, about to take his head off. But a hand shot from behind the door and, for the first time ever, held me down for protection. It was Solomon. 'Please, Sir?' he whispered, standing behind me. 'Please? Is OK, is OK.' So I stopped and, within that second, I looked around me. Instead of a dismembered thief there lay a scattering of shredded-up rabbits. 'What the fuck?' I said, now freeing myself from Solomon.

'These fucking dogs!' Hugh barked. 'They've been at my rabbit hutches during the night. Now look! What a fucking mess! They've had the lot.'

I walked over. They were the same rabbits, all right – my rabbits. I looked over at Solomon, who smiled with his eyes before bowing his head. Just then Hugh went to hit Jimmy again, who was now cowering behind the other two. But he didn't. Instead he threw the whip at them like a spoilt child throwing a toy and walked out, tears near flooding his face. I looked up to say something to Solomon but stopped short. I think I'd got it. He was never a prophet and he owned nothing in the world but it seemed that he'd drawn a line too, and he'd prevented Hugh from crossing it.

Earlier that morning something had happened. Either Hugh had found his rabbits gone and blamed me or found something in or around the garage that made him twig about the day before. Either way I was in the cross hairs before Solomon framed the dogs. I looked at him to smile but said 'thank you' instead; my face muscles had long since forgotten that movement. Solomon nodded, then, without any fanfare, began to clear up the garage, which by now resembled an abattoir more than a place built for cars.

If I'm honest, part of me was disappointed. I'd been let off by an act of kindness but it was too little too late. The time for heroics was then, not now. I'd wanted the confrontation; I'd wanted to feel his anger. I'd even wanted him to lose himself and attack. It would have been his last time. I wandered back to the house through the kitchen, where I grabbed a beer from the fridge and a bowl of mashed potatoes, which I'd slung together in a mound rising way beyond the rim – a major rule infraction. I kicked off my shoes and left them at the door, where they'd sat before my Berlin Wall was built, and within ten steps I more lay than sat along the replacement couch over the substitute rug. I ate like a pig and, like a careless love cheat, I hoped to be caught. But I wasn't. I thought he'd be on the prowl but, after an hour, and with my mound now a ripple, I dozed into a daydream, reliving the day before in every detail. It was then that it happened.

Within that space I got it. You can't put a price on being understood. To hear somebody say 'I get you!' is rare, but to truly understand someone else is rarer. A'luta had consumed us in so many ways but somehow we'd drowned in a lake that was frozen over. And it wasn't him who'd broken the ice. My mother could never get past the need for 'why'. It was a rhetorical question that repeated in her mind like a stuck record. She needed an answer. Instead she died. Hugh was a cowardly victim who kicked down to push himself up and, like a panicking swimmer, was steadily drowning the lifeguards – my stepsister being the first. And then there was me. I was in trouble and I knew it. My deep loathing for humanity was crippling and my affinity with the animal world a worry. But, of all people, A'luta had shown me the way – the way to get by. Soon I'd develop a life that thrived on complexity, yet, from the grand to the small, my goal was simple: to get through the day while carrying my mind as an anchor. I was no longer a boy, yet was struggling to be a man. I knew my life was changing but, like a caged animal set free, the hardest step to make was the first one through the doors. As I lay within my daydream, staring without seeing, I suddenly had a thought that made me focus my eyes. Then I saw them: the encyclopaedias, including the one I'd meant to read all those years before bedlam had interrupted. I sat up and negotiated my way around the glass coffee table – the only relic to survive the fires. I remembered it was open at L but not the word that had caught my eye. Still, I figured I'd recognise it when I saw it.

Their covers were clean and shiny, while their tops, partly covered by the shelves above, lay dusty and discoloured from years of sitting idle. I ran along the bound leather volumes with my hand until I hit the right section. Then, gently, ensuring not to rip the spine from the tightly packed book, I took it like a secret find and made for the table. It was old and dusty, and on turning the pages and sneezing I saw Hugh walk past the glass front to the garden. I stopped, but this time, instead of leaving it for another day, I took it up the stairs and into my mother's room.

As I turned each page, and on seeing the illustrations and paragraphs, I began to feel my blood bubble. You can't miss what you don't know but almost every entry was new to me. Finally, after several minutes of being distracted by other words, I found it, all on a page of its own; it was the word 'lycanthropy'!

I read it once, then twice. Then, after the fifth time, I placed the book down at my feet and, for the last time in my life, I cried. It read: 'In folklore lycanthropy is the ability or power of a human being to undergo transmogrification into a werewolf. The term comes from Ancient Greek: *lykos* (wolf) and *anthropos* (man). The word lycanthropy is often used generically for any transformation of a human into animal form.' It went on: 'There is also a mental illness called lycanthropy in which a patient believes he or she is, or has transformed into, an animal and behaves accordingly. This is sometimes referred to as clinical lycanthropy, to distinguish it from its use in legend.' Further down it continued: 'the essential features of the were-animal is that it is the alternative form of a living human being, while the transformation may be voluntary or involuntary, temporary or permanent. The were-animal may also be the man himself, whose activity leaves his appearance unchanged, or it may be the messenger of a human, a real animal for example, whose connection is shown when any injury causes a corresponding injury to the man.'

At that I wiped away my tears, slammed the book shut and walked through the dust cloud. My mother had died and Hugh had drowned – but there, all alone, at the age of 6 ft, I was convinced I'd got it and so had set myself free! But I hadn't. In all reality, real freedom would take 50 years and a true understanding a lifetime. '*A'luta continua*!'

IV

THE TRAIN TO NOWHERE

I could read. I could write. And I could just about count.
But beyond that I knew fuck all about anything. Taking
pain came naturally, inflicting it, a pleasure, but as I sat
on the platform awaiting my train, I soon found that
getting by was a challenge and a skill yet to be learned.
For all my coming and goings, rights and wrongs, there
had always been food in the fridge and my dinners had
always been cooked. Until now earning and work were
words, money was paper and the notion of value needed
a social understanding – the most alien of all.

That morning I was overwhelmed, standing at Salisbury
(now called Harare) station in Southern Rhodesia like an
institutionalised 'lifer', 20 years in the making. I missed
home. I missed the certainty. I even missed the Hugh! Under
the baking sun I stood sweating. My trousers were inches too
short, my jacket too tight and my boots, Oliver Twist style,
were old and buckled and done up with odd laces – one
coming from a dress shoe and falling well short. I looked
a state and people were staring. But what did it matter? I
was too dumb to feel their contempt.

My belongings were few. My intentions were fewer. In my bag, now dumped in the dust, were what clothes I had, my British birth certificate, a roll of pound notes, mysteriously placed in my drawer, and a kukri knife, sharpened so fine that it could cut paper under its own weight.

I'd never expected him to plead with me to stay but a good-luck handshake wouldn't have gone amiss. Instead I got nothing. Like a guard with a backhander he left the bolts off and my exit was made easy. I hadn't even known that I had a birth certificate – fuck, I didn't even know what one was for – but, sure enough, all that I needed for my escape kit just seemed to materialise. His only decency was not to have stuck them together with a label saying 'For you to fuck off'. But the message was clear anyway.

It took me the best part of an hour to get my shit together. I walked one way, then another, and then went to buy a ticket for Bulawayo, the only name that came to me when I was asked. I knew Bulawayo not just because it was the second-largest city and the capital of Matabeleland, the tribal area to the south, but because Tobacco Man, my stepsister's boyfriend from years before, had his farm there. I figured, in my innocence, that I'd look him up, maybe stay with him for a while, or some fucking thing like that. At any rate I needed some kind of plan. The ticket man, a stern black man with an Oxford accent, pointed out the platform with a gesture that shooed me away. Then, when I heard the price, I shooed him away. Well, I told him to get fucked. Standing looking at what I had and comparing it to what he wanted gave me my first impulse to cheat.

After choosing my moment, I climbed aboard the steam-pulled carriage. I'd never been on a train before – well, not that I could remember – and so found the basics a bit confusing, to my detriment. Considering I was trying to dodge the fare, sitting in first class was like sprinting with a fag in my hand. No sooner had I settled in than an angry hand lifted my collar and, with little explanation, booted me up the arse and onto the platform. I protested – well, I called him a cunt – and had it not been for my kitbag still being in the carriage, I'd probably have slashed him to fuck. But as fate would have it, a sympathetic passenger chucked it to me when the train was moving. And for that, my life was spared 'life' – a life sentence.

Now, though, I was known as a chancer and if I was getting anywhere for nothing, it wasn't going to be like that. Calming myself down – no easy task – I started to leave the station for something to eat but had my eye caught by a slow-moving wagon that began pulling in behind the Bulawayo express. This one was a goods train – made pretty clear by the stink of cow shit wafting through the wooden slits, followed by tongues as long as my arms, which prodded the air like tentacles. I was fascinated but only for as long as it took me to roll underneath and onto the other side, where, like a scene from *The Great Escape*, I frantically searched for an empty wagon or at least one I could get into. But it never came. Instead, two from the end and sandwiched in, was an open-bucket trailer, empty but for a few inches of rain water that had collected at the bottom from an earlier shower. Without much thought, and figuring that all rail lines were a straight road with no turn-offs, I clambered up the rusty access ladder and, as if scrambling a fence, heaved myself over the side and down into its basin and waited, then waited, then waited some more. Finally, after some of the livestock had been offed, swapped or loaded – I couldn't have known from my blinded bunker – we were off, my feet now ankle deep in water and my legs knackered, after having to lean backwards to support my back against the angled wall of the container. But for the first time that day I felt good – well, I didn't feel so shit and fucking helpless. And as soon as we'd cleared the station, I leaped up to look over the rim and, like the cow tongues earlier, began sampling the dry breeze, which mixed with the smoky steam before me. This was to be my first taste of adventure.

Realising I couldn't stand all the way to Bulawayo, and seeing that the sun wasn't setting in a hurry, I hung my slacks on a rusty rivet along with my kitbag and, near bare arsed, sat down in the murky, lukewarm water and thought about food.

Africans alike have a culinary weakness. It's called biltong: a dried, salted meat that the rest of the world knows as jerky. Unlike jerky, though, biltong can be made from any fucking thing, ranging from beef to ostrich. My favourite, and that of my old family home, was kudu biltong, cut from the flanks of an antelope. It tasted great and was the perfect food, especially for these conditions, given it was salted and couldn't go off. So naturally I'd brought some with me. After my satisfying fill I sat looking in the only direction I could – up – while listening to the engine chugging its way through miles and miles of cloudless Africa. Soon I was drifting. At first I slipped between daydreams and sleep, then, as my heart slowed down from its usual high-anxiety pace, I breathed easily and, for the first time in years, slept with both eyes closed. I could say that I was dreaming of the sea but, as I couldn't remember it, I'd be lying. I was dreaming of water, though – probably me splashing about in our pool or jumping in puddles when the rains came down. In any case when I woke up it was dark, which freaked me out, because I was cold and my skin was shrivelled. Standing up and shaking myself down on the ever-moving train, I saw the sky as clear as ever and full of stars. In my bag I had an old watch, which I'd stolen from Hugh. I tried to see its face, but between the glare of the moon and its weathered glass I couldn't make it out. This occupied me for a long time, as, like a cricket bowler, I incessantly spat and rubbed then spat and rubbed, before finally giving up with a best guess of eight-ish.

I had very little idea how long it should take to get to Bulawayo. I mean I'd seen it on a map and I'd heard it being talked about as a day away, but then what did that mean? A day as in the hours of daylight? Or a day as in 24 hours? And in any case a day by what? Car? Train? Fucking donkey? Fuck! I felt my anxiety rise as my situation began to dawn on me. It wasn't like I could ask the guard or my fellow passengers – and even though we've all seen the cowboy films, this train was half a mile long and walking along the roof to the driver was stupid. So, standing in my bucket, I tried to figure it out but couldn't. Soon the moon became obscured, as did the stars, which plunged me into a darkness I'd not yet seen. But it was only when the air really cooled that I knew what was coming – a storm, and it fucking belted me.

I later came to know an expression that I found quite suitable: 'It never rains but it pours'. Before then I'd become well accustomed to the idea that, as life was so shite, it might as well have been super shite. It was difficult back then not to feel a victim, like fate had singled me out for an extra helping. And that night I did that, but this time with a difference. At home I'd always been able to blame other people: my mum for being too weak, my stepsister for being too vain and A'luta or Hugh, no difference, for any amount of things. But as I sat drowning in my container, now waist deep in storm water, and with no end to the journey in sight, I cursed the absurdity of it all but could find no one to blame but myself. I tried scrambling up the side but couldn't get a footing. My hands were tired and cut, while the wind and rain were determined to keep me down. In the distance forks of lightning smashed into the ground, while the roar of thunder more exploded than rumbled around me. The train went from fast to slow to fast again, each time jerking me forward then shoving me back and under the water as it fought its way through the elements and the rolling gradients. I tried walking the bottom rim where the sides met the floor in an attempt to find a drainage hole, which I did. But after several blind dives I found that the blockage was more rock than muck and so I concentrated more on keeping me up rather than the water down.

Finally, after what felt like hours, the rain let up and the storm clouds cleared. As I stood there in relief, gasping for breath and wiping my face down, I began looking up – again in the only direction I could – and it was beautiful. The stars were stunning again, more stunning than ever before, as was the moon, which fathered over them in a way I'd never yet noticed. In my night reverie it spoke to me and my lesson was learned.

Until then life was a conveyor belt with no way off. Whether I opted for one thing or another, it had no bearing on my trajectory as, like this train, the tracks went in one direction and the only way off was death. The knowledge of this had always been compounded by my passive belief that things should be better. But in truth they shouldn't. That's when I got it. Things are what they are, not how they ought to be. I found that true solitude and helplessness were my catalysts and not my hindrance. The sky, the land, the air around me were the constants and I was a guest – a minion, a fucking nothing. No one was watching out for me. Why should they? It wasn't what hit me that caused my suffering; it was the shattering of my expectations. At that moment I hated all humanity. I hated the very form I was guesting in. I hated every piece of meaning that a human had ever given the world. I hated every preconception of how living should be. To me, and at that moment, I saw that the natural state of life was suffering and what causes us to move, to fight, to fuck was not comfort but the need to relieve ourselves of this. But we can't. Suffering doesn't follow us but rather we walk, talk and breathe amongst it. That is our condition, our cross to bear. And if I was to know myself, I needed to appreciate my capacity to tolerate it – that was my edge and something I'd long earned through attrition.

By the time the sun broke the blanket of night I'd near emptied my bathtub. In some ways I'd zoned out on the task and, deep within my own introspection, had almost forgotten myself. My clothes and kitbag were soaked through and if my watch wasn't fucked before then it was now. After a breakfast of biltong and a re-energising from my new sense of self I got it together and waited for Bulawayo – but Bulawayo never came. Instead the rising sun became the midday sun and, when that began to sink and create a golden hue, I realised that something was seriously wrong.

Soon the world turned red, as the rusty bush landscape became a lush green, while in the distance, instead of more dust, were trees – so thick that their canopy met the horizon. Only when we reached it did the train finally slow then stop in a town that I saw as just a few streets. Deciding to jump, I slung my bag over my shoulder and began pulling myself up, but stopped short. The animals were being unloaded but, with a half-mile of train to choose from, some farmer bastard had parked his arse just feet away from my wagon. It wouldn't necessarily have bothered me but the sight of his shotgun proved unappealing. Looking back, I should have just jumped. A white kid looking like me jumping from a wagon in the middle of nowhere was unlikely to be scolded. But then the problem was me, and my intense hatred of everything that moved. There were no sheep in my world, only wolves.

I fumbled about and my heart began racing. I might have been naive to the world but I wasn't stupid. If the train pulled off again with me on it, fuck knows where I'd end up. Fucking Europe? By now the dust being kicked up by the animals was swirling around us like a sandstorm and soon voices shouting and yelling commands to the beasts and themselves filled the air like ghosts in the wind. My throat was dry and my body was aching. I knew I couldn't last another day and, for as much as I loved my salty biltong, it sure rattled my water. In any case the decision was made for me. Under the rumble of dust and hooves a truck had backed up against my tub and moments later I could hear the rusty mechanics of its struggling gears, which made me grab my stuff and jump for it.

Picking myself up, I scrambled through the dust until, like a right fool, I walked straight into a belly: farmer fucking Joe's belly, shotgun slung over his shoulder, other hand fumbling his no-doubt sweaty arse. I bounced off him and waited on his scorn but, to my surprise, he smiled and, with a refreshing indifference, walked straight past me. Feeling like I was in the clear, I bolted out of the station, which in part resembled an industrial plant, and soon found myself standing in Wankie (now called Hwange), a coal town that I'd later find was just south of the Zambezi and Victoria Falls. One way or another I'd done some kind of dog-leg on the railway as I'd gone south from Salisbury to Bulawayo – had been sleeping or too stupid to get off at my destination – and so ended up heading north-west. What an arse!

Just walking about made me feel free, almost as if I'd achieved something. But it didn't take me long to see that I'd just swapped a shit city for a shittier small town. So, after approaching a few people and being told to get fucked, I decided to move on – well, after I'd sorted myself out.

It didn't take me long to see that the blacks here were different. Instead of the passive, all-smiling, all-smoking Shona tribe, this lot, the Matabele, the cousins of the Zulu, were a bunch of vicious bastards who weren't afraid to show it. With tribal markings slashed in their faces, they walked tall and, even though they knew their place standing next to the white man, like in a prison there lay an uneasy peace where the guards knew that the cons could take it at any time of their choosing.

By now, though, it was pitch dark and the few shops there were long since closed. I walked down one street, then the next, not really knowing what I was doing or where I was going. I could see through the white picket fences and into the glow of the living rooms. I could see and sense their comfort, their lives of ease, built on the back of other men's slavery – and I was jealous.

Up in the distance I saw a couple of people leaving their home, then, after some fumbling about, get into a four-door Morris Minor saloon and head off. I walked past where they'd come from and, unlike most of the other houses, the area was in complete darkness. So, being me, I jumped the fence and within a moment was pressed tight against the front door, which opened. The house inside was big and the floorboards creaked, and even though I treated the floor like a minefield, every movement I made seemed to echo in the rafters. But the darkness told me the house was empty so, after a few minutes and using it like a cloak, I began to relax and set about the kitchen. Like ours the larder was well stocked and, as I was rifling the house for survival, food was of more use than bone china. So, after a good feed, I finished stuffing my bag and turned to leave – when bang! Some fucker whacked me right across the shoulder, just missing my head and sending me tumbling. I turned round and in the darkness hooked the shadow that was now trying to choke me – but he kept on coming.

'You dirty Kaffir!' he shouted. 'You try to rob me again, eh?' And with that I caught the glint of steel flashing about in front of me; the fucker had a knife! Now I was in a fight to the death so, holding on to both his wrists, we tumbled back and forward, forward and back, as I tried to kick him, bite him, then kick him again. But fuck, he was like a bear. The strength on him was overpowering, and all the time he's calling me a Kaffir! A Kaffir?

'I'm no coon!' I shouted back, as I kicked his balls, finally sending him down, at which point I laid into the shape on the floor like a kick-bag in the corner. Time and time again I booted, connecting with hard then soft, then hard again, while still crying out, 'You call me a Kaffir, eh? You dirty fuck. I'm no Kaffir!'

I only stopped when I ran out of breath. Sweat dripping, I stumbled back onto a chair and sat there gasping. Next to me was a long table, whose white cloth hung half-on, half-off down to the ground, which was now covered in smashed glass and debris. I took a hold of it, sending what was left on top crashing to the ground, and whipped myself down. 'I'm no Kaffir!' I kept saying, but more to myself than to him, who was now whimpering in the corner. I stood up and felt my way along the wall searching for a light switch, which I found – but it didn't work. So I felt the other way and, where the door wall hit the window, I found another but that was dud too. Then I heard him. 'There's . . .' He stopped for breath. 'There's no lights in here. If you want one, you need to use the oil lamp next to the main door.'

'What?' I barked at him but he didn't answer. I paused then slowly stood up. I don't know why I didn't just run away but I'd seen the unusual lamp on my way in and I suppose I was curious. 'If this is a trick,' I said idly, 'I'll stick that lamp right up your arse. Got it?' And with that I moved back down the corridor, got the lamp and lit it.

The naked flame pierced the darkness and before three breaths I was back in the kitchen. 'What the fuck?' I said on entering.

V

COLOUR BLIND

In the dark the kitchen was just a kitchen. But in the dim light of the oil lamp it seemed like a madman's cell. The walls were peeling, the sink was festering, the furniture, so normal before, was crooked and dust ridden while the plates, once white, were stained yellow with a lifetime's nicotine. I glanced over at the heap now moving in the corner. I went to say something but stopped. The window at the far end was draughty and as opaque as my watch face. As I struggled to see through it, I noticed the bottom pane was smashed, while the glass still lay scattered on the floor below it. It had been smashed from the outside.

It seemed, then, that I'd just stumbled into someone else's saga and, at that, I turned back towards my attacker. I thought about killing him and in fact had the knife in my hand. There was no way I was getting caught for this. All I wanted was some food and this dark-living weirdo had jumped me. I lowered the lamp and myself and timidly crept towards the corner. His face was mashed and his left arm cut, no doubt from him trying to slash at me. And I half-expected him to attack again. He was a bull of a man with a bull's strength and wasn't likely to sit there. But he did just that. I expected him to at least say something. But he didn't. By now I was less than a yard away, while the light shone directly into his face, but even though his eyes were half-open he didn't react. 'Oh well,' I said, 'fuck you!' And with that I raised the blade to stab him hard, hard into the neck and down through the lungs and heart – a lesson learned from one of Hugh's drunken 'I'm a hard man' routines. But an inch away from his neck I stopped. What kind of fucking weirdo was he – someone without fear? 'Are you off your fucking head?' I said, now shaking his shoulder with my knife hand.

He breathed deeply. Then, from his pulped-up eyes, I saw a lone tear journey the length of his lived-in face, negotiating the lines before collecting on his chin like a stalactite. 'Fuck you!' he barked with a mouthful of blood that caught my shirt.

I slammed the knife handle right into his shoulder. 'Fuck me?' I barked back and was about to stab him when again I stopped. His eyes were open but he wouldn't look at me. I lowered the lantern until it was almost in his face but he still looked away. Then it dawned on me. 'Are you blind?'

He gave a choking laugh. 'Who else lives in the dark: fucking moles?'

I couldn't believe it. 'You're a big mole,' I answered, before the inquisitive child in me awakened. 'How did you go blind?'

'Fuck off, you nigger!' he belted out again with the last of his strength.

I was about to protest my whiteness to the blind man but stopped. I'd just found a way out of here without setting off a lynch mob that would no doubt track me down and hang me. If I bolted now, they'd be looking for a black man who'd just robbed a house instead of a white robber who was also a murderer. And the few folk I'd already bumped into might suspect that the scrawny wretch who'd been walking about had something to do with it. But then he slowly raised his hand and, before I knew it, he was feeling my face – though, as a daft kid, I never twigged why, until . . . 'You're no Kaffir!' he shouted. 'What the fuck are you doing?'

It seems strange to say but until that point I'd never felt shame. I mean I'd felt every other fucking thing – bad as that is. But shame? I said nothing. 'Tell me,' he kept on, 'tell me you're no Kaffir.' I stayed silent.

It's since been said to me that it doesn't matter how you come to realise something, just as long as you do. But right there, in front of my blind victim, I felt so horribly ashamed. Not because of my actions but because I'd behaved as a black, and in my world, in that era, that was a line never to be crossed. 'Nah,' I said sheepishly, 'I'm not.' He waited on an explanation. Well, he waited on something – probably the knife that he couldn't have seen before he felt it. 'Eh, well, I was, I was hungry.'

'Hungry? Where you from, boy?' And at that he began shuffling about to right himself.

I went to help him but on resting my hands on his shoulders I said in no uncertain terms, 'You try anything and I'll cut you – got it?'

'All right, tough guy, all right,' he muttered and with that I manoeuvred him so that he sat back, straight against the wall. 'So, why are you blind? You in the war?'

'Yeah, I was in the war.' I could feel his anger at having to justify himself to a snotty kid. 'Normandy. Right the way through with the Grenadier Guards.'

'The who?'

'Never you mind, you little fuck. You're not even worthy to say their name.' And at that he started shuffling about again, which pissed me off. He was my prisoner and I was feeling the power that had pulsed through my body the year before with the road worker. It was the God feeling, I suppose – in that I could take his life or allow him to keep it, that I could help him or not, that either way it was my choice and it came from a position of power, which he didn't have.

He started to laugh to himself. 'You know, I went the length of the war, I fought like fuck for king and country and you know what? Not a scratch! Not a fucking scratch! I had to come home for that. That fucking . . .' He stopped.

'Fucking what?'

'Fucking . . . fucking Kaffir that blinded me. And now . . . now this. I stood proud against the best that Hitler had but lost it all to a thieving nigger and a wretch like you!'

'Well,' I said, sitting down some feet away and placing the lamp firmly on the table. 'I know about the wretch. What about the nigger?'

He took a breath to right his slumping body but wouldn't answer. So we sat. Then, as the minutes passed, I began to realise my situation. I was sitting in the middle of my own crime scene and now seemed determined to get caught. I started to stand up.

'See that window?' he said, stopping me with his words. 'Bastard came in there, through the back while my wife and me was sleeping. I heard the noise of the glass breaking so I came down the stairs. But well, you've seen the floors, the boards aren't exactly quiet, so when I got to the door there he, well, I just felt this pain in my face, like a fire in my eyes, and I couldn't see, not a fucking thing. Well, he . . .' He paused again, then sat for that moment, obviously reliving it. 'He went up the stairs and, like I said, the boards are like piano keys, so I knew where he was. He was in my room, our room, in the room with her. She sleeps heavy – slept heavy.'

I was no counsellor so, with an immature fascination, I blurted it out: 'What – and he shagged her?' He didn't answer. 'Where's she now?'

'England. She went back. I mean I brought her out here. She blamed me.' Then he added, turning his head in the direction of my voice. 'We could have made it, you know. We almost did, what with our little secret.' I felt a shudder. I knew all about secrets. 'But then, well, then she missed her period and we knew exactly what that meant. What were the options? Try to live round here with a goffle kid? No chance.'

'But you're fucking blind!' I laughed. 'What was the difference to you?'

He ignored my stupidity and carried on. 'She did it herself.'

'What?'

'The termination. She used a bicycle spoke and did it herself. Damn near bled to death. And you know what the funny thing was? We moved here because she'd suffered so much in England as a kid. Her whole family had got it during the London Blitz. She saw the lot of them killed when a bomb hit their Anderson. This was our new start, the chance to get away and have a shot at happiness.' He brushed his hands through his uneven hair and shook his head like he was shaking away the memory. 'Go and get me some water, would you?' I shrugged my shoulders at his command but then nodded my head and made for the sink. 'Nah, I don't drink that water; it's lethal. Here, next to the door there's a jerrycan.'

'Fuck!'

'What's wrong?' he asked, keenly interested.

'Nothing,' I said. 'Nothing. Just, eh, just that . . .'

But he finished my sentence for me. 'Just that you've drunk the water, right?' He began laughing. 'Did you, did you drink from that tap? You did, didn't you? C'mon, tell me you drank the fucking water!' He began to laugh like a madman. 'You little shit – you've drunk that water!'

VI

SAVED BY THE WILLIES

Cholera? Dysentery? I would never know. But I do know
that my arse gushed like a storm drain, while I vomited so
much that I near choked on my own stomach. For the rest
of that night I slipped in and out of my very own delirium
cinema. Being nursed, being kept alive, are dream images
that I remember as feelings, occasionally triggered as déjà
vu when I least expect them.

It's funny how quickly the wind can change, and African
winds can blow both ways at once. That night I went from
playing God to playing dead, while my hostage became
my keeper – less guard and more guardian. I suppose the
water hit me some time after he stopped laughing. He knew
what I was in for, probably from past experience – the dirty
bastard in his dirty house! He probably stopped caring when
his wife went. I suppose he let go. I knew about that. The
people I'd seen leaving his house that night turned out to
be missionaries, a couple that lived some 50 miles deeper
into the lush bush, parts of which would later become the
Hwange National Park.

I don't know what the old guy told them the next morning

when they came to check on him. Seemed they'd stayed in town that night before heading back, as the roads weren't the safest by night. Now believe me when I say it: he was bashed to fuck and looked it but somehow, and for some reason, he'd gathered himself together, blind, and hauled my vomiting carcass through to his lounge, where he'd slung me on a sofa. Then, giving them some bullshit excuse, he convinced them both to keep me alive – diarrhoea is lethal if you're not given the right hydration solution. They offered to take me into their mission if I wanted, where I could work for my keep.

Well, beggars can't be choosers, especially when the alternative is a nasty death or at best a day in court and a lifetime in jail. And as to why he'd helped me when he should have killed me, that was something that would only become apparent later. In the meantime I was given a groggy Land Rover trip along a bumpy clay road to a hamlet of huts and homes that unexpectedly rose from the dirt, like a lost city suddenly re-emerging. But by the time I got there I was so drained that I nearly collapsed and so was taken straight to bed – in a room that resembled a hermit's cell more than a bedroom.

My room, as I'd later see, was off the kitchen. The kitchen was in the middle, while the rest was beyond that. And the word was humble. If I'd thought that all whites lived in the lap of luxury, I'd soon see that the rule fell well short when it came to this crowd. On their side were a few more rooms: their bedroom, a spare of some sorts and a living room that sported a collection of books that ran along the sparse, whitewashed walls, reminding me of my mother's room when she withered away. Outside their house was a small square, with broken, neglected washing lines in it and a large outside sink with a yard of cut hose for a nozzle, which constantly hissed and was of more interest to the dogs than any people. Thirty yards beyond the square was what

I'd later find to be an orphanage, while the new washing quarters had been slapped onto the side of that and were constantly buzzing with movement. At the entrance to the compound, completing a triangular shape, was the mission hospital. Well, it was more of a clinic than a hospital, offering rudimentary care, but compared to the 'bush medicine' alternative it was nothing short of space age.

As for my hosts, well, they'd certainly met me but I couldn't have recognised them from Adam. When the next morning broke, I half-hoped to still feel ill. It wasn't that I was averse to working or to getting back on my feet but there's a certainty in illness, like a holiday from life where there's only one focus, and that's getting yourself better. I heard them stirring in the kitchen, while outside my window, one I'd yet to look out of, I heard arguing in a local language; the argument came to an end with a thud. I bolted up but felt too faint to look, so instead I slowly got dressed. Somehow the clothes I was in hadn't made it, which was no great loss, considering. But my bag was in the corner, while its contents, the few shirts I did have, were neatly pressed and placed in another corner underneath a crucifix that dominated the room, especially given its lack of aesthetic competition.

With a deep breath I slowly prised open the door, to find a silver-haired man sitting back drinking tea, while an aged German shepherd sat by his feet underneath an old wooden table. 'Athol,' he said, gesturing me over with a smile while leaning forward to push a chair out from the other side. 'It's good to meet you at last.'

I sat down and wiped my face, like a kid who'd just woken up. Then I yawned before replying, which didn't impress him. But I soon rescued the first impression with an emphatic apology, a routine I'd had well polished from the 'impossible to please' Hugh days. I shook his hand and he shook mine firmly. 'Thank God you were there!' he said to me.

I looked at him. 'Eh?'

'Thank God you were there at the Woodwards', when that awful man tried to rob Tony again!' The penny dropped. 'Tony said you men put up quite a fight.'

'We did,' I said slowly. 'Some fight, let me tell you . . . bloody Kaffir!'

He looked down his nose at me. 'Now we don't say those things here.'

Again I was emphatic. 'Sorry, sorry – I forgot myself.'

'So how long had you planned on staying with Tony?'

'A couple of weeks,' I said, while seeming unsure of myself.

'But you're a boy. Where else would you go after what happened to you? It's just terrible.' He was now losing me. The fight story I could get, but the rest was beginning to annoy me. The silver-haired Jesus man might have been getting off on his altruism but I didn't need saving, and even if I did, it wasn't to be through him.

'Sorry,' I said. 'What happened? What did that Tony tell you?'

'Your parents were killed. He's your father's cousin, right?'

'Oh . . . right,' I said, coming round again. 'I hate to talk about it. I just can't. I was here to stay with Uncle Tony but I don't think he's up for having company. I suppose that's why I'm here, yeah? Thanks for that. I mean, really, thank you for taking me.' And at that I began to eat the eggs and bread that had been placed in front of me by a less than courteous domestic.

I was just about to ask him some stupid question in an attempt to break the silence – silences made me feel awkward – when, from a door behind me, a woman appeared from what seemed to be a cellar. She was in her 40s and a bit fat, and I soon saw that she was talking to two cats, which seldom left her feet, as if they were humans. After adjusting her dress – a long garment that crossed Joan of Arc with Big Daddy – she sat down at the table while wiping her hands on a hot towel that had been put there by the angry servant. To be honest, from the moment I saw her I hated her. The way she looked at me was more in keeping with a Victorian workhouse mistress than a church sort. She asked me stupid questions but didn't listen to the answers, while she made points that seemed unrelated and more about herself than anything to do with me. In all she had styled herself as a no-nonsense woman, on a mission from God, and her purpose was to be the great white saviour of Africa. So, with her confidence as her shield and her arrogance thus justified, I'd see her speak to the locals like shit yet weep before the cross at night – mad. But then she did get things done, and for that she flourished.

'Dave' the silver haired was the vicar, while she was the doctor and wore the trousers. Dave begrudged that of course, and having another male in the house to witness his daily castration changed his world from one of anger to humiliation. Like his sermons his excuses were thus frequent but thin, as he rationalised it all to himself, while justifying it to me. This of course made me laugh, as his head might have been in heaven but his arse remained firmly on earth – and belonged to her!

The orphanage was run by hired hands from the area and had 20 kids at most, who she graced with her presence each day. The hospital had about 15 beds but often made use of floor space when the going got tough. It dealt with anything – and in those days that meant anything. Smallpox still lived and other outbreaks were as numerous as the lists of diseases were long. I'd been spoilt in Salisbury; it sat at nearly 5,000 ft above sea level and so mosquitoes and malaria were never a problem. Down here it was different. The hospital was staffed by African medics, while now and then you'd get the odd European doctor touring the badlands to get their

'jump wings' before specialising back home. Apart from that
a string of labourers and helpers made themselves busy on
whatever Her Majesty commanded, while others – a black
and anonymous mass – sat hanging around. There was a
lot of that.

Matabeleland was definitely the short straw for a
missionary. Whereas the northern lot had an easier time
of it, being in Mashonaland and beyond, the Matabeleland
missionaries found the locals were in no hurry for salvation,
a later 'freedom struggle' commander stating, 'If the Jews had
not killed Christ, I would have done it myself.' Nevertheless
they tried and, encouraged by the size of their flock, they
soldiered on. African tradition, though, didn't just compete
with medicine and Christianity; the 'bush creed' was an
altogether different animal. Some of it was harmless ritual,
while other parts were just plain stupid, but beyond that
there was a side to it that was downright sinister, and I'll
come back to that in a moment. Anyway, like the rest of
the area, the compound worked for as long as the locals
saw fit. And that was that.

My first job, then, was to sandpaper old hospital beds.
Smelted down and cast some time before the Boer War, the
beds had found themselves coming north and now, after
facilitating more writhing deaths than I'd care to imagine,
were being stripped and repainted by me. The hospital
buildings had a quadrangle in the middle: an airless sweat-
hole where the beds were stacked like a primitive scrapyard.
That was my space. As soon as my introduction to Queenie
was over, I was off, scrubbing my fingers to the bone in
a heat that was debilitating. By midday I was fucked. I
knew I could bolt whenever I wanted. I'd already seen an
old motorbike propped up against the wall of the laundry
building and I figured that the jerrycans kept in the shade
were full of fuel. But instead I found myself genuinely trying
to do a good job. I cared little for my fellow man but I

had developed a sick interest in masochism, and the more the heat and pain from my lingering illness got to me, the harder I worked.

Anyway, some time after midday but before lunch Mrs Jesus – I'll call her Alice – walks in. She asks me how I'm doing, then rubs her fat fingers the length of the sanded frame I'm working on. She looks at me then looks at the bed. 'You should do it properly!' she says to me, now trying to scrape the rough edges with her nail. I said nothing but my blood began to boil. 'You should do it properly. You're here to work, otherwise you should just go for a walk or something!' Then she turned, manoeuvring her blubber between the frames, and fucked off. Now believe me, I was less than a second – no, I was less than an impulse – away from head-butting that fat bitch into next week and sending her to whatever illusory spectre she prayed to, when, out of the corner of my eye, I caught a glimpse of some light brown hair and suntanned flesh. I stopped. Then, through the window pane, which was more reflective than transparent, I began squinting. I couldn't see shit. So with that image in mind I kept on working, but, like a sentry on guard duty, I was constantly jumpy. The reason, of course, was that as I fast approached 16, I'd never had it. Although I'd been sexualised at a young age and developed my own alternative sexual interests, I'd never fucked a girl – a white girl. In fact I'd never really talked to one, never mind had a kiss or a feel.

At lunchtime I made a few discreet enquiries after a lengthy grace. I didn't want to ask the Bible bashers who the bird was in the hospital, in case puritan Alice shipped me off to some morgue, if they had one. But I did find out that there was a young nurse from Bulawayo called Sarah staying for a while. Now I had a reason to be here.

I found lunch difficult. They talked non-stop about God and attempted to talk about the tragedy of my parents, which, of course, I declined to respond to. I also soon realised I was their latest project for conversion, which annoyed me. But that wasn't the worst. What really fucking got to me was the way they treated their animals like humans, in particular the cats, who she referred to as her children. The dog, King, I could handle – well, for obvious reasons – but I still hated the idea that he came into the house. I'd grown up with dogs – albeit evil murdering bastards – but still, a golden rule was that they never came into the home. And this one stunk. The cats, though, were vermin. I hated the look of them. I hated the idea of them. I hated the idea that they could be anywhere – hidden, like cats do. It made me uneasy, and uneasiness was bad for my mania. Later that evening, after a day's work and a fruitless search for my mystical nurse, Sarah, I took a wash outside and made for my room. But a few feet away from the door one of the cats, the ginger one, came out of the basement and stopped. Then, for no reason at all, it hissed at me and spat, before making some fiendish noise that made me shit it. As I then stood there quite startled, it simply fucked off with its head held high, like it had marked its territory and beaten me.

At dinner then, half an hour later, I was in a world of my own. I'd expected to be thinking about a girl I'd just seen but I was right back with the rabbits. I couldn't think of anything but hurting that cat. Like a nut I had invested that cat with a mind, a will, and the ability to use reason. In all I'd taken a hairy fucking rat and made it my adversary. Soon I began to sweat, which they noticed. So I put it down to my illness. Alice then made a feeble attempt to praise me for working but I barely acknowledged her. She could iron her guilt out later, in front of her cross – a cross I could now so easily have rammed up her arse.

At that moment the vicar tried to say something but I interrupted. 'So your cats,' I said, looking firmly at Mrs

Jesus. 'They're gorgeous. Tell me about them.' Alice smiled before clicking her fingers. It seemed both God and cats were her thing. The ginger rat bounced onto her knee and nestled in, making that purring noise that contented cats make, which sounded to me like nails down a blackboard. Then she pulled it up, held it like a newborn baby and began nuzzling her face into its fur, her breath parting its soft hairs each time she exhaled. I looked at it: it had a snow-white face with sky-blue eyes and a little pink nose. It looked so cute, so lovely. It looked like a small fur ball, which made me tingle. But by God that tingle got me racing, as, set against my hatred, those contradictory feelings gave me a sweet and sour sensation I could hardly explain. I just knew that I had to hurt it – no more. I had to break it – break its will; break the spirit I had given it. It had to know its place and my mere presence had to paralyse it.

'She's got no claws.'

'Sorry?' I said, shaking my head out of the fantasy.

'She's got no claws,' Alice repeated, holding up one of her paws. 'See, we had her de-clawed when she was young. I wanted her to stay in the house with me and they can ruin things, you know. He's not, though,' she said, nodding her head in his direction. 'Jack, he's a real tomcat. We let him out to hunt. He even brings back small birds or mice. He leaves them just out there on the porch.' She sniggered.

When I say that the cat was smirking at me from its position of power, I mean it. My affinity with the animal world meant that pecking order was everything and at that point I was lagging. As the days went on, then, I'd kick the two of them, which cultivated their hatred towards me. But they still stayed aggressive, like the fight was on – in particular the ginger. And so, when the 'Holy Willies' weren't about, I'd chase them and try to terrorise them but I never got the calm in my mind that I craved. Even after beating them and smashing them with brooms, I'd still fall short. Ultimately I needed to be alone with them. I needed a chamber and for them to be my guests.

My attentions were distracted when, one morning, about a week and a half after I'd got there, Dave the vicar came running through to the lunch table, crying as if a bully had just stolen his dinner money. Alice, as Christian as ever, told him to get it together before asking what the problem was. It turned out that he'd gone to his wardrobe to try on a suit – he was off to some missionary do in South Africa – and had found it had gone. Straight away I knew this spelled trouble and that I'd be right in the firing line but luckily the racism of the time was all pervasive and if they didn't say the words 'thieving coon', then they certainly thought it. Within half an hour she had the entire staff standing to attention in the small square. Then, like Heinrich Himmler, she marched along the lines, eyeballing each one before announcing the deal. In essence some cunt had thieved a suit and probably swapped it for smokes – well, probably for food to feed his starving family but I was going with smokes, because I was still pretty new here.

She then explained the deal to them, starting off calm and controlled then getting harsh and bitchy. At first she offered to buy it back. No doubt whatever money they'd got for it was well below the value of having it replaced. When that fell on deaf ears, as did the promise of an amnesty, she turned to the Lord – well, she turned to the Devil by suggesting that the suit thief was hell-bound. I found all this to be quite funny, of course. You can't threaten people who've already got fuck all with losing it all, nor with hell, when their daily lives are just a stone's throw away from the brimstone you're describing. In any case this wasn't the army and there was a limit to how long she could have them standing there. Soon, then, it was over and they went back to their jobs, while I went back to mine.

Later that day I nicked my arm on a rough edge. The wound was short but deep and, after my poisoned-water experience, I'd taken a new interest in parasites. I wandered through to the clinic to have it scrubbed – and there she was, when I least expected her, my mystical nurse. She was young, 20-odd at most, and was pretty short – well, petite. And she didn't really pay me much attention, which made my spirits sink. One of the black doctors then came to see me but I stood up and left like I'd forgotten something. Then, seeing he'd fucked off, I went back. She was nice to me: she smiled; she treated my wound. She asked me how I was getting on but not my history, which I thought strange. I tried telling her how I knew the Holy Willies but she just seemed to look at me in bewilderment. After a few more words that was that. I was cleaned and out. Our germ date was over.

To be honest I left without any specific feeling about her other than an unusual familiarity, as if I'd already dreamt her. But understanding the impossibility of the whole situation, I was glad. I was a kid, after all, and she was a woman – a trained nurse, in fact – and not short of attention. I, on the other hand, was the fucking weirdo that scraped beds – hardly a mover. But that wouldn't last. Soon I'd see that those boundaries were the domain of the sane, while reason and rules were merely suggestions – suggestions I'd later choose to ignore.

The next day I noticed a lot of moaning amongst my black brethren. I didn't care why, they were all whining bastards to me, but when I went for lunch I soon saw the reason. Stood at our doorstep was a nanga, a fucking witch doctor, for those in the dark. He looked the part and spoke the lingo, and could put the shits up a ghost if needed. He was covered in bones, stones and animal skin, and was setting about some ritual, spitting in corners and drinking red stuff, no doubt cow blood. Straight away I clicked. It

seemed Mrs Christ had decided on a new way to flush out
the suit thief: by using black magic.

Now, once again, I found this all to be quite amusing.
I was under the impression that she was here to give the
dark continent her light. If the local beliefs were all shite,
how come they suddenly had value? If I'd known the word
hypocrisy back then, I'd have used it. Instead my word was
idiot. That was her.

Again she put them in rows but this time they all listened.
The nanga then did his stuff and within minutes some
woman fell over crying. Everyone looked for where the
noise had come from, as the woman in question was 20
yards away and not even part of the line-up. She was one
of the 'hang-abouters', the wife of one of the orphanage
cooks. Well she'd immediately sold the suit and so, in a
spirit of Christianity, the Holy Willies sacked her husband.
And that was that. Well, not quite. The problem was, and
in later life I'd fully understand this, that for every action
there's a reaction. 'Nanga Joe', or whatever his fucking name
was, was one of a handful of witch doctors in the area. The
Willies had, in their ignorance, just grabbed the first bone-
wearing native they could find and slipped him a few quid.
But it turned out that he was their version of Rasputin: a
real evil bastard. Once he'd outed his victims, he'd cursed
them, then muscled them into buying themselves out of his
curse, which they couldn't afford because they were skint.
So, driven mad by his bullshit, the suit-stealing woman killed
herself and her infant. Then, after her five year old died
– no doubt unnaturally – the cook was left all alone. In a
fix, and now coming down with some illness, he went back
to Nanga seeking a cure, which was – and this is fucked – to
rape the arse off a white woman. Sound familiar? Now in
later days, when the Aids thing first hit Africa, that was top
of the macabre cure list, but the seeds of that madness were
being sown even as early as then. I've often wondered how

Alice the Christian reconciled that chain of events as she sat in front of her cross. I could have rationalised it quite easily but then I am without any conscience. But her?

I heard an old story one time that resonated with me – it's about a snake in the cold and I find it to be very apt. An old woman spies the dying snake and takes it home. She heats it, feeds it and nurses it back to health. But when she goes to release it, it turns around and bites her. So, lying there, death taking her hand, she asks the snake, 'How could you bite me? I found you. I took you in. I saved your life.'

The snake replied, 'Yes, but when you found me, you knew I was a snake!'

VII

IGNOMINY

Two days after the nanga visit, but weeks before the saga's unfolding, the Willies announced they were off soon. They were heading to Pretoria in South Africa for a conference, or get-together, or whatever the deal was that the vicar wanted his suit for. They said they'd be away for a week and wanted me to take care of the cats. I almost choked on my porridge. 'Sure!' I said, with a bit too much enthusiasm.

Later that day I got talking again to my nurse. It seemed we shared the same views regarding the Willies and the nanga. Well, we shared them because whatever she said I agreed with. I asked her if she was married, to which she sheepishly said not yet. Then I asked her if she had any hobbies, which sounded so creepy that I should have just asked to put salt on her forearm and given it a good gnawing. She said no, of course, to the hobbies and so left me feeling like a five year old. But later that day I was passing through the main attendance room on an unnecessarily long detour when I saw her and she smiled. It sent a spark through me that I'd never felt before and, for the rest of the day, I floated on a cloud.

I suppose the strongest things in life take time to build. It wasn't love at first sight. It wasn't even love on the second. But the more I saw her and heard her and spoke to her, as hopeless as I was, the more she became engrained on my soul. She felt like a missing part of me and, now that she existed to me and I didn't have her, she was nothing short of a limb that was separated from my body. I couldn't wait to see her and when I did the world stopped moving. Then, when I left, the craving kicked in and the cycle began all over again.

To say we had become close was a lie but she knew I had feelings for her – and she wallowed in it. I mean, if nothing else, the flattery made her feel good and, given where we were and what we were doing, my attentions, as lame as they were, sure helped her pass the day. One day I gave her flowers, which made her uneasy and left me feeling sick, but later on she came by me and thanked me by putting her hand on my shoulder and kissing my cheek. I spent the next day and a half analysing it. So the day after that, filled with certainty, I turned up after lunch and, wearing my best shirt and polished boots and brandishing another bunch of flowers, went round to the entrance with the intention of asking her . . . something, out, on a date – something beyond a hello. But when I got there, she walked out dressed in her civvies, said hello and jumped straight into a motor with some guy driving. And it hurt.

My head spun as I struggled to keep a handle on it. And, while the sweats hit me as I became consumed by the devil, jealousy, I more stumbled than walked back to the house, where I flopped onto my bed like a victim with the plague. It's taken a lifetime but I now know my mental make-up. My emotions, my moods and so my mind are less individual strains and more of a tangled ball. To most people one button pressed is one button lit, but to me one button pressed lights everything. After the train journey I was so sure of myself. The world was as I defined it. I was no longer a victim but a player – and that was empowering. But now, on the receiving end of something new, something uncontrollable, I felt helpless. And of all my states that seemed to me the worst.

The next day she wasn't there but the day after that she was. It was also the day that the Willies were leaving. My inability to have her was now pressing down on me. I couldn't eat; I couldn't sleep. Everything I did or thought came round to her and every action was engineered with meeting her in mind. I made idle talk with the locals – something I'd never done before – as just talking about her eased my head, which was now like a pressure cooker.

After lunch the Willies packed up and were off. No sooner had they gone than, with a smoke in one hand and a beer in the other, I ventured down to look for my nurse. This time she was sitting out, just yards away from the end of the square, sunning herself during her lunch break. I sat down and she smiled. Her nurse's blouse was unbuttoned and her hair was let down. I tried not to look but couldn't help staring. For the first time I saw her legs: they were soft, smooth and golden. Her ankles were perfect, as were her feet, and between the heat and the beer I sat in an atmosphere that I can still see like a painting and taste like wine. It was another sweet-and-sour moment that I'll never let go of.

She couldn't know it but she had a strong power over me. And although I loved her, I hated her because of it. Like a puppet-master with his strings or a zookeeper with some food, her being was dictating my life. I began to speak but, like squeezing a pool full of water through the plughole of a bath, my attempts were strained. How could I communicate my world to her in those moments? The words 'I love you' were labels, labels to drawers she'd never be opening if I fucked it. And that was more pressure. I wanted her to feel for me, to pity me, to worry about me, to worry about a boy who she'd only just met, the boy who was the weirdo who scraped all those beds. I spoke a few words, and then a few more, but before I knew it I'd blurted out the lot, everything, including how I'd come to be beside her. Then I stopped. She listened. She listened to it all – but fell silent. For the first time ever I'd laid myself out there and now, exposed to the world and while the clock ticked, I waited. I waited on an answer, on something. But nothing. Instead of a mothering I got a firm shaming. She was only a kid herself and could never have cared about me. In any case I'd done it all arse over elbow as, with nothing to start with, she had no emotional investment in me. She didn't even know me. I'd used my past as a lure, as a crutch to gain favour by pushing myself up, but had only pushed myself off. Now I was no different to the patients in her beds: a case to be cured, or labelled and binned. I wanted to be a strong man, like the survivor of a lion attack, but had fallen short, no more than a waster.

Minutes later she'd leave my company like she'd chanced across a sideshow and flicked in a quid. Stunned and empty I packed up my story and shuffled off. I was embarrassed. I was down. I was ashamed . . . I was home.

I was due to work but could hardly stand. The tension inside was explosive, while the shame stunned me like a deer caught in the headlights, transfixed by its own imminent death. I wanted to be a warrior, a tough man who she'd feel safe with. But I wasn't. How many times had I fantasised about being her hero, about the lance in my side draining my life away while she wept at my passing? But with the buzz came the bump, which always snapped me back and made me feel childish.

I instinctively reached for my kukri, which sat under my kitbag. I pulled the steel from its scabbard and held it up to draw strength from it. Then I pushed out my arm and slowly began cutting. From my wrist to my elbow I drew the blade down and watched myself bleed. I felt the warmth on my arm as the blood flowed downwards, finding its course through my hairs, round the curve of my elbow and onto the ground, where it formed a small puddle. It was a release and it was my secret. But beyond that it was my world of self-harm that only I'd come to know as my numerous 'mini suicides'.

An hour later I felt eased. But each time I imagined her laughing I was sent backwards. I walked into the kitchen, where I expected to see the staff. But they'd gone. Seemed they'd taken advantage like me and so had fucked off early. I walked about, looking for my smokes, which I found. Then, from behind a closed door, I heard a small noise. It was the cats. Right then I felt my heart jump, like I'd just seen my nurse. I closed the kitchen door and shut down the blinds. Slowly, like a literal cat burglar, I joined my soon-to-be victims. I grabbed Jack first and, by the scruff of the neck, chucked him the ten steps down to the cellar. The basement was dark and damp, and was the same size as the kitchen. It was unusual for those houses to have one but the vicar had insisted on it. Two seconds later I was back with the ginger. Straight away it hissed but this time I loved it. I hissed back, only louder, which made it spit. Then its hair stood on end and it puffed itself out, which made me feel angry, as the once-cute fur ball now looked like a snake. And for that I felt hatred, which made me lunge but miss it. It ran, but with nowhere to go it wedged itself between the sofa and the wall. To its shock I moved the sofa out. Then, two seconds later, I had a sheet from a bed, which I threw over it and wrapped up tight. Now, like Santa, I slung the sack over my shoulder and marched down to the fun room.

What was I to do? At a loss I punched it. Then, time and time again, I pummelled the lump in the sack like a boxer using his speed-bag. When it fell onto its side, I pushed down on it hard, squeezing its neck, nipping its stomach. Then, taking a hold of its tail, I tried to swing it, which didn't work, so I picked it up and threw it against a wall. There was a crack and it fell, and then, stumbling about, it scrabbled into a corner. So I sat there and, enjoying an erection, I lit up a smoke and began breathing its fear.

I tried to figure out my next move but knew that I couldn't kill them. The Willies would lose it and my nurse meant too much to me. I understood the fun to be had with their torture. I'd done it before. But this time it was different. Killing was simple but often a luxury, and an accidental death was a technician's failure. These cats, then, were to turn my hobby into a profession.

Looking about, I found a cut length of clothes-line. I fashioned two loops and joined them together by less than an inch of cord. Then I slipped the loops around their heads and fastened them, leaving their bodies free. They would live like that for the day, I decided. I stubbed out my smoke, opened the top kitchen door, then began shouting. They tried to run, one way then the other, but banged into walls and kept hitting each other. Then Jack, the stronger one, began dragging the other around like a ball and chain. And I loved it. They moaned. They screamed. Then, exhausted, they flopped and just sat there cowering. So I kicked the two-headed beast back down to the basement and chucked in a meat scrap, hoping that they'd fight for it.

That night I slept happy. I loved the idea that they were stuck down there struggling for life. I imagined their pain, while reliving them running about, heads stuck together, over and over again. The next morning I got up with the sunrise as usual and began to get ready for work. Like a kid with presents under the tree I kept getting tempted to have a look at them but, by resisting, I gained a satisfaction from denying myself the pleasure. I decided to keep it up till lunch and so headed off to the clinic and the beds I had left. I had little intention of doing much work and as soon as I got there my need to see nursey was stronger than ever. After an hour I saw her, passing a window without looking out. So I followed her and passed her in a place that I couldn't justify being. She forced a smile, which was a dagger in my heart, then, when I asked what she was doing for lunch, she said she was busy. At that I went back to my sweat-box and scraped the beds.

Half an hour later I was thinking about the Willies. Being here was meant to be an escape but I'd gone from the frying pan into the fire. I was thinking about leaving, just heading off into the distance like a love martyr and imagining Sarah distraught at having missed her chance, when I heard laughter – it was a man and I was sure that I recognised it. I stopped my scraping and wiped my head down with my shirt. Soon the silence surrounded me, as even the usual banter of the clinic had subsided. I took a few steps before hearing it again and this time the words that came after it sent me searching. I walked through the open door and past the toilets. I turned left before right, then, after a narrow corridor, I broke into the reception, where I saw them. The black nurses and doctors were huddled in a group around a white man, who was now holding court. I stood there listening. He was talking about marriage and was busy cracking jokes. He was taller than the rest of them and had a confidence that I envied. I tried to see his face but it was partly covered by a leather bush hat, which he wore pulled down and at an angle. I took a few steps closer but, to my horror, my nurse, the being of my life, walked into the middle, put her arm around him and laughed. I heard her say yes, and that she couldn't wait – meaning get married – then they gestured to the door and made to leave.

In a rage I turned around and bolted back to the house. I took hold of my kukri, stuffed it in the back of my shorts and pulled down my shirt. Within a second I was straddling the motorbike and, cap open, I rocked it back and forth to check there was enough fuel, which there was. I was off. By the time I got down there, they were away but, determined to find him, I pinned my ears back and throttled the bike, near killing myself twice. Within two minutes I could see the dust ahead, as the Land Rover he drove churned the bush dirt into a cloud that rose behind him. A minute after that I was on to them. I kept just out of view for an hour until they stopped. I pulled up short, convinced they'd seen me, but from behind my tree trunk I saw that he'd only stopped for a pee before carrying on, at which I followed again. The road now was long and the longer it went, the longer I had to question myself. My face was now sunburnt and my lips were being chafed but, as the dusty wind sandblasted me, any sense that had rolled in was soon pushed away again.

It took another 20 minutes for us to enter Wankie. Then it got weird. This time I saw the mineshafts. And where I once saw a few streets and imagined that was all there was to it, I now saw a town built on the back of some bloody hard work. The Land Rover slowed and I recognised the street. It was Tony's – the blind man, my once hostage now saviour. They finally stopped less than ten yards away from his house, got out and walked straight past his gate and in through the neighbour's. I pulled up some yards away and waited. I tried to figure it out but I couldn't. I had tunnel vision and my red mist had now descended into a rolling fog that consumed me. I reached backwards and took hold of my blade – but paused. The sun was up and the street was lively. The few cars about seemed to be driving one way then the next, like they were taunting me. I made to stand up but once again stopped short – fuck!

The minutes now became an hour as I sat there transfixed. I hated the idea that they were in there, together, my girl being touched by that man. It felt personal, like a betrayal. I was now moments away from heading straight in there when the door finally opened. Then, after a pause that suspended me in time, my hat man walked out and jumped into his Land Rover, before hitting the horn twice and taking off.

I was now at a fork: follow him or try to get her? If I went after her . . . well, I knew what that meant. And it would fuck up any real chance of getting her. No – clearly he was the problem. He was the obstacle and the focus of my hate. I kick-started my engine and, with less than no savvy, I tore down the street after him, near-missing a wagon.

The chase was back on and it lasted until the tar road became dirt, before the dirt turned to gravel. Then, after another half-hour, he turned off to a five-mile stretch of farmland. I sat back and, when the tight turns opened out onto an avenue, I pulled into the cropland and turned off my bike. I suppose it was all simple. I'd cut him up, feed him to something, then fuck off home – back in time for tea and medals. So I wandered through an orchard until I saw the opening to a house. It was white and grand and reminded me of home. The bushes were trimmed, the flower beds well watered and, while no one was about, it was obviously well staffed. I wanted to run in, to just get it over with, but no bird wants a jailed man and a frontal assault would end me. So I sat.

But soon my friend was upon me: the calm. I thought about him in there, with his nice lifestyle and money. He had it all. I had fuck all. But I did have the power, over his life and limb. Taking a breath, I thought I heard crickets but it was just imaginary white noise – I heard that a lot. So I more stumbled than walked, then broke into a run to keep myself upright. I went round the back but startled a dog. It barked like fuck, which summoned another, then another and another. But, just as I thought I'd be shredded, they stopped and, like a pack of rabbits, sat licking their balls and doing fuck all. Seemed Hugh had a point after all.

I didn't know who lived there, nor how many of them there were. But the tunnel I was in kept forcing me through and so forward I went. Within a second I was standing on a carpet: a long one, like you'd see at the Oscars. It was ornate and red and ran the length of the hallway, passing a grand piano that was covered in framed photos and running on to the front, where it ascended the stairs in one direction, tacked down to each step with precision, and hit the marble floor of the front double doorway in the other. To my left was an opening that gave way to a living space – more of a reception for entertaining than a sitting room. To my right were the kitchens.

This time the floorboards were solid, while the carpet silenced my every step. Each room was lit and, like a museum with exhibits, each contained well-mounted and illuminated displays. The oil paintings, the sculptures, the silverware and gold were all the trappings of a rich man who'd soon lose it all.

I surveyed the rooms but came up with nothing. Then, with my kukri in one hand and the other pressed down on the banister, I ascended the staircase. At the top I had choices. The doors were all closed and the landing lights were turned off. I tried to see which had life beyond them but the plush carpet left no gaps under the doors. So, starting on my left, I walked the corridor, my ears pressed tight to the doors, trying to hear movement, but nothing. I was about to lose patience when finally, at the end of the corridor, face on to it, was a grander door that was part-hidden in the darkness. Above the carved frame was a bust, which sat watching me. I pressed myself against the door and heard pages turning. I heard the strike of a match, then the rattle of a drawer. Then nothing. I steadied my breath and waited. I saw myself moving. I saw myself killing. Then, in a sudden rush, I bashed through the door and screamed like a nut.

'Athol!' I heard, before, crash, I sunk my foot right into his balls, which buckled him down and onto the floor. 'Stop!' he yelled. 'Stop!' But I'd already swung down at him, the blade missing his head and nicking his neck before splintering the floor and sticking there fast. Like the wounded shit-bag he was he cried and crawled towards his bed, while I wrestled with the blade and snarled at him. Finally it popped free of the wood, as I watched his long silk dressing gown, once white, slowly turn red. I stopped to watch his shocked and panicked face. But on seeing him lie on his belly and reach under his pillow, I jumped and landed my knee in his back – hard.

'Face me, you fuck!' I screamed. 'Face me!' And at that I stamped down on his spine, again and again, before leaning in and pulling his head up by the ear, which nearly ripped off. His throat now exposed, I stuck my blade to it, but fuck! His forehead! His forehead was missing. Well, the skin was off and instead lay a rough patch where whatever remained had healed itself over. So, righting myself, I more kicked than threw him back to the floor, where he lay facing up. I couldn't believe it.

'What are you doing, Athol?' he pleaded in terror.

It was him. It was Tobacco Man!

As I stood there, his willing executioner, I had nothing to say. My rush had just hit a massive speed bump and I was plummeting down fast. 'Is that you?' my lips shaped, but I wasn't able to speak.

'Athol, it's me, mate. It's me. You remember?'

I nodded. 'Yeah, I remember you. You left my stepsister for dead and now you're fucking my girl!' I raised my blade.

'No – what? She's what? Athol, that's my wife. Next week we'll marry. I've been with her for two years! Please. I helped you. I saved you!'

'You what?' I belted out. 'Saved me? Saved me from what?'

'Jail! I saved you from jail. Athol – fuck – how do you think you ended up at the mission?'

'The blind cunt. I screwed his house but got sick. He helped me!'

Tobacco tried to laugh but his nerves got the better of him. 'No, you fool. He wanted to turn you in. It was me that saved you. When you got sick, he dragged you to his living room – but thinking you'd die, he called the nurse from next door before getting the police. That nurse was my girl – a coincidence, I know – but she sat there all morning with you. Mate, you were out of it! So when I came to see her, to tell her she could work with the missionaries I know, I found her with you. I couldn't fucking believe it. And I didn't – but your birth certificate, it was in your bag!'

'Fucking shite!' I belted out. 'You're talking shite, dead man!'

'No!' he cried, now desperate. 'Please, Athol, think about it. How did the missionaries know about your parents? They did talk to you, didn't they?'

I felt cold. I stood there reliving the whole month in my mind. Was it possible? 'Nah, that's rubbish and you know it. My uncle – the blind cunt said he was my uncle.'

'Right,' he conceded nodding his head. 'Right, but that was me – I mean him, him through me. See, when I saw it was you, I told him everything – I had to. Athol, he wanted you dead, for fuck's sake! I told him the whole story, to try to get him to have pity. Christ, he'd been through it himself so I knew I could do it. All he had to say was that he was your uncle – you know, to justify you being there.' I was silent. 'And as for me – my head, look, I did this to myself.' He smacked his forehead. 'With a bottle of whisky and a razor my marking was gone. Fuck – that's how I met Sarah. She helped me get over it. She was working at the hospital in Bulawayo at the time.'

'Shit!' I shouted. 'Fucking shit!' And at that I took

two steps and kicked him like a football. He winced but, struggling to stay with me, he kept pleading.

'Athol, please. We were just trying to help you. We all were. Think, mate, think about it. We all knew the story. We were trying to give you a home. We all were. The missionaries knew; Sarah knew; I knew. We thought you'd start coping in your own good time – fuck, you're just a boy! She told me you talked to her . . . the other day at lunch. Mate, she didn't know what to say. She already knew it all – she didn't want to let on. She knows you like her but, Athol, she's two years shy of thirty – and you're just a kid.'

'Thirty? She's thirty? Thirty,' I repeated, as my voice became a whisper. 'She's thirty.'

I stood there. I stood there unable to move and in my stillness I hid. There's a beauty in truth. There's a perfection in logic. And when they both come together, they just seem to make sense. And right there, in that perverse moment, I saw truth and the picture became clear. I thought I had the power. I thought I'd even held the cards. But in my arrogance I was blind – blinded by my own endgame, where I was the king and the rest were my pawns. But I was wrong. Instead of the technician I was only the lab rat. That I found was unbearably humbling.

And humbling soon became humiliating. While his actions would have been truly noble to most men, to me they were unsettling. I smiled, which perked him up, then I leaned down and suggested a hospital, which perked him up further. He was pale and had lost some blood but he was more shocked than fucked – and so I got him into his Land Rover passenger seat and started the engine. My kukri needed adjusting, which set him off again, pleading as we went. But I enjoyed that. I enjoyed his fear. It made me feel strong. With an admirable concern he'd set up my life but what I'd thought was my own free will had all been an illusion.

We came to a stop at a long, narrow bend. Then the engine stalled. I turned the key once, then twice, then, with less speed than I'd intended, I leaned for my knife and slashed him a fucker. I aimed for his head but got his arm instead. He squealed like a pig before scrabbling the door open and running out. He could have gone left but he chose to go right. And so, instead of being in darkness, he found himself in the full beam of the front headlights, where, ten yards on, he collapsed in a heap. He got up. He ran on. He fell down. He got up, ran on, but fell down again. And each time I kept up, just one pace behind him, with my kukri drawn in my floodlit stadium. Finally he stopped and, at the last gurgle of his voice, I slammed the blade deep into his back and at last it was over. Now I owned him.

So I stood there that evening, knife edge dripping. I leaned in, then bent down. I felt his face, his chest. I felt his skin. I felt the heat of his body leaving slowly. It felt comforting for me to be there. He wouldn't say no. He couldn't say no. And for that I loved him.

Standing up, I took my knife and went to cut him. But I wanted to make sure I wasn't caught and to enjoy him before daybreak. I picked him up and carefully placed him upright in the passenger seat. Then we drove back on ourselves before, like two lovers, we went off-road and onto the flats of the bush at the other side of his orchard. We continued some 20 minutes, carefully noting our direction, until we reached just the right spot and finally stopped. I pulled him out and gently laid him down. I removed his dressing gown and spread it out like a picnic rug, and then sat down beside him. His eyes were open and they stared right at me, giving me their undivided attention. I'd never seen a human being look more beautiful, so much more than my nurse had ever done, as she'd always looked past me and made me feel invisible. If her life had near killed me, it was in death that he made me feel alive.

I sat there for hours and dreaded leaving. This was true love, I thought, but I'd have to get moving. Africa's kind to a murderer – and the times we were in kinder still – so I spent an undisturbed hour butchering his body. My knife was sharp but it wasn't serrated. Lesson learned. I took his legs and arms and wrapped them up with the belt from his gown. Then I sat his head on his torso and folded the robe around them. I thought about burying him right there. But luckily I got wiser. With all that space and even more animals my choices were as endless as my mind was trouble-free. So I righted his house, made his bed and cleaned up his motor. Then I enjoyed the calm of an African morning as I fed the wildlife on my way back home. It was my first night out.

VIII

CONGO BOUND

'No way!' he said to me and I couldn't believe it. Some
bastard in a clown suit was telling me no. I only wanted
a piss, not a five-course dinner, but because my face didn't
fit, or my wallet wasn't big enough, he was now a barrier
that I hadn't even known had existed. Back home my
skin was my currency. White was the colour and my credit
was good. Here, in London, the currency was green and
I was well short.

If I was questioning my future then, the hotel doorman
had given me the answer. The Scots Guards had taken me,
trained me and made me a man. But I was never in it for
the service and now, four years on, my time was fast spent.
I was young, immortal and all fucked up. And while a
deployment to Kenya had seen us neck high in Mau Mau,
who had continued to fight on long after their uprising had
officially ended, it wasn't the Congo – that's where the money
was. In Nairobi I'd heard of some jobs that were going: a
couple of the older lads had been in Uganda, next door,
and had met a recruiter, a mercenary recruiter, which they'd
gone for. They'd been with the 2nd Battalion since it had

moved to the German Rhine in 1953 and now, faced with a pension and not much else, Colonel 'Mad' Mike Hoare's mercenary exploits in the Congo were their last-ditch chance at some cash before their retirement.

Rhodesia to me was now but a faded memory. I'd left in a hurry and had gone to the UK but, between signing up and shipping back out to Africa, the adventure had only continued, without ever giving me a chance to catch my breath. But I did now, and what I was breathing in was poverty, as money had suddenly risen in importance in the UK from something to everything. I had nothing.

I'd heard that the Salisbury and Johannesburg papers were now teeming with situations-vacant ads. 'Fit young men looking for employment with a difference . . .' and so on. That was me. Another guy I knew down in South Africa, who I'll call Steve, had been contracted through Patrick O'Malley, the mercenary recruiter there, but had bottled out after his wife had threatened to chop his cock off if he went. That wouldn't have stopped me, though, even if it meant going with my cock in my pocket.

After getting the details off this guy, I bought myself out of the British Army with what little I had saved and was now en route to BAKA, or the Kamina Military Base in the Congo, as a 'gun for hire'. It's not my intention here to give a blow-by-blow account of the conflict but only to set down my experiences with it and, most importantly, my second reason for being there, which I'll get to. So, for those in the dark, here's a quick summary so that you'll know what I'm on about.

The Congo war of 1964 was an open revolt. It masqueraded as a cold war skirmish but was more about colonial stupidity and the short-sightedness of its natives and their backers, left fighting over the scraps. After the Belgians split, the place went from bad to worse as the newly independent nation's 'government' tried and failed to unite the country. The Simba (Swahili for lion) revolt began small but went large as government misrule soon pushed people over the edge and into rebel control. In August 1964 the rebels seized Stanleyville (now called Kisangani), a major city by Congolese standards, and took 1,600 whites hostage.

That said, the government did have 1,500 Armée Nationale Congolaise (ANC) troops stationed there but, as 1,500 shit-bags, they ran when faced by 40 Simba rebels led by witch doctors waving palm branches. Worse still, they left behind their weapons, including mortars, armoured cars and a variety of small arms for the rebels and the *Jeunesse* – youth gangs – to gather up. The Simbas then celebrated in the traditional way: with ceremonial cannibalism and anarchy. That was the Congo.

Stanleyville, meanwhile, had over 300,000 inhabitants, while the whites included missionaries, teachers, traders, doctors and foreign embassy and consulate staff and their families. The Simba bastards hated the American and Belgian inhabitants the most, blaming them for everything that was wrong with their country. Many of the whites were rounded up and held in the Central Prison and the local jail but, as time went by, the Simbas moved them around, the bulk of them ending up in local hotels under close guard. One of the Simba leaders, a real vicious bastard called Christophe Gbenye, suggested that the hostages would be tied to oil barrels and set on fire if any attempt was made to rescue them – something that would play on the mind of Colonel Mike Hoare when push came to shove, as it delayed his final advance. There were estimated to have been between 2,500 and 10,000 Simbas holding them.

Those allied against the Simbas – the Congolese government, the Americans and the Belgians – then pissed in the wind for 111 days, trying to negotiate. This was a tall order given that one of the many groups the Simbas would target for slaughter were the intellectuals, which, for the Simbas, applied to anyone who could read and write. Several contingency plans were proposed, before finally the Americans and Belgians came up with Operation Dragon Rouge, or Operation Red Dragon, followed by Blanc, Noir and Vert for other cities where whites were being held.

Beyond that the Congolese government also organised a ground force to at least suppress the rebellion before it swallowed the whole country. This force of course included ANC troops but was spearheaded by the 5th Brigade of white mercenaries, led by Colonel Hoare. I was one of 'Mad' Mike's mercenaries.

The goal was simple: to drive north from Kamina towards Stanleyville and Paulis and liberate as many towns as possible, while stamping our mark on the conflict for all Simbas to see. We were well under way when Dragon Rouge was launched and, as far as we were concerned, were ready to spank fuck out of Stanleyville, overseas airdrop or not.

In any event the drop happened and it was truly an international affair: Belgian paratroops were flown in American Airforce planes, using the British Ascension Islands as a staging base; the air support consisted of B-26s flown by Cuban-exile pilots trained and operated by the CIA; while we, the renegades, were British, French, Belgian, German, Italian, South African and Rhodesian.

On 24 November at 0600hrs the first B-26s flew over the airfield and drew no fire, and so disappeared to seek other targets. The first wave of paras then dropped onto the airfield and the golf course to take control of them. Several platoons were allocated to secure the control tower, which the Simbas defended. Others struggled to clear the barricades from the tarmac – the Simbas had placed 50-gallon drums filled with oil and water on the runway, as well as scrapped cars without any wheels. Almost immediately the paras came under fire from the jungle. But by 0700hrs the runway was clear and the troops began to land. These troops included the recce elements, with their armoured jeeps and AS-24s – large motorised tricycles that could carry weapons and four men. The lead elements then headed into town.

In the city itself the Simbas had begun to round up the whites and herd them into the streets, while the planes buzzed overhead. Their command structure, if they'd ever had one, soon broke down and, while some of them wanted to use the whites as human shields, others, and in particular a horrible bastard called Major Bubu, who dressed in a monkey-skin robe, wanted them killed. The not-so-brave Christophe Gbenye had already bolted and, when his car had been grabbed by the paras near the Sabena Guest House, he wasn't in it. By 0740hrs the paras had reached the city limits and pressed towards the central hotels and prison. By 0745hrs the Simbas had opened fire on the hostages, killing 18 of them outright. And by 0750hrs the paras had reached the site of the massacre and begun killing the Simbas. The running battles raged for the next several hours.

We had been moving towards Stanleyville all through the previous night. Although we'd been hit three separate times and had taken heavy fire when crossing the Lualaba River, we'd made good time through the torrent of rain and streams of mud. By 1100hrs we reached the city, where we linked up with the paras. A bastard of a fight then ensued for the Ketele Military Camp before we fought our way through the city, allowing the Belgian paras to fall back to the airfield, which was then coming under heavy fire. Meanwhile the hostages, battered, bruised and terrified, continued to pour onto the tarmac and were given medical attention before being loaded onto C-130 transports, which lifted them out. The last Simba attack on the airfield was at 1745hrs: a mortar barrage preceded a 150-strong charge, led by their witch doctors. This time they'd chosen to charge the paras, instead of daft natives, and were consequently cut to pieces.

At the end of the day 33 hostages were killed, while over 1,600 had made it out. We later found another 28 dead on the city's Rive Gauche, which was still in rebel hands, bringing the total to 61. The Belgians lost two paras, with five wounded, while the Simba casualties were unknown but high.

After the operation the 340 paras were given a heroes' welcome in Brussels on 1 December. The idiot parts of the world reacted with demonstrations in Moscow, Nairobi and Cairo, denouncing 'American imperialism', while we, the mad, marauding bastards that we were, chased the Simbas from pillar to post for another three months.

So now back to me. Shortly before I'd boarded my flight from Johannesburg into the Congo, I was stopped by my old friend Steve – the man who'd chosen his cock over his liberty. Steve was the eldest son of one of Hugh's rare friends and was the man who'd helped me get to the UK after my subtle exit from the mission hospital. Steve was a funny guy. He was highly intelligent, softly spoken and well mannered – certainly not what you'd expect from someone who'd soon be at the heart of South Africa's torture apparatus. I nearly drafted him in for the Olof Palme job that I'll be revealing in detail later, had he not come down with septicaemia. Anyway, he told me that, in amongst all the geopolitics and sabre rattling, a multitude of personal tragedies was readily unfolding. One of which was for the Banda family.

The Bandas were somewhat unique for the time. They were from the Chewa tribe, a Bantu-speaking people of Malawi who are also located in the now-named Zambia and Zimbabwe. In any case these guys lived in Europe – France, in fact – with close ties in London. By all accounts they were

very wealthy and three of their sons had attended Eton.
They also had two daughters.

Now the story was that the youngest daughter had
managed to land herself in Stanleyville when the rebels
took over and so hadn't been seen in months. Steve said
she'd been visiting relatives, some of whom ran a supply
business to the hotels, and was last known to have been in
the European part of the city, from a telegram her father
received before she went missing. The rest of her family
was said to live in Mangobo, one of the three sites within
Stanleyville where the native Congolese lived. Her family,
then, were sick with worry and feared the worst. They placed
little hope on any impending Belgian action as, even if an
intervention took place, only the whites would be evacuated.
And besides, although she had a French passport, her papers
may well have been taken and that would have been that.
Anyway it turned out that Daddy Banda was offering a
wheelbarrow of cash for whoever could find and rescue his
missing princess. Steve had jumped at it when he'd got the
call from a security-services firm in London – but, like I
said, his wife would rather have him than another extension
on their already extended house. So if I was interested, I
could have the job.

Now succeeding in this mission would be no mean feat.
In fact, given the circumstances, it was near impossible. To
begin with I'd have to keep my mouth shut. If the others
got wind of me trying to run my own show under the radar
of the main event, I'd be shot. Secondly, if anyone else up
there found out and did some digging, they could grab her
and take the loot, and I'd still be shot. But, of course, both
of these paled into insignificance when it came to the main
problem: how the fuck was I going to fly a thousand miles,
fight for two hundred more, find an African who was either
hiding or dead and then, in the middle of a war, with no
support, essentially desert my unit and march me and her all

the way back to Johannesburg to collect my wages? I put it to Steve. He paused, then squinted and cleaned his glasses, as if trying to fathom an answer. Then, after a minute of me looking some more, he held out his hands and shrugged: 'Well, you're fucking going up there anyway, aren't you?' He had a point.

IX

BITE HARD AND STAND FIRM

If the British legacy in Africa was infrastructure, so the Belgian gift for the Congo was town planning. From the major towns to the hamlets, wherever they had an influence, so a bounty was left – for the Congolese to lose. And they did. The Kamina base was just that. Erected as a NATO foothold in Africa, the Belgians spared no expense. There were tarmacked runways, an air-training school and billets for thousands of soldiers, while beyond that lay an entire support town, with everything from cinemas to post offices. This base was as shiny as you get anywhere and a real jewel to behold – until independence, that was. In those few years the blacks had taken a chocolate and made it a shit. There was no water or power. And no sewage. The wiring was stripped, the fixtures and fittings were looted and the whole place was stinking. It was another testament to the spirit of the Congo, the sooner accepted the better.

I met Colonel Hoare on my first day there. He was no doubt an inspiring leader and a fearless man but to me there was more. He was a true mercenary, whose natural state was

in conflict. And for that I admired him – as I saw the same
thing in myself. Sure I'd come for the money – but, as I'd
later see, I'd stay for the way of life. Serving a flag has many
things to recommend it: duty, camaraderie and a grateful
public, to name just a few. But to be here for hire? What was
that about? That status did not carry honour in the minds
of others. If I lie once, then I am a liar – but only for as
long as I'm a stranger to the truth. But if I rape, then am I
forever a rapist? And if I murder, am I a murderer for life?
And does the same apply to being a mercenary? Ultimately
the answer to all of these questions is that these words are
only a label – a tag to be assigned by those who draw the
moral line. But to me, at that point, it was a privilege, a
once-in-a-lifetime chance. Like amateurs making it to the
World Cup, it was all or nothing, villains or heroes, and
all on the turn of a dice. For that one episode in history a
group whose only loyalties were to a pay cheque and their
own survival would be an orchestra on the world stage,
conducted by the Colonel, a true maestro of war.

We stood there that day getting our pep talk. He tied it in
to the greater struggle of East and West, of saving hostages
and of defending our own backyards – this part was aimed
at the Southern Africans, I figured. But I didn't care. I was
thrilled to be here and if I could save my young Chewa for
a sack full of gold as a sideline then all the better for it.

What I didn't know was what I would see in my fellow
fighters. In all they were a pretty mixed bunch. They too
had come to make money – but why they needed the cash
was more revealing. Although previous military service was
preferred, it wasn't essential. Sure there were some real heroes,
who I'll come to, but the Colonel had his work cut out to
shape us in time and weed out the shit. Surprisingly enough
that started early, when a group of ten or so asked to get
out – seemed things had looked better in the Johannesburg
brochure and they certainly hadn't expected to be shot at

or killed. Others were preoccupied with questions about contracts, which was fair enough, although we'd later learn that the Colonel himself was working at the behest of some Congolese admin body and so was in little position to answer. In all he'd wanted around 1,000 mercenaries. So far he'd got about 500 but, within a few days, that number had dropped to around 340 and, of those, most were fit for the purpose.

In any case the training was hard and the comfort was little. But, as was commonly said, any fool can suffer; it takes a soldier to make the most of it. Finally units were drawn, leaders appointed and some uniforms arrived. Now we were an army, known as 5 Commando. Well, almost. At first we had to make do with old Spanish FNs (the first 5.56-mm rifle made by the Belgian manufacturer Fabrique Nationale) – a batch of semi-automatics that were once destined for the blacks. But by the end of October the new versions came straight from Brussels – though that was too late for me and a friend of mine.

A couple of weeks before we were off, I was sitting with a group of Italians, sharing a memory or two. The Italians were agitated because we'd just heard of our plan to push north for Stanleyville, liberating the towns we encountered en route, one of which was Kindu. Now Kindu was a place that no red-blooded Roman was forgetting, as, two years previously, a UN flight had landed with its Italian crew and they were arrested by doped-up Congolese soldiers. For no good reason they were then hacked to bits with machetes, paraded around the town and subsequently feasted upon, while budding photographers captured the moment for their grandkids. The bastard in charge that day was a Colonel Pacassa, whose entire battalion of shit-bags had then deserted to the rebels before justice was ever served. Now, as you'd imagine, news from within Kindu was thin but we had heard of a scene more in keeping with a medieval crusade than a 'civilisation', as a daily ritual of torture and mutilation was played out like a spectator sport for all to see. The rebels, as I said, hated all intellectuals, as in the literate, they hated chiefs and they hated the well off, those not half-starving. And, as such, this lot were the first to be chopped by the head of torture, a 14-year-old kid.

When I heard this story, I wasn't disgusted but was strangely jealous. His daily ritual took place in front of the Lumumba monument, an icon erected in most rebel towns. This despotic teenager would run the length of the condemned, hacking at whatever he fancied: a foot, an arm, a neck or a head. The choice was his, while the crowd, his true captives, were mesmerised. Then, like the thumb up or down at the Colosseum, he'd give the order and a bullet would finish them. Or not. In fact some shots were deliberately aimed low, so as to wound and not kill. This added an epilogue to the matinee, as the men, women and children were tossed in terror to the mercy of the Lualaba River. The whites, meanwhile, around 250 or so, had been moved to a lock-up and were being held there by guards.

Anyway, on listening to this, and me fantasising about getting hold of the boy, I heard shouting and arguing coming from 40 yards away, where some of the local levies were sitting about cooking a roast. We stood up and saw there was fighting. Some mad Scotsman – only a Jock can swear like that – was trying to take on the Congo bare-handed. The dust settled and we walked over. But before we could place our bets, the show was over and the curtain was down. We began to speculate about what had just happened but, seeing the natives were well rattled, we fucked off before they tried to eat us instead. Little did I know, that would be my first proper sighting of Rod McLean – the only man I'd ever call a friend.

Two days later we were off. As misfortune would have it, the Simbas weren't waiting on us getting our shit together and so pressed on in the north, almost sinking the country.

When the good citizens of Gemena, the home town of the Congolese brass, heard the sharpening of their machetes, they demanded action. Hoare, at their behest, threw together 40 men under the command of 2nd Lieutenant Gary Wilson and flung us up there to plug the gap. Called 51 Commando, we were a collection of the well trained and the dispensable, and for that we arrived with nothing, some of us even standing in the clothes we'd come in. But that all changed at Ndjili thanks to the CIA – another story – and soon we were off, charging through the jungle to Lisala, determined to take the country from one set of blacks and hand it back to another.

After some thought our young lieutenant, Gary Wilson, soon decided it better to keep the pressure on them rather than sitting about waiting. It paid off, as, at the head of the useless ANC troops, we thrashed the arse out of the Lisala garrison and 1,000 Simba warriors had fled, leaving 160 to perish. And that's when the real fun began.

Some of the Southern African guys were moaning. It seemed to hit them that all they'd done was swap one African country, where the blacks knew their place, for another, where they didn't. And so they began to express that with bullets. I could see their point but it wasn't a worry to me. The longer I was spending in country, the more I was thinking about my African 'princess', as in our midst were all the skills necessary to at least have a shot at the impossible. The thing was that the main thrust into Stanleyville was coming from 5 Commando to the south, with Hoare at the head, fighting for each town. I was worried that I'd miss Stanleyville altogether and end up spending my time chasing shadows up north in the jungle. Oh, and the fucking jungle . . .

See this place was cruel enough even without war. It was stagnant swamps, red clay dust, man-grabbing vines, bamboo thickets and 10-ft adrenalin grass. It was unbearable heat with constant humidity, while its two seasons, roasting and dry or roasting and wet, were interchangeable, like annoying twins with different clothes on. It was home to rats, bats and gnats, leeches, lizards and spiders, the malaria mosquito and the tsetse fly, the bamboo viper, bush viper, baboon viper, burrowing viper, saw-scaled viper, rhinoceros viper, river jack, green mamba, puff adder, horned puff adder, cobras, pythons and a multitude of other constrictors that were so big they'd surely had a sprinkling of gamma rays on top of their breakfast. And then there were the diseases: malaria, black vomit/yellow fever, dengue fever, hep A, hep B, rabies, cholera, dysentery, typhoid, pneumonia, tuberculosis, leprosy and Ebola. And all that before Aids. In all, this was the one place to be shoulder deep in shit and still have the dirt kicked in your eyes. But I loved it.

By the time we were fully acclimatised, we were actively patrolling outside the city, hoping to shove the rebels back towards Bumba, a city further west along the River Congo. But after a string of ambushes and us taking casualties, a more aggressive plan was needed. The young lieutenant wanted us to break out of the pocket we'd created and smack head on into Bumba on the Bumba–Aketi axis. Hoare, after mulling it over, gave him the go ahead and so it was decided that we'd take a village en route as a staging point. And we were put on a 12-hour notice to move.

I remember that later that night we were sitting about readying our kit. I was sharing a stolen bottle of Belgian spirits with a man – I'll call him J.D. – who was once in the Black Watch but had fallen out of favour after an alleged rape back home. He tried for the French Foreign Legion but wasn't taken – that should say it all, especially given that the guy was fearless. Anyway, next thing another boy from 51 Commando came over and asked if we'd heard about what was happening in one of the hotels. Seemed that one of the Simba leadership had been captured with his family. J.D. said he had, which surprised me, given that he hadn't mentioned it. He said the Simba had stayed because his kids were sick, or his wife and kids, or something like that. It all seemed a bit off to me. I mean who brings their family to war, for fuck's sake? So, after finishing the bottle and making my excuses, I went for a wander to see for myself.

The hotel was less than a hundred yards from our position and was every bit the picture postcard, with its whitewashed walls and well-maintained roof tiles. It must have been white-owned before the Simbas took over. I got to the door but stood aside as one of our boys bundled out, soon followed by a high-ranking ANC officer. They looked pissed off and walked like they had somewhere to go. I could hear shouting, then screaming and then the thud of someone being hit. I passed through the reception area. It seemed like a family home that had been deserted in a hurry. The guest book was still open but the clocks were all stopped. Behind the desk and above a board where the door keys hung was a calendar, still open on the day that the Simbas arrived. I walked past the dirty walls. The pictures were smashed and now lay amongst the broken glass, which crunched like snow beneath me. A cool breeze blew through the kicked-open shutters and across my skin, which was damp from a day of sweating, sending cold shivers down my spine. Then I heard screams and more thuds. I looked up at the ceiling and saw mists of plaster falling to the thumping beats and covering the furniture like a layer of icing sugar. I made for the stairway. It seemed inviting. All up the walls ran pictures of scenic Belgium, ascending in line with the steps, while a portrait of the owner hung facing the gable end. I looked at it. It had been knocked down, smashed and stood on but someone had hung it back up, damaged as it was. The owner was back – at least in spirit.

I made it up to the landing, where a half-opened door

emanating light seemed to beckon me in. So with a steadied breath I pushed it open. And I was there. It seemed odd at first but what had evidently been a bedroom was now stripped of furniture, while sitting in the centre was a black man strapped down, while one of our lot – I'll call him A.B. – was beating him senseless.

'Tell me, you bastard!' And smash, A.B. back-handed him across the jaw, before an ANC boy who I'll call Benoit spraffed the translation out to him in Swahili. I took a step in and they looked at me. But, though I'd discovered them, it wasn't a private event.

'This bastard can save us trouble!' A.B. said to me. He wasn't an officer but was probably more respected. I looked at the prisoner. He looked like a boxer after 30 rounds of sparring. His eyes were mashed and his jaw was broken, while his nose, now even flatter than nature intended, was a bloody dimple that poured when touched.

'Who is he?' I asked.

'He's a collaborator,' said A.B., turning round with a fist clenched.

'A collaborator?' I said, before whack, he smacked him again, causing his head to drop, like he'd been shot while tied to a post.

'Oh, fuck it!' he said, now realising he'd knocked him out cold. 'Yes, he was collaborating with the Simba. He was pointed out to us by some of the locals as being responsible for gathering the names for execution. He'd give the rebels a list each day, they'd round them up and then . . . you know.' He signalled a throat-cutting by drawing his thumb across his throat.

'So what does he know?' I asked.

'What does he know?' A.B. echoed, wiping his bloody hands on a smock jacket from the corner. 'Bastard knows the lot: their lines, trails, supply routes, garrison strength at Bumba. Fuck: even which villages are sympathetic on the way.'

I looked at him as I lit a smoke. 'So he's from here, from Lisala?'

'Born and bred. His wife and kids are in the next room. Oh, and he's smart. I mean he was a bookkeeper or something, right?' he said, turning to the ANC translator for a nod. None came. 'Anyway, I'm telling you, Athol, this guy's a fucking gem. But he's a stubborn bastard. Look, I've thrashed fuck out of him – and nothing.' I looked at the near-dead man. He was buckled over, battered and bruised. He'd no doubt had a hiding before the locals had handed him over for another one. I looked under his chair; it sat amid a pool of urine that extended out like an ever-filling moat. He was finished.

Now I could say that me getting involved stemmed from a need to further our cause. But I'd be lying. Even if it did, it would soon be assigned to the backstage. 'No wonder he's not talking,' I said to A.B. 'You've knocked fuck out of him. He doesn't know what decade he's in. Have you never had a beating? If you want him to talk, it's got to be done right.'

A.B. looked at me and shook his head. 'What are you going to do? Shag him for it?' He sniggered, before saying, 'Whatever. I'm done. He's all yours.' And at that he shook off his jacket, wiped the blood into smeared streaks and took off, leaving myself, my subject and my ever-eager translator to our business.

'Benoit, get me a bucket of water,' I said, miming the action. 'Oh, and wait: a length of rope.' He looked at me. 'Oh, fuck, eh, a length, a length of rope. A *longueur de corde!*'

His face lit up. '*Oui, monsieur.*' And he left. That was the limit of my French.

I didn't know exactly what I was going to do but I knew the area I wanted to play in. When I'd been at the mission, I had continued to torture the cats. I did this right up until I left – some two months after my killing. My methods would get ever more adventurous, technical and, of course, cruel, as I'd spend hours thinking about it yet a fraction of the time in the execution. I knew that I had to keep them alive at all costs, and so I became fascinated with the notion of one cat inadvertently hurting the other in an attempt to save its own skin. Of all, I enjoyed these experiments the most. And of all these experiments one in particular stood out.

Down by the clinic there was a small workshop. One lunch time I took a plank of wood, screwed in two small bed wheels a yard apart and threaded a string through them, creating a simple pulley system. Back in the basement I'd place the plank, wheels down, across two chairs, tie one end of the string in a slip knot around one of the cat's necks and tie the other end in a simple knot around the second one's neck. Now what was important was that the rope was too short for both cats to sit comfortably but not so short that they were instantly being hung. In fact the length was such that each cat could only stand on its hind legs in a stressed position. I watched how the noosed one would never pull, as whatever movement it made would only tighten the cord. But the knotted cat would jump and tumble before finally figuring out that it could pull down and away to alleviate its pain. And in doing so it would slowly strangle the other. At first I would swap each role around. But I found that the male, with his claws, was stronger and could easily lift the weight of the ginger one. I loved the way that it would then fight, its white paws kicking for ground but finding only air, until its eyes would roll back and, with a few final kicks, it would slowly go limp. I became an expert in knowing at what point to stop and how to resuscitate a cat. One Sunday when the Willies were away preaching 'the word', I hung the ginger cat five times and on the fifth had to pour whisky down its throat in order to bring it back. The problem for me, though, was that, as calming as this was, I had to invest the animals with a conscience to get the most benefit out of their torture. I had to pretend that, while one cat strangled the other, it knew what it was doing in order to save its own neck. But, of course, it didn't. How could it?

Five minutes later Benoit walked through the door to see that I'd already assembled the subject's wife and three children in front of him. Thankfully they were already tied up and so easy to manhandle. When I threw the water in his face and he shot back to life, instead of an evil white man he saw a lovely black woman and some beautiful children. Now I had his attention. His first child was a boy of ten and his second a boy just younger, while his third was a daughter. She was probably around three years old.

With little thought I got things started by throwing the rope around the rafters and making a noose. Then I placed it firmly around the middle child's neck, before sitting him on his older brother's shoulders. Benoit, who seemed to get the idea, now warmed to his new handler and pulled out the slack. Quite simply the middle kid's life depended on his brother's ability to stay standing up. I bent down and glared straight into my subject's eyes. He was awake now – no doubt! He made to say something but I stopped him. I looked up at my assistant and smiled. 'Not yet,' I said to my dark friend, before turning back to my victim to place my finger across his pulped, shut lips to shush him. He'd say anything at that point. I knew that.

After a minute I stood up and walked around my macabre totem pole, once, then twice, then three times and each time the sobs increased as they expected worse but hoped for the best. Then I removed my buckled belt and, with a venom that surged in me like a drug, I began whipping. Whack! Whack! I hit the boy's legs time and time again: on the thighs, on the knees, on his hips and his ankles. And he took it. With his hands tied behind his back and with his brother crying and pissing down his neck, he stood there like a statue and suffered. Soon his mother screamed. His father raged and Benoit laughed. But while the two heads cried hysterically there was only ever going to be one outcome. Finally he went, and as he crashed to the ground, his battered legs scrambling, his brother swung and choked from one side to the next, until his eyes went blank and his face became bloated. He took a minute to be still but a half-hour to die. His mother was beaten down every time she tried to help him and his brother's legs were ruined. Benoit ended up having to pull down on the swinging child, eventually breaking his neck.

'I want to know where the leaders are. And I particularly want to know about the *Jeunesse*, the youth gangs,' Benoit translated, I think. Then, without prompting, he began unfolding a mud-coloured map from his top-left pocket. He held it up but I couldn't have cared less. It could have been Blackbeard's treasure map and I wouldn't have cared. Instead I bent down and grabbed the older boy's arm. 'Stand, you fuck!' I snapped. 'Stand!' And he did. His knees were like footballs, his legs a dark purple, but he made it to his feet. Then I turned round and took hold of his sister, like I was hauling an animal to the slaughter. At my word Benoit cut down the dead boy, his corpse crashing to the floor, where he lay bent double and limp. Now, with the same length of rope, I tied a tight knot around the three year old's ankle and, like a piece of meat, strung her up to the height of the ceiling. I looked at my subject and saw him writhing. Benoit held up the map again like he was justifying my actions but dropped it slowly when he saw my disinterest. Now even he was trying to figure me out as I suspended the child 14 ft high, ignoring her piercing screams. She managed to work her tiny hands free and, like a spider in a sink, thrashed her limbs from side to side but couldn't catch anything. She was completely helpless. So, with everyone's attention and the rope in my right hand, I walked over to her mother, who was still sat on the floor with her hands tied up, and shoved it into her mouth. 'Bite tight, my dear,' I said. 'You don't want to let go!' And at that I backed off.

Her eyes were livid as she clenched and wrestled a weight that wouldn't stop shifting. I watched the seconds become minutes, then the blood pour from her lips as they were slowly forced apart, before finally the white chips that came springing one after the other from her mouth as her teeth began to fail. But she wouldn't let go. She frothed, she foamed, she screamed and fretted and cursed me with her flaming eyes before her mouth gave way and her little girl went crashing. The noise was nauseating and you could almost see the sound. Her head, her neck and back were all crushed as she found herself lying, her legs twitching and her voice box groaning, until she finally went with a death rattle. Now she was silent, while the room was in chaos.

The screams were like audible wallpaper and, as I sat basking, Benoit once again feigned a military intention and shoved the map to his face. This time the subject, realising the limitations on his time, began spouting in Swahili, on and on and on, until more than a minute passed before he stopped to breathe. Benoit, then hastily taking a pen from the same pocket, began scribbling words, marking lines and circling names. But I still couldn't have cared less. Benoit looked at me like we'd done it. But I hadn't even started. I was deep in thought over my next ruse when I heard boots stumbling through the door below us, followed by a load of blacks shouting and arguing like they'd just been stung out of money. They had.

Leaving the happy family where they were, my trusty sidekick and I bolted down to see an ANC man lying bleeding on a table while five others stood shouting and not one paying him attention. So we walked right through this little scene and out, Benoit telling me that they'd been arguing over betting and one had stabbed the other.

Anyway, two minutes later and we were standing in front of the powers that be, witnessing the formation of yet another new assault plan, this one based on our debriefings, his in the local language to the chief native and mine in English to the chief white. They never did ask how we'd got the information, only if we were sure it was true. We were.

When I got back to the boys, I didn't know whether to hide my face or make a point of it. In any case I shouldn't have worried. Nobody knew what I'd been up to and if they had, only a few would have bothered to act. Besides we were off the next day, and the prospect of jungle life without a town to haul up in was no doubt all-consuming. I looked for a perch and found one next to J.D. He hardly looked at me and was in the midst of sawing down an American M14, while the rest of them sat like a gang of Cub Scouts, watching and learning. Apparently, as we heard, when an M14 is fired on semi-automatic using certain trigger manipulations, it sounds exactly like a 50-calibre machine gun. And in dense jungle, no soldier – not even a trained NATO officer – can tell the difference. 'This is effective,' announced J.D., in his few words, 'because it creates confusion. Fifties are only encountered in large units and even then are usually track or jeep mounted. To hear one in a mountainous jungle would put the shits up anyone, making them call for a witch doctor, break for a brew or even dig a deep hole to shit in.'

As interesting as that was, I began foraging for the last of the bottle but found it empty. So, on searching, I found another, half-full, sitting by a sandbag that was filled with maize. I went for it but a hand shot down and grabbed my wrist. It was J.D. I went to pull away but, with a machine's strength, he held me firm, glared in my eyes and smiled through an unshaven grin. There's something consoling about seeing yourself in another man. It's reassuring to think you're not the only person to have turned out that way. As J.D. looked at me, I could tell he knew what I'd been up to. So he put down his rifle and reached for a mess tin. He poured less than half into it and gave me the bottle. He swigged it down and didn't say a word. Then he got up, walked in the direction of the hotel and disappeared. A minute later I heard three shots from a 50 cal., which rattled the night and for a moment stopped us all cold. It would take me the longest to warm back up – though I soon slept where I'd stood.

I get this dream sometimes and it's paralysing. I'm in a bedroom. I guess it's my own but I can never recognise it. I take the same route up the stairs, over the landing and into the room, which is small but L-shaped. I turn left and there's a window, and the window overlooks a garden that is constantly changing. On the windowsill sits a figurine. It's plastic, about 7 in. tall, and is of Henry VIII – the old English king – and he's on a plinth that doubles as a money bank for putting your coppers in. Every time I walk into the room, I feel the atmosphere change. It gets heavy, then heavier, and by the time I see the garden the figure has always started smiling. And then it happens. At that moment the air becomes like water, which forces me down and spins me around, all out of control. And a noise. It's so disturbing that I scream. I scream until my lungs hurt but I'm powerless and I know it, and that's when it comes. I call it the blue ghost. I've dreamt it so many times but I've never come to know it, though it's always the same. The ghost comes from the air and is part of the atmosphere, the pressure – it isn't separate to the room. So the room then is the ghost and just waits to reveal its face. But why do I walk in every time? Is it to see the garden? To see the face? I just can't seem to stop myself. Even though I know what terror lies within, I am as powerless to fight against entering as against the ghost itself.

In Stockholm in 1986 nobody would wake me from this dream but here in the Congo I was jolted from my sleep by A.B. He was walking around kicking us up, as the blood-red sun made its first appearance of the day. J.D. was already awake, filing down and blowing the rough edges from his bushcraft muzzle. A.B. had saved me from the blue ghost but J.D. would soon take me back.

A.B. explained the deal. He said they had information about one of the Simba's main men. I say men – the guy was the head of the *Jeunesse* and so probably 13 or 14 at most. Anyway, they knew where he was and it was a village en route to Bumba. Now these guys were bastards and spent their days chewing a bush root called *dawa*, and, like a Glaswegian on Buckfast, it was not a favourable combination to deal with. I looked at J.D. but he seemed in another world. He just stood there, looking without seeing, and when I said something, something stupid to get his attention, he just grinned again and looked right through me. It seems easy with hindsight to suggest that he knew something about that day or about that village before we set off. I mean, Christ, there have been times when I've been convinced that something was going to happen. But, like most people, for every hundred times you've got a feeling about something, ninety-nine of them are nothing. But back then I really think he knew.

Back on the move the jungle was as unforgiving as it ever was. We slid, sweated, got stuck and got stung, and before long almost forgot our purpose, as we fought our way along a path of dense foliage that reluctantly yielded to our blades. The air was heavy and completely humid, and, like a sequence of mini déjà vus, my blue-ghost dream would flash before me, at least as a feeling if not through a vision. Two hours later we were separated into three columns and each column tasked with a different route, to rendezvous later that night before hitting the village first thing. At that I stopped to drink and to mop my porous brow with an already saturated hand towel. I knew where I was and perhaps what lay ahead of me but felt powerless to stop. And I entered.

X

THE SOUP'S OFF

The heavens opened up on the way to our rendezvous. By the time the downpour's fury was spent, its damage was done. A creek bed that we were meant to cross had become a surging, impassable river. We were forced to change our route and then dig in for the night, abandoning our plans for the link-up and the village in the morning. During my nightwatch the sound of the jungle's creatures slithering, crawling, padding, eating – normally a constant backdrop in the hours of darkness – suddenly stopped. All I could hear were the raindrops filtering through the leaves above me. I was relieved by Rod McLean, who pulled the 0400hrs to 0600hrs watch. He'd hardly had any sleep beforehand, between the constant rain and the leeches crawling up his legs. As dawn broke, an overcast sky was revealed, with a ceiling so low you could touch it and a fog just waiting to drop. As we readied the troops, A.B. sent three of us out on a recce. We came back in one piece but saw how close we'd been to an ambush. Seems the Simbas had fucked off during the night, not wanting to give away their position with their muzzle flashes. We set out and advanced in formation through their abandoned man trap. Our radio was fucked – a result of the previous contact – which gave us a new worry: being shot by the column behind us as we cleared through the undergrowth. A.B. decided on a white-faced point for our squad. He decided on Rod. I laughed. Rod was a lion, no doubt, but he was having trouble adjusting – letting go and embracing his new self: Rod the mercenary. Still, fate would soon change that.

As he took the front, the fog came down. The temperature dropped and the jungle was quiet. With every step we took, my legs got heavier. My dream visions were now a taste of dread in my mouth and for no special reason my heart began racing. Soon I felt death upon us but was powerless to fight it. I fixed on Rod, a shape in the distance making one sure step after another, crouching, alert and full of aggression. He was 30 yards in front. I looked around, I looked forward again and he was gone, swallowed by the mist. I paused and within that breath made another ten yards before the jungle revealed its secret. A white man was slumped against a tree. Rod approached to within five yards and looked straight into his eyes. He was dead. He didn't check his pulse. He said he didn't need to: the dead look dead. All around our feet were scatterings of spent .45 Automatic Colt Pistol (APC) and Tupeolov 9 mm casings (the Tupeolov was a Russian-made pistol). The fighting here had been close. I walked on further but already knew where I was.

The fog rose from the lush green ground and lingered all around us. Moving one way, then the next, it swirled past us, chilling our necks, as if the jungle was breathing – perhaps even waiting? And as the atmosphere began to crush me, we – the willingly condemned – walked into the arena. To the thousands of eyes upon us the matinee show had begun. At first I wondered why there were so many slabs on the ground – there's no symmetry in nature and these seemed to be designed. I took one step, then two, then in the clearing I saw Rod drop to his knees and glance back. He stared at me. They were bodies – and they were ours, our first column. Scattered like kindling, they festered and stank, while their faces, unrecognisable, left us in no doubt of their fate. The hunters had been hungry and so had sought out their prey. Their hearts were gone; their kidneys taken.

The others moaned and fucked about, then fell around like Victorian women. But I knew where we were and could feel my blue ghost upon me. We stripped the dead for bounty but they had stripped us for 'muti'. Or that's what A.B. was saying when he first saw them, but I wasn't so sure.

Muti killing isn't about making a sacrifice to any god but about harvesting body parts for bush medicine, meant to strengthen the 'persona' of the backwards bastard who takes it, enabling him to excel in money, power or war. When a victim is identified – kids are a favourite – they're either 'bought' or abducted, taken to an isolated place and mutilated while conscious, as their screams of agony make the medicine more potent. Body parts excised mostly include soft tissue like the lips, scrotum, labia, eyelids or ears and are then mixed with plants. This, though, was an altogether different animal.

A few of the boys were now openly vomiting, while another was weeping and mumbling about God. So I kept on walking, from one body to the next, carefully negotiating the many parts that were stripped clean and down to the bone.

Then I heard: 'Bastards! Evil fucking bastards!' And I shot over to where Rod was standing. It was J.D. He was tied to a tree and, by the looks of it, had been eaten alive. His flesh was ripped and covered in a frenzy of bite marks. All that remained was a macabre mask of white flesh around his eyes. We stood there stunned. Except Rod – he was shouting and snarling and wanted to go after them. So I stopped him. We would, but in time.

When the shock subsided, they began to bury our dead. And so, with them, I went through the motions but, like a priest in a brothel, my condemnation was paper thin. This work was done by kids. I knew that much. Probably the *Jeunesse*. As a strategy of war magic's got a piss-poor record of enhancing success. But then, and still now, scores of young natives line up to answer the witch doctor's call – 'magic warriors needed!' The Congo's rife with the dangers of the faithful. Those believing they can affect a battle with paranormal powers are in no shortage. To the Southern Africans amongst us this came as little surprise, although we were a bit side-swiped by its intensity. But to your average white boy from Europe, this was the stuff of nightmare and legend.

Dressed in monkey skins and not much else, these teenage fucks hailed from a primitive society rooted in animism and witchcraft. The child soldiers amongst them genuinely believed they were immune from death because of their magical ability to repel bullets after being anointed with ampoules of protective water by their witch doctors! They even figured that heavy weapons, like mortar shells and grenades, would bounce right off them.

And how was this done? Because the magic men of the village assured the stupid bastards that all projectiles would turn into water, which is why they chanted '*Mai-Mai!*' (Swahili for powerful water) when they went into battle. In fact we'd later learn that such was their belief in the sacred water's protection that they'd march into battle adorned with water-related objects, like shower hoses – even fucking drain plugs. And while we readied our dead, we found all sorts of other things, like crowns made from vines, which were worn to make them invisible. Despite that, a contact head-on with this lot was usually favourable: bullets had a habit of taking their heads off and their emphatic belief led them to charge open ground like it was Waterloo. And what were the excuses given to the living by the witches for all the deaths? That the dead coons in the monkey suits had failed to observe the necessary rituals, or that they were killed accidentally, as friendly *Mai-Mai* bullets can't be stopped by the same magic.

That said, the *Mai-Mai*-shouting Simba warriors were ideal recruits for the charismatic shit-stokers of the Congo. The kids were stupid, unworldly and entirely irrational. They were ritual cannibals and merciless killers who were usually singing and dancing when they engaged their enemies, secured by their magical protection. But as we stood, the graves dug, our dead buried, I figured that, irrational or not, fear and confidence must play as much of a role as bullets and brawn – a lesson I'd carry for the rest of my life.

It didn't take long for A.B. to give us a heads up. He was a South African ex-Nazi straight from the Third Reich and so had washed more brains off his boots than an Italian butcher. By the time the third section moved in on us, the shock was rapidly turning to rage – especially when our lot recollected what had happened to J.D. His death was a turning point for many of the lads. There was no doubt that the war was real: we'd fought; we'd died; we'd fought again. But with characters like J.D. and A.B. leading from the front and standing tall when the rest were eating dirt, we all felt invincible. They were our magic-water bottles. And, unlike witch doctors, they worked.

Later that night we were off, pushing towards the unnamed village. If before we'd assumed that it was a bastion to the *Jeunesse*, then by now we were convinced. After snaking along our course all night, we stopped for the last two hours of darkness and made ourselves ready. A.B. was now using the third section's radio and information was being barked back and forth. He then plotted our position on a terrain map that would have confused a cartographer. Finally he sent out a recce, which came back in record time to say that all was quiet but that they had seen a couple of armed kids floating about near the outhouses. Within half an hour, then, we were lined up with the rising sun and made ready to advance.

As we lay face down in the grass, where the thick cover met the clearing, our pulses were racing. All along the line you could hear the sporadic sounds of vomit, either through nerves or the onset of malaria – or both. I looked to my right and saw an ANC face. I recognised him, not by name, but after what I'd seen him do the day before. It seemed that the African men had their J.D.s as well.

Then I heard a splutter and raised my head over a clump of grass to my left. The splutterer was a guy I'll call Pat Simmons. He made me laugh because he'd only signed up after having a row with his bird back home in Pretoria. He'd said one thing, she'd said another, then, as a threat, he shouted that he was off to be a fighter. She said, 'Go!' He hadn't expected that. Anyway, a week later he was sat on the Johannesburg tarmac in his DC-4, half-expecting his bird to come racing down the runway and beg him to stay. But she didn't. So a week after that he was paddling up Lake Tanganyika on Operation Watch Chain – a story so fucking insane that it put the 'Mad' in Colonel 'Mad' Mike Hoare's name. Now he was next to me and I could tell that he'd gone. I mean he came out as a boy, grew into a man, but now – in amongst this madness – he'd become an animal, addicted to a drug that few knew existed. I went to say something but saw him wiping his face down – probably tears. He was lucky; he could blame someone for making him this way. And, right or wrong, I knew he would. 'Hey, Pat!' I whispered over when I saw he'd finished. He locked his FN before looking back but it took him a second to recognise me. That was common. 'You ready?'

I said, nodding. There was a pause. But before he could open his mouth, the whole damn line opened up. 'Fuck!' I shouted, scrambling to ready my rifle. 'I thought he'd have at least whistled.'

Crack, crack, followed by three heavy thuds that came closer rather than heading away. I tried to see a target but, between the dirt, dust and debris, what was previously a village had become a moving wind, swirling away like a brown tornado. So I fired twice, then jumped to my feet and headed on in. '*Mai-Mai!*' I heard the bastards cry – voices in a dust storm. But no sooner had their first water boy been smashed than they shat it and tried to bolt, and instead of the jungle they careered straight into our ANC line, which was flanking an irrigation channel to the west. Soon the dust settled but the screaming kept up. And while villagers darted from one spot to the next, so the turkey shoot began. The rifles rattled and bayonets were blooded – only to be answered by sporadic pops and the blind-faith cry of '*Mai-Mai*'. But it couldn't last. And so no sooner had it started than A.B. blew his whistle and the game was over. 'Ceasefire! Ceasefire!' he screamed, each time getting louder until his 'Fucking stop!' was finally obeyed. And at that came an unholy calm as the storm passed over, leaving us with the eerie laments of their distant wounded.

A.B., now seeing that the village was routed, began to organise things. And so, slinging his FN over his shoulder, he pulled off his cap and mopped down his brow. We all focused in, sweating, pulsing and out of breath. 'Right!' he said. But bang! Before he could start, his head exploded like a hammered-down watermelon and A.B., the father of us all and the Third Reich survivor, was gone, covering Pat from head to toe in his brains. In shock we scattered like rats from a cat and soon found a kid in a doorway, brandishing an old Mauser rifle. It was an ANC boy who shot this kid, followed by another one who then emptied his clip after booting him so hard that it vocalised the air left in his lungs. And that was that.

It's difficult to say how much A.B.'s death contributed to what then happened. The guys were already in a bad way. What they'd seen the night before was unimaginable. And the bodies weren't random: they were our friends, perhaps something stronger than that. In any case it wasn't down to us. The ANC were out for revenge and, whether or not it was these *Jeunesse* who did it, they'd pay for it. And so the killing began.

There's a notion in Africa that the cure can be worse than the disease. And while some of the ANC boys rounded up the *Jeunesse* who were still alive, others, directed by a few of our lot, began cleansing the village. The first man to die was stabbed in the back with a bayonet. His silent panic near set off a frenzy, as he dropped to the floor and spent his last pulses of life grasping in desperation at Pat's trouser leg. Pat did nothing.

Then an older man was picked up, thrown down a well and a grenade lobbed in after him, which fragged his wife as she leaned in crying. Ten yards behind me a group of 20 older women who had gathered in a circle were all shot in the head and left there to rot. In a small square at the top end the separations intensified. To begin with it was the men of fighting age from the rest, as intended by A.B., but now groups of women were being singled out and led off.

From the western side they rounded up a mixed group of 50 or so by a ditch. I saw Robby Van Heusen, a South African, call Rod and send him and four ANC boys over to them, before being called away himself by Pat. Rod, now standing there, looked at his condemned down the barrel of his gun but did nothing. Five minutes later an irate Van Heusen was back. 'Haven't you got rid of them yet?' I heard him shouting. 'I want them dead. Fucking waste them!' The ANC boys began firing into the group from close range, making a bloody mincemeat out of their limbs, torsos and heads. I saw a woman stand up and bolt with a kid under her arms. I could have thrown her further than the ground she made, as the unforgiving bullets ripped her to shreds. She hit the dirt, spilling her babe like a knocked-on rugby ball. When the wall of noise stopped, a two-year-old girl, miraculously still alive, ran from the ditch like a startled rabbit but Van Heusen simply picked her up, threw her back in and shot her. Then Rod raised his rifle to shoot him. But I yelled him over and told Van Heusen to get fucked. Rod's morality was useful to me and I'd rather he died helping me save my princess in Stanleyville than for killing that prick. Besides, I'd hoped to slaughter Van Heusen at some point myself.

Five minutes later I strapped my weapon over my back and began wandering about. I walked one way, then another, but in every direction lay something I wanted to be a part of. Everywhere women were being raped and their husbands tortured. While they were forced to watch their wives, and fathers forced to watch their daughters, I realised that these rapes were less about aggression and more about destroying these people's spirit, stamping out their souls.

In the square the remaining group of about 50 or so were in the hands of the ANC. These were the *Jeunesse*, the worst of the worst. The whites were now drinking a jungle juice that strips copper with their new Congolese soulmates. They jeered, they toasted, they egged each other on. And while their orgy of sadism developed, so did their ingenuity – each trying to compete in a tit-for-tat game of brutality.

Meanwhile the 50 children and teenagers were stood to attention in lines. As the hours went on, the kids began to drop. The ANC had told them that if they fell over, they'd be brought to the front and beaten to death. Which they were. But soon the game changed when a large oil drum was brought to the front, filled with water and boiled over a log fire.

Straight away two of the kids bolted but were caught by the drunken ANC and thumped about until they lay down slumped. They bled and cried but weren't killed. Ten minutes later one of the ANC soldiers walked the ranks like he was inspecting the troops. At each kid he would stand there staring, while they, knowing full well what was coming, dared not look or breathe and, hanging their heads, hoped to be passed by. Towards the end of the third rank I saw a scuffle and then heard screaming as he parted the first two rows and dragged a boy over, near wrenching his arm off. He was their man. In fact he was more than that: he was their leader, and was no more than 14 years old. I heard cheering amongst the ANC. I thought it was just part of their fun but I'd learn within the minute that they'd been after this guy since Lisala had fallen. Seemed I had done something right after all in getting us to this forsaken place. So, pleased with myself, I went from being a spectator in the gods to having a ringside seat. A moment later I could feel the heat of the fire on my face and its sweet smoke stirring the hairs in my nostrils as the screaming youth was dumped down next to the pot like a chicken for killing. The chief man kicked down on him, then spat, before taking a drink from a broken clay pot. He turned to the rest of the *Jeunesse* and said a few words in Swahili. They all pointed. They pointed at some other young guy up front, who again tried for the jungle but was caught, kicking and screaming, before being hauled over and flung down too. I lit a smoke.

There's no doubt that there's a bad place in every man's heart, which few people ever reconcile. And even though we bury it, reshape or relabel it, that dark stone is always lurking. Some call it curiosity. But it's not. It's our reaction to modern life keeping us removed from death and the unpalatable. Rubbernecking a car wreck, watching a fight or getting your sales up when tragedy falls: from the small to the large it's all shades of the same black and in it we take pleasure.

No sooner had it become clear what was happening than some of the whites who'd been otherwise busy dropped their entertainment and began to walk over to the show. Just then two ANC boys came to the front and, on the chief man's orders, they stripped the first boy of his monkey skins and held him out naked. The moment was heavy – I'd been here before. I tried to think about what he was feeling, to get inside his brain and, for even a moment, share that experience. They bound his feet and hands, then held him up, one man supporting his arms, one taking his feet. The drum was huge, more of a cauldron, and the water, boiling furiously, spurted and steamed above the rim with a captivating anger. Two steps to the side and they were holding the squirming child above it. They looked at the chief man; he looked at the assemblage, then he nodded down. They began to lower the boy slowly but he twisted and kicked so much that the man holding his feet lost his grip, plunging him into the scalding water up to his waist, the spillage hissing like doused coals in a sauna. But still he wriggled and turned, and now, like a sport fisherman wrestling in a marlin, the man at the top fought to keep the boy's head above water. There was a process to be seen to and death would come as his blessing. His pain, though, was theirs to enjoy.

Soon his scream was a gurgle as he twitched uncontrollably before his head flopped back and he began to lose consciousness. When he did, he sank under and disappeared like a sinking battleship. The system can only handle so much shock but he still lived a damn sight longer than I'd expected. Now there was a silence. But through it drifted the sombre tears of the second boy. He was also bound and lay in the dirt, sobbing with an acceptance that the first boy never knew. What can someone with nothing offer a man with everything for the gift of his life? Two minutes later the chief man took a long pole that was used for grinding maize and began prodding, almost stirring, the broth beneath him. Then he summoned his two helpers, who fished the boy out and held him high. Fuck me, what a sight! He was almost stripped bare and was shrivelled like a fig. They threw him with contempt towards the second boy, almost landing him on top of him. Instead he finished up next to him and they lay side by side, still bound, like two lovers in bed exchanging glances.

I heard laughing and turned around. I expected to see a gallery of white guys, all standing about, eating their popcorn. But they'd gone – well, apart from a few like-minded individuals. For the others, it seemed rape and pillage: yes; horrific acts of brutality: not so much. But that was the whites. The laughter was coming from the big black guy who I'd been lying next to some hours before. We'll call him Cedric. He'd been brought up an orphan by Belgian missionaries near Yakoma, just north of Lisala. He was a bright guy and surprisingly friendly. But as the black version of J.D. – a compliment – he was a real fucking animal. Big chief man called him over to talk, then argue, and while they went at it about something no one could understand, I decided to get myself a drink. Two minutes later I was back and, a minute after that, big chief man shoved Cedric, who stumbled back and tripped over the fig boy, next to his writhing lover. He jumped back up, heard everyone laughing and, with little self-control, pulled his bayonet and ran it through chief man, right through his belly. He stopped, withdrew and took a step back. Big chief man, his face in shock, put his hand to his gut and fumbled with his camos, before holding them up to see his own blood. But Cedric was ruthless. At that sight he darted at him like a shark to blood and stabbed him time and time again until the two dark warriors were down on the ground rolling about on top of the kids. Nobody got involved. Nobody dared.

Cedric stood up and wiped himself down. He looked round for a reaction but none came. I looked at his soldiers, to see them looking at dirt. Cedric smiled, nodded his head, then picked up the old chief man's hat and placed it firmly on his own head. He was the new chief in town and everyone cheered him.

In the space of these minutes I'd just seen a coup – African style. Cedric now wasted no time. Whereas chief man before was slow and deliberate, Cedric was an impulsive brute. He looked down and near stood on the fig to take hold of the live boy. Then, with little effort, he picked him up and dunked him head first into the drum and walked off without looking back. I watched the legs dance and the feet twitch but within a few seconds they stopped. They would stay there until the fire burned itself out and the water went cold. At that I decided I'd spent enough time with the blacks so I wandered off. By this time an air of militarism had descended. Some of the guys had organised sentries, while others set about contacting Kamina. But I did my own thing.

Now there are, of course, certain things that a man can reflect on: impulses that came over him, some bad, some good and some terrible. Of these some are befitting of print while others, when told by the perpetrator, are not. So, as for what I did next, I think it better to leave the details unwritten here. But there are some things I can say. I remember once, while at the mission hospital in Rhodesia, I saw a kudu antelope being strung up. One of the local farmers had shot it to make biltong but had had to leave for the UK at very short notice and so, rather than leaving it to rot, had given it to the Willies, who then gave it to the staff.

The orphanage cook hung it up by its hind legs in the square and, with little thought, slit its belly, making its innards fall out. Then the cook reached his hand in, rummaged about until he'd taken hold of what he was looking for and yanked it hard, as if he was starting a lawnmower, causing the rest to come tumbling out. Now I remember being strongly aroused by this, by the revelation of the hidden workings that keep a being moving, neatly packed within their casing when all is well but now bloody, messy and scattered all over the ground. Perhaps the only way I can convey it is by comparing it to the enthusiasm other men have for strippers. Beneath the clothing lies something secret and the excitement lies in the act of revealing that, more than just the sight and shape of the end product, the naked female body. Now I know that it's wrong and strange but to me, in my mind back then, it not only made sense but was perfectly normal to have this curiosity. So while the rest drank themselves to oblivion in this hell-struck Congolese village, I set about fulfilling my very own fantasy.

It's difficult to explain what a certain type of power can feel like. Perhaps only the Nazis at Auschwitz could understand that utter godly feeling of having someone's life in your hands and choosing whether to kill them, spare them or something else. A'luta had chosen something else. We, his chosen few, would walk the earth forever bearing his mark on our foreheads, unable to forget him. So as I turned one corner, then the next, I came to a hut where I found a group of four women huddling in a corner and I knew I'd struck gold. The hut was quite central but it looked like just a ruin, as the back half had collapsed after a grenade had exploded less than 5 ft away. Now they sat there and shook, saying nothing. I raised my weapon but didn't have to fire.

I'm not wanting to harp on about cats again but I'd trained on them and now, self-taught in my nurtured obsession, I knew the feelings that I wanted to explore. I remember chasing the ginger cat around the house one day when the Willies were out. I had closed all the doors and blocked up any hidy-holes, and so had created a circular arena in a four-cornered room. I chased it and terrified it until I opened the basement door and it shot down the stairs. The basement was dark and, instead of flicking a switch, I took down a torch and steadily crept about after it. I looked under all the places I knew it could hide and after ten minutes was completely convinced it was magic, as it was gone. I went back up the stairs and closed the door. But, unable to get the thing out of my head, I soon found myself back down there, searching again. After another few minutes I looked in a place that I'd already checked twice but now, on my knees and with my head jammed tight between the space and the wall, I shoved the light into the gap and saw its eyes reflecting back at me. I couldn't believe it! At once I felt aroused. It was like a stripper taking off her last. The cat was frozen stiff and now sat in an increasing puddle of its own urine as it had lost its bladder control from the terror I had instilled in it. And I understood then the nature of fear. Humanity and the animal world have the fight or flight response, no doubt. But there's also a third and it only comes when you are truly broken. If the other two don't work, all that's left is to find a space and freeze in it. Even though the cat heard me, smelled me and now saw me, it sat there like it hadn't been found, hoping I'd soon go away. That space, then, is as much mental as it is ever physical.

So there I was with my four women. I didn't have to tie them up; they'd done it themselves. Constrained by their ligatures of fear, they just sat there. I walked over and held out my hand. Then I leaned in and took one, and, like a blind woman, she followed my lead, to a spot less than 4 ft away from the rest. I had my way. Perhaps, if there is justice in this world, in this life or the next, they will have theirs.

It lasted over an hour and, at one point, Rod McLean broke through the door. He was raging. He looked at me in despair and, like a parent hunting a lost kid, his crazed eyes shed tears but were as wide as saucers. He raised his hand and I saw an axe. A huge fucking axe! And he was about to chop my head off when . . . it's funny: I could lie and say I did something but I was in the middle of an organic mess and couldn't respond. So I simply bowed my head and, frozen stiff like the cat, hoped that he wouldn't. He didn't. And a second later he was gone. I later heard that someone else had got it off him. That night justice had paid me a visit but had chosen not to stay. When the sun set, I lit a small lantern and lay down amongst them. I owned them and they had become one.

A moment later I decided to leave my macabre harem. I was sorry and would miss them, as I'd taken a blank canvas and made something more beautiful. Standing up, I lit a smoke and took a step outside to breathe the cool fresh air. It was alive and I felt like I'd just wandered out of a tent at some outdoor festival or something, and now, with noises and smells beckoning from every direction, I felt spoilt for choice. So I headed back to the square. It was a sight! The *Jeunesse*, if that's what they were, were struggling – struggling to stand and so stay alive.

Some of the ANC boys were sleeping, their rifles lying feet away, their hats covering their faces in shame. Others were too into the game to stop or under orders from Cedric and so marched an imaginary wire, which kept the prisoners locked in. The kids had begged for water and to go to the toilet. But Cedric had added talking to the list of capital offences, so they were now quiet. At some point they'd made three of them beat a fourth to death – not to be granted their lives but only to not have been killed at that moment. Now they stood back in the lines. Once straight, they were now broken and staggered like black parapets on which the battlements kept falling, one by one. In the distance I could hear drumming. The jungle telegraph is no myth. These guys actually communicated that way. No doubt they knew we were here and so soon, I thought, it would be their move.

I thought it best to use the downtime properly. We wouldn't stay here long – a day at most – and, with the bigger target in sight, we'd be moving to keep the initiative. So after a few minutes of wandering around I found a spot and stuck my head down. I slept well.

It's very difficult sometimes – almost as if humanity rattles me but I refuse to answer. My eyes were open as the sun began to shine but it took a minute to see it. In the distance, between two huts, I saw a kid of four shaking his dead mother, trying to wake her. He was crying and she was bloated. And, though that innocence was a tragedy and I could intellectually grasp it, I didn't feel sad or appalled. As if I was looking at a still, I felt remote and uncaring. In later life I'd truly come to understand that my detachment, and that of people like me, those few per cent of bastards, was the most dangerous thing of all. And so I sat there challenging myself to cry, to feel sad or to want to act. But nothing. And at that I knew it: I had empathy but no sympathy; I understood but couldn't feel; I lived in a world of glass walls but didn't know they were there to break them; I knew and admired the human spirit but had total contempt for humanity. But beyond these there was something else – and that was what drove me. Above all I was uncomfortable to be alive and so pushed everything to its limits. And in that pushing, those like me would always create hell. If hell needed defining, then this was it. It was a helpless place of suffering where we – the devils, the Satans by our actions – stoked and fed off the fires of the innocent. I was beginning to transfix on the trauma in front of me when a pair of boots kicked at my calves, which jolted me. I jumped to my feet.

'Athol, is it not?' asked a large black man in a washed and pressed uniform. It was Cedric.

'What the fuck?' I blurted out, still annoyed at the kick. I wanted to kick him, the black bastard!

'Athol, I was wondering if you might help me.' And at that he beckoned me over to the square with a gentle coaxing of his arm. I almost fell over. The whole village was cleared. It was like an army of ants had come in during the night and cleared the place out. No bodies, no debris, no sign of life, as most of the whites and all the blacks were sound asleep in the huts. A minute later we arrived at the square. Where there had once been hordes of young faces, either fucked or soon to be, a handful still stood. The rest had gone with no trace. 'I want you to show them how to shoot,' Cedric said to me, as if he was introducing his children.

'You what?' I said, not sure if I'd heard him right.

'To shoot. These ones are the winners; they made it. The rest, well, the rest as you know are . . .' and at that he nodded over to the western ditch, where I now saw smoke rising into the cloudless sky. I walked over to the kids. They still stood there, in their spot from the night before. They were withdrawn. They didn't look, smile or cough. Their ankles were swollen, their knees were shaking and most had a fever. But they stood and it seemed like a bomb wouldn't have moved them. 'You see?' said Cedric. 'You see how strong? That is why they will join us. They are our brothers now.' And he said something in Swahili. But they didn't move. Even though he'd probably told them they could and that all was now well, they stayed firm. He then summoned one of the ANC soldiers who, with another one, was attempting to remove the body by its legs from the water-filled oil drum. He arrived promptly and Cedric took his water bottle. At that he passed it around the boys, who, out of need and not trust, gulped it down like a Jock in the desert. 'Please,' he said to me, 'you teach how we work. Yes?'

I looked at him, thought about it, then saw an angle. 'Sure,' I said. 'No problem. But I think you and I should have a talk later. I've got something that might interest you.'

XI

A SAFE EXPLOSION

As a punishment from the gods in the underworld Sisyphus was compelled to roll a huge stone up a steep hill but, before it reached the top, the stone always rolled back, leaving him to start all over again. This cycle would continue for eternity. I'd always drawn a lesson from the myth. I'd often lie awake at night visualising it. I'd see the man scrape, struggle and sweat from the bottom to the top, time after time, until the rock rolled relentlessly back down to the bottom. And it was clear to me that the stone rolled back because the peak wasn't flat. It was an impossible task and the gods well knew it. Yet Sisyphus must have hoped that just once the hill would be flat, that on reaching it that one time it might be different. But it never was. People are like that. They take the role of Sisyphus inadvertently, willingly and blindly toiling for their masters, while these masters, the powers that be, take the role of the gods.

I personally wavered between god and Sisyphus, controller and toiler, every day. I'd long since decided that the basic condition of life was toil and suffering, yet I'd hypocritically react to personal hardships by regarding the universe with spite. A part of me expected to have balance in my life, an equal amount of fortune and misfortune, and the longer a run of bad luck continued the more I was owed fortune. If that didn't come, then I wasn't playing any more and I was giving up, like a spoilt kid. My life, then, was and still is a constant battle between who I am and who I believe myself to be. I find comfort in atheism and my disbelief in the supernatural but I'm the first to look skywards when things go wrong.

I trained the kids that made it. It took a day. They were strong and ruthless, and now, wrapped up in his own power, Cedric led them all the way to Bumba. En route I'd managed to befriend him, or at least get to know him. I needed a team for the rescue job and he seemed just right. He knew the place, he knew the people and, above all, he commanded authority, which was invaluable for getting people to act without any questions. My side of the bargain, though, was riddled with problems. He was nobody's fool and demanded to see everything I had on this secret mission. Before leaving Johannesburg, Steve had given me a small envelope with all the information he had. It contained two photos of the missing daughter, one head shot and the other with her family. It had her name, the address she'd been staying at and all the stuff you'd need to know about her family's Stanleyville business. On top of that it had her African name – used as a middle name while in Europe but a first name over here – and that was important.

The amount of cash her dad was paying was huge. I mean it wasn't millions in today's money but I saw it as a way to get myself a house – a base, which I so badly craved – with a few quid on top to keep me out of trouble. Cedric wanted to know the lot. He even wanted the envelope, which was never going to happen, but his insistence and arrogance began to annoy me. I hadn't told him who was paying the wages; I had said she was wanted in London. I certainly didn't say how much the job was worth, though I offered him about a twentieth of the bounty – which was fair enough, given he was a bush man, unlikely to see middle age.

Another problem I had in the beginning was that I didn't have a load of money to grease people's palms with. This was the Congo and favours from my fellow mercenaries were unheard of. And so, left with nothing to offer them but meaningless promises, I was soon disheartened by their continual rejections, while my failed offers were fruitlessly drawing attention to myself and my mission. No doubt when I got there, I'd be watched and potentially clobbered if I found her. In any event I did have some luck. On one of the Simba boys we'd thrashed in Lisala, I'd found a roll of francs in a blood-soaked monkey pouch. It was just short of 35,000F (150F to the US dollar) and I'd hurriedly shoved it down my jungle boot, before some other predator could make a grab for it.

At Bumba Cedric called me over. He was sitting in an old, busted-up French Ford Vedette Sunliner, holding court with two others. By now the rest of my group, war fatigued and mad, had degenerated into a ravenous pack of bastards who seemed hell-bent on causing trouble and wasted no time in looting. I, on the other hand, had had my fun and was now ready for business. The new big chief man had decided it better not to try to intimidate me like he did the others and instead now maintained a certain air of respect. He managed this with some ease, given that he was brought up by white Belgian religious types and so was every bit the white black man you'd see on American TV.

Bumba was en route to Stanleyville and, although he couldn't have known it for sure, he figured that we'd be smacking the place head-on in no time. And he was right. Like an overgrown kid behind his dad's wheel, he sat there turning it and pretending to drive. He put me in the back and, like four goons at a Mafia meeting under a bridge, we sat and plotted. He introduced me to two other blacks. One was a local from Stanleyville and the other, he declared with pride, a Chewa. With such a coup he then figured his share had to be increased and so began haggling for more money. I offered him a new amount and let him dispute it. I still had over three-quarters for myself and I always figured he'd get killed at some point, given his reckless disregard for personal safety.

So in this surreal setting we began talking as the sun began to dip. The town was now quiet, empty almost, only to be interrupted by the occasional crack of a rifle round, the breaking of glass or the distant screams of some poor bastard getting it. At first I felt good. It seemed like I'd picked the right man at the right time, and in turn he'd chosen the best men for our job – a job he was now taking seriously. But unfortunately that was all very short-lived. The Chewa man was in fact a Bemba and I could tell by the stories he was casually sharing that he knew little about the tribe he was impersonating. The Bemba have their own religion. They believe in a god called Leza, who doesn't live in people but in the sky and controls thunder, women and weird shit like men's fertility. But above all he is a source of magical powers. These bastards had me for a fool, sitting there talking about how Leza would help us find her. Then he went on about how he'd been disgraced in his family, an extended lot that comprised all the generations. 'There's no ceremony for boys at puberty,' he told me, 'but there is for girls.' The ceremony, called *Chisungu*, starts when the girl's breasts form and she's put into a hut for three months to train and so on. But if a girl gets pregnant before this, they get banned. Well, according to my lustful friend, he had single-handedly got four out of the seven girls in line for it banned and so in turn was banished himself. Though he was puffing out his chest like a young boy bullshitting his mates, I soon saw that my problems were mounting. They were trying to sting me and get as much info as possible before hitting the city. The thing they'd obviously forgotten was that, apart from my skin and my disbelief in sorcery, I was every bit as African as them, and knew the difference between a Chewa and a Bemba. At that I was raging and was so mad that I wanted to gun the bastards down where they sat. But sense prevailed, luckily, although I kicked myself when I realised I'd passed round her picture and the Bemba man had stuck it in his pocket. If I wanted it back, I'd have to kill them – all three of them – and at that I'd be dead myself. So I held on but, as usual, fate took a hand.

By the end of October things were going from bad to worse. The local folk hated us liberators more than the Simba and, while some showed their discipline, others lived like there was no day called tomorrow. It didn't take long before Hoare called us back to Kamina and its routine and order. I was pissed off. I had never imagined in a thousand years that we'd be flown back to where we'd started – the other end of the country – when the goal of everything was just over the horizon from where we were sitting. But it was worse. Left in Bumba was a fully equipped, trained and motivated ANC force, and, worst of all, three of them knew about my Chewa. I told myself over and over again that, even if they got her, it was useless to them. But I was wrong and I knew it. It wasn't like they were capturing treasure or an obscure artefact whose only value lay in knowing who wanted it. She would talk. She would tell them where she came from. They'd find a way to get her home. And they'd take my prize. I was fuming.

A few days after landing in Kamina airbase, a few of the guys were summarily dismissed. It was shameful, as the man who was fingering the looters and rapists was as guilty as the rest of them. I'd personally seen him in the village knocking fuck out of a youth with a drunken rage that even the worst of the worst would have been proud of. I, on the other hand, was lucky. It seemed that the canings were being carried out purely on our conduct in Bumba, and in Bumba I'd been a good boy, while in the village I'd been a disgrace but at least discreet. I also realised that my intelligence-gathering skills were soon to be coveted and so, regardless of my actions, I was seen as worth keeping. In any event Hoare was at Kindu in the fight of his life. Reinforcements were called for and that meant us. Twenty one of us were dispatched and my game was soon back on.

Kindu is a town based on the banks of the Lualaba River, between Kamina and Stanleyville. The river rises in the highlands of Katanga, where it's known as the Luapula, before becoming the Lualaba at Kongolo – the place Hoare had taken off for just before we'd arrived back in disgrace. Finally the river becomes the River Congo at Stanleyville, before snaking back round to where we'd just been brought from and where my new competitor was no doubt plotting with our replacements, 52 Commando, who'd lead them along to Paulis and then down to Stanleyville. As it stood, though, Kindu was to be the staging garrison for Hoare's main thrust, as they'd fought and died their way from Kongolo, where they'd first picked up their vehicles. And so now, sitting in amongst an ever-enlarging formation, I fought to get my bearings and establish a place as I'd gone from a big fish in a small pond to just another crazy competing for fight time.

The column, known as 5 Brigade Mechanised, consisted of over 200 vehicles. The lead was taken by two Ferret scout cars, three Scania Vabis – shit Swedish armoured cars – and a mad pathfinder Frenchman, De la Michele, who carved up the jungle like he owned it. Behind were the rest of us. First were the three white mercenary groups known as 55, 56 and 67 Commando, a communications headquarters in a customised Dodge pickup, and a mixed collection of jeeps and five-ton trucks. Finally behind that were the ANC soldiers, a rabble I'd yet to see fight, and a Belgian Army bridging unit as ingenious as the Ancient Romans themselves. Although Hoare was in command of his units during the battles, the overall command of the column was given to another colonel.

Soon, then, the column had slashed its way through Simba-gained lands and now, blooded for action, steamed for the outskirts of Stanleyville. We knew there was pressure to get there – something that clicked when night came and we failed to stop, as night fighting in column warfare, putting it simply, shouldn't be done. With every advantage of speed and stealth thrown to the wind, as 200 vehicles cut through the night air, headlights and muzzle flashes glaring, we were open to ambush from even the most amateurish tactician. And this duly happened. The approach was scattered with small villages, all of which were hostile and so spewed out bullets from their blankets of darkness. If I said that the scene came straight from the Wild West, I'd be putting it lightly. Finally, after we'd taken a serious smashing – the worst yet – they halted. The lead Ferret scout, 'Frenchy' and a sack of others lay dead, including the infamous CBS reporter George Clay, who'd come along for the ride. He was shot right through the head and died where he stood. That night it rained and rained and rained and, as morning broke, everyone was up for a battle, if for no other reason than getting out of the jungle.

At 0635hrs the Belgian Paras dropped from the sky and by 0700hrs the slaughter of the white hostages began. Only the day before, *Le Martyr*, a newspaper owned by the cowardly bastard Christophe Gbenye, had lambasted us on its pages: 'We shall cut out the hearts of the Americans and the Belgians and we shall wear them as fetishes . . . We shall dress ourselves in their skins.' And only that morning Radio Stanleyville had repeated over and over: '*Ciyuga! Ciyuga! Ciyuga!* Kill, kill, kill all of the white people. Kill all the men, women and children. Kill them all. Have no scruples. Use your knives and your pangas!'

And they did. Many of the Simba shits were out of it from a mixture of booze and hemp. According to some survivors the signal to fire came from the deaf mute ex-boxer 'Major Bubu', who'd served as a personal bodyguard to rebel defence minister Gaston Soumialot. Still, whoever gave the word, the rebels started firing into the assembled hostages with rifles and automatics. The firing wasn't random, as they deliberately chose women and children as their first targets. It lasted just four minutes. By 0900hrs we rolled in and four kilometres later we were sitting at the centre, in the Lumumba square. We'd made it, we thought, while in reality it was just the beginning.

As the Simba occupation of the city had continued, the nature of the bloodletting had gone from spontaneous slaughter to a ritualistic madness. The favourite location for these murders was the Lumumba monument, where dozens of men were murdered and mutilated while mobs stood cheering. This would continue until, in the interest of avoiding mass hysteria in a population of over a quarter-million, they were moved to night-time on the Tshopo Bridge, where the victims were thrown alive, dead or dying into the cataract below, the crocodiles taking care of the bodies. Thousands were disposed of this way.

By 1230hrs the 51 Commando diehards, including me, were in defence of the forsaken place but were constantly sniped at and mortared from the other side, known as the Rive Gauche, which we still didn't control. Finally, after the commander Graham Horgan had charged us over in an effort to improve our untenable position, losing Van der Westhuizen, a South African lad we all knew well, to the bullets and with two others wounded, we consolidated where we could, before I was pulled back into the town after taking a concussion from a mortar impact. It had landed just feet away but, by the grace of somebody, every piece of metal had zipped right past me.

My misfortune soon had its merits. Hoare and his band of marauding bastards were now in charge of the entire city and so had the perilous task of crossing the river on a number of rescue missions, each one penetrating further and further into rebel-held lands. The city had been surrounded by church outposts and missions – some Catholic; others Protestant – and for months now few had been heard from, so the worst was feared. The worst was soon realised. In the beginning the shorter hops were quick, with few casualties, although the hostages found were utterly sorrowful, as murder, mutilation and ritualistic torture were as commonplace as the greenery around them. The guys I'd been saddled with at the bridge were now part of these stealthy liberation columns, while I, in my convalescence, was based in the city, manning crossroads and maintaining 'order' – that's to say order Congolese style.

The Congolese have a tradition called *ratissage*. It's the act of brutality towards the vanquished. And there could be no better setting for this barbaric display than that of Stanleyville. I don't know what I'd expected to see when we first rolled into town. I'd never been the liberator of such a major population before and so had imagined a Stalingrad idea where decimation, rubble and twisted columns of metal and timber rose from the city's dying foundations, like a last-gasp hand from under the quicksand. In fact Stanleyville was an unusual sight, instead reminding me of how a teenager might wreck his parents' house after an unsupervised weekend. The streets were filthy and quiet, except for the few jeeps that buzzed around like pollinating bees. The rubbish lay foul and the animals foraged, while the bodies, in various stages of decay, lay sporadically placed, like blasted-out debris. The stench was thick, as was the silence, which was at first interrupted only by distant cries and momentary shots, some at people, others at the starved, rabid dogs who'd work away at the decomposing limbs and bloated faces. Death was everywhere and caked the landscape like a layer of dirt. But the buildings still stood. The windows were unbroken and, apart from the odd crater, the only restoration needed was a bloody good clean. That, of course, was all about to change.

The city was soon feeling the side effects of its liberation. The ANC were rounding up the collaborators and whoever else they didn't like the look of. I saw a line of prisoners, clerks from the Hotel des Chutes and others, being marched past me on their way to a fate I was yet to know. They were beaten and blood soaked and, while they passed, they stared right at us. We'd set the wheels of their deaths into motion but were ironically their last chance at life. I turned to my two new crew mates and smiled but they weren't laughing. They had fought their way up the column but, unlike us from 51 Commando, were as yet to sample *ratissage* in action. It was an acquired taste that few learned to savour.

Still, for no other reason than passing the time, we got talking. The man next to me, who I'll call Konrad, was in his early 20s. He was tall and tough looking and by Christ was a racist. He hated the blacks – something made pretty clear by the few words he said but more, as I'd soon see, by the way he treated them. Behind us, swinging about on a mounted 50-cal. Browning, was a black lad. I'd assumed he was from South Africa but, after talking some more, he started going on about his early life in the copper belt of Northern Rhodesia (now called Zambia), particularly in Kitwe. Straight away I thought he was another gift from the gods – Kitwe was as close to the Chewa as I was likely to get – but before I could recruit him we'd got sidetracked when he'd started on about why he was out here in the first place. In fact Chizyuka, as I'll call him, was a fair bit older than us and had been working in the mines as a blaster.

He was another soul on the run after being accused of having an affair with some white man's missus. Not rape or anything but just that she was up for a bit of black cock – and Chizyuka had done her just fine. It wasn't like he was going to get lynched, I don't think – I mean this wasn't the deep south of the States – but he had chosen to fuck off with a box full of her jewellery and so had burnt his bridges forever.

Two minutes later we were summoned to head off and relocate some three streets away, where we'd been told there were looters. When we got there, we found a bunch of ANC boys hacking away at a shop door while tanning in its windows. There was no way we were going to stop them, even if we wanted to – we'd be hacked to bits as soon as looked at. But when we saw them, about ten of them, huffing and heaving before finally overturning a huge metal box that nearly crushed them, we suddenly got interested. It didn't take long to see it was a safe. It weighed a ton or more and so nothing short of a crane was moving it. We stood there laughing. I mean it was funny, as a bunch of stupid fucks tried everything from shooting bullets to smashing it with rocks in an effort to get the damn thing open. It was designed to be robber proof. And it was. But as our laughter became a gobsmacked silence, we heard a voice from behind us: 'I could open that in thirty seconds!'

We looked over our shoulders. It was Chizyuka. 'Thirty?' I said.

'Yup – thirty.' And at that he flicked out his smoke, jumped down from the back and came around by my side. 'Thirty seconds,' he continued, pointing over with a smug grin. 'That's all I need.' We were silent. I looked at Konrad, who narrowed his eyes in response. We looked back. Now we were listening.

As soon as the sun set, we were off, explosives and Chizyuka on board. The streets were all but deserted, the only signs of life being looters, fools and the soon-to-be victims. In the distance, around the corners and up the streets, came the constant sounds of pain and suffering. The pleads and screams almost blended in with the buildings by day but by night, under the blanket of stars, they stood out, individual and acute. We drove one way then the next. Then, after a wrong turn and a near run-in with an ANC mob, who took us for two whites with a prisoner, we made it through to the bank of Stanleyville, where we stopped, open mouthed and nervous, just yards away from it. We salivated before our prize. Like the bunch of useless amateurs we were, we'd psyched each other up about the riches inside, even figuring how we'd escape the country – that night if the bounty was big enough. And I was serious. I was off if the money was right and so had prepared my kitbag accordingly.

Konrad dropped the two of us off and made a quick scout of the perimeter. The night was as humid and muggy as ever but, with a lull in the chaos, it seemed eerily still, like a web had been spun and the spiders were watching. So I wiped my brow and made myself busy, shifting obstructions and clearing out the bricks and mortar that surrounded the safe, while Chizyuka, a man in his element, set about with a quarter-pound block of TNT and a sequence of wires. In less than a minute he took hold of my collar and didn't let go until we were crouching down low, behind the parked-up jeep. Immediately after Konrad had joined us – boom! It went up with a thump that shattered the stillness and lit up the night. The smoke billowed out into the road but instead of rising it stayed low, as the humidity channelled it down like a creeping fog. Taking a breath, we hurried in and, with two flashlights and a whole load of fumbling, found our metal. The box still sat there and the door was buckled – but off. We were in. Our Chizyuka was a master and I wasted no time in telling him so. But no sooner had I sang his praises than we stood there dismayed. It was empty.

Cunts! We would have stood there all night – it wasn't like the police were coming – but Hoare had expressed an order that looting was theft and so a criminal act, punishable by something unpleasant, although not to be death. So we fucked off and, down but not out, resumed our posts at an intersection two streets south of the American Consulate.

Soldiering can sometimes be a boring existence, interrupted by moments of intense mania. A mercenary life, however, is often an existence of sheer madness, only interrupted by periods of monotony and solitude. So as we sat there in the calm after the storm, we waited on something to happen. But nothing did. And nothing continued to happen. So I tried to get chatting but Chizyuka was already curled up snoring, while Konrad wasn't up for saying much else. In these times, alone with my thoughts, I can easily slip into an introspective trance, which often leads to my crazier moments, as the questions are endless and the answers few. Both cause me problems that only chaos can calm. Konrad then said he was going for a wander. Feeling like his lottery numbers had come up only to find that his mate hadn't bought the ticket, he sulked about like a lemon-sucking woman.

At that I was truly alone. Beyond the tension I'd always seen the mercenary life as an expression of my freedom. As a child I'd had none. But as a man surely I did? I'd defined my coming of age as my ability to make choices. I could go and do what I wanted, whenever I felt like it. And, for as long as that novelty had lasted, I had lost my burden and had broken free. But at that moment it was choice that was causing me pain, as with it comes accountability and with accountability comes judgement – not by others, but by me, judging myself. There's a moment, I found, when all men entertain fear – not of pain or even of death but worse: of uncertainty. I had committed the worst and had justified it all to myself as a product of nurture but that grace period was long since gone and the days of 'no other choice' were all but a faded memory. Now I was an actor in a world that had despised me but I still spent my time making decisions, usually passively, by taking the path of least resistance. But I continued to suffer. I could, like most people, have done that forever, until the only meaningful choice would be that of survival – like a man who needed to starve before ploughing his field for food. And by then it would have been all too late – the boat would have sailed. I'd always thought that by being a mercenary I was being proactive but I wasn't. I was only being a piece in someone else's game, while I was only borrowing control when I blew out a safe or planned to rescue a girl who didn't want rescuing. In all I was a fool to be sitting here, wasting time with two people I hardly knew, to protect a road I'd never live on and to secure a people who I didn't even care for. I started to feel mad. I was living a life where tomorrow was the big day and so pacified myself with an inbuilt morphine tap, which I'd trigger whenever I felt breathless. There's a comfort in seeing the rail tracks in front of you, even when you know that the bridge is out just two miles ahead.

I had seen civilisation. I'd lived in the UK and had been in South Africa. In moments of sanity I'd even thought about my future but had scorned the typical lot of the masses. I had vowed to either make it big or not make it at all. Fuck the pension plan, the mortgaged house and the pretty wife who gets a fat arse after a string of little bastards. When it gets to this point, what is the point? Most men self-medicate with sports, beer and porn. Like a neutered house cat they live longer but this living has to be done vicariously, through information fed to them about the outside world, where the choices are real and not the ones that you're given.

I'd always seen myself as better than that but, at that

moment, I wasn't. I had chosen to join the army and now I had chosen to come here, and here was the arsehole of Africa – fuck. Why I'd done that had a number of answers, each one depending on how honest I was being with myself at the time. I didn't want to be part of something bigger or help to solve other people's problems. If I did, it wouldn't be here, where one bunch of blacks was just as bad as the next. I did want to savour human experience and this was definitely the place to touch base with its more extreme limits. I did want an environment that suited my skills and strengths, while allowing me to continue on my often macabre journey. But most importantly, as I sat there in the city of suffering, two juxtaposed intentions became obvious. If I was here for the future, then sitting about was achieving nothing. While, secondly, if I was here for the experience, for my own unique flirtation with a world that only a privileged few ever enter, then my preoccupation with the future itself was imprisoning me behind the bars of my own expectations. Either way I was intending to have both but accomplishing neither. In short I'd never get rich working for somebody else and, when it comes to the personal human experience, the only rule book to use is the one that you've written yourself.

It seems strange but it wasn't until that very moment in Stanleyville that the true man in me was born. Choice, I considered, is everything, while real freedom can't be given, only taken.

'Hey, blast man!' I said, jumping in the back and kicking Chizyuka. 'Wake up. We've got work to do!' Two seconds later, as he sat up rubbing his puffed-up eyes, I started the engine, at which a startled Konrad came tearing round the corner, thinking he was getting left in the badlands, on foot and all alone. 'That's not the only bank in town, is it?' I said, already halfway down the block. 'Besides, we might as well get hung for a sheep as a lamb.' They were reluctant but found they were bound by the choices I'd given them.

We crept round the side of the Consulate and, with the lights out, backed the jeep up to the quartermaster stores and relieved them of another quarter-pound block of TNT. A quarter-pound block packs a fair punch – a grenade has two ounces – and would certainly blow the arse out of most safes, particularly the ones in the Congo. We soon found ourselves running the gauntlet again, this time from our own troops, as much as from the ANC and Simba remnants. Finally, after a series of false leads and hopes, we struck upon what looked like an old colonial post office on the far end of a square. In the dark, and with nothing but the moonlight to illuminate our work, the white, filth-covered building shone, almost glistening, like a cleaned white tooth in a dark, decaying mouth. We circled, then backed behind the gable end and waited for a group of drunken ANC revellers to pass, before slipping back out again quietly, like an attack sub off to war.

Finally we parked up, before Chizyuka and I slowly crept in and through to the back, where a strong box sat behind a counter. It had already been hacked at and was no doubt earmarked for another looting team that was yet to arrive. I legged it outside, FN in hand, and waved to Konrad to scout the next street over, before he took up post on the other side of the square and mounted the Browning to cover us. We knew the routine by now and so once again I helped Chizyuka with the necessary items, before I cleared his escape path away from the fuse. I turned to look at him and he gestured me away, so I dashed back outside to see the silhouetted jeep against the whitewashed walls on the other side of a green. No sooner had I made it over than bang! Once again the place went up. This time the debris and smoke blasted out like grapeshot from a cannon. 'Fuck me!' I shouted to Konrad, now picking myself up from an unexpected knee buckling. I patted myself down and turned round to see Chizyuka but . . . 'What the fuck?' I said. 'Chizyuka?' He wasn't there. 'Where is he?' I shouted to Konrad. He looked blank. 'I thought he was right behind me!' But before he could answer, the two of us were tearing back over and into the dust-filled cavern.

'Oh shit!' said Konrad, as in fumbling around blind he felt what he thought to be Chizyuka. It was. He was lying and let out a steady groan, in all kinds of pain. He knew what had happened. It was a freak accident, a million-to-one shot that demolition people are all well aware of. A malfunction in the time fuse didn't give him any delay. And so, in a blinding flash, our trickery had come crashing down upon him. I felt my way over and now, taking a shoulder each, we pulled him the length of the shop floor, out and onto the wooden veranda. He was a mess. Besides losing his right arm at mid-forearm, he'd lost his right eye, ruptured both eardrums, severely damaged his chest and had a wound to his stomach that you could put your fist into without touching the edges. In fact, as we tried to attend to his injuries, he could only lie there gasping in the darkness before passing away with very little protest.

We stood for a moment, quite unsure as to what to do. But it didn't take long before we were right back in there, feeling for the safe, like junkies scouring the floor for a clumsily dropped fix. This time I found it and, although the door was still on its hinges, such was the force of the blast that it had punched a hole right through the locking mechanism, allowing us to prod about inside with an outstretched arm. After a moment I could feel paper at the bottom but only at the tips of my fingers, so I stood up, took off my shirt and this time stretched and stretched until I managed to grasp a handful of it. I pulled my arm out and Konrad lit a match. It was francs. We almost fell over with excitement but still we couldn't reach all the way inside. So we sat back and tried to think. Konrad wanted to go back for another quarter-pound. I said no. That was just stupid. Between the explosion, the fact it was fast approaching morning and the now dead Chizyuka, which we would need to explain, getting grabbed was a distinct possibility. And believe me, I wasn't worried about the consequences of either the crime or the accidental death while committing it. I was totally concerned about our new-found riches. I wasn't sharing them with anyone, least of all some black who we'd have to pay off just to keep silent. I stood up and walked back towards the front door, almost in desperation, half-hoping to see something jump up from the debris with a 'use me' sign, like a pinch bar or a blow torch. Behind me, Konrad leaned back towards the strong box and, in a moment of frustration, pulled on the bastard – and the door sprang open. I couldn't believe it! But bastards!

We thought we'd struck gold but once again it was all to be short-lived. The safe was full of paper but it was just letters shoved in for security. We did find a few gold coins, which were definitely worth something, and about 500,000 francs – more after recounting – but as we hauled ass back towards the Consulate, with a dead Chizyuka strapped to the front, I couldn't help but blurt out my Chewa rescue story in a moment of weakness. And so, of course, no sooner had I said it than Konrad was in.

XII

C'EST LE CONGO

We had only been here a day and a half and the town was not yet won. Outside and across the Rive Gauche the battle was still raging. I was acutely aware of the race against time. I could easily be pulled off into one of the many columns that were gallivanting around trying to find lost missionaries. And while I was still concussed and confined to guarding occupied space, I was in no way doing my bit and so could hardly justify saying no if ordered. But apart from that my main concern was that there would come a time when the young princess could simply walk out of the city on her own. Indeed the airport was now open and medical cases were being flown out, while reinforcements were being dropped in – another reason why the city would be consolidated before too long. I knew, then, that if I could only get to her and present her back in London, then whatever the climate was over here her dad would still have to pay me. And besides, I had recently figured out a way to do it.

Rod McLean, my new acquaintance from 51 Commando up north, had completely fucked himself during a personal struggle with another of our soldiers during the now infamous night in the village. In fact he'd hurt himself so much that he had been flown out of the jungle and had made it all the way back to Leopoldville (now called Kinshasa), where he now sat in a rather lengthy convalescence. I knew this because one of the guys who'd brought in a load of supplies from Kamina had been talking to him while he was down there. Rod was the kind of character you were unlikely to forget. He said he'd broken his leg or something and so was having to rest up before being able to go back to the UK. I thought it ideal. If I could get hold of this bird, I could get her flown down to the Leopoldville hospital, where I could get Rod, for a cut of the money, to escort her back to London and collect. It was perfect for me for three reasons. Firstly it cut out having to go back to South Africa. Secondly I knew that, of all the evil bastards out here, he'd protect her from getting her arse shagged on the way back. And thirdly if I let him in on the deal, he was gentleman enough to take his slice of the action without stitching me up and spanking the lot.

I therefore tasked Konrad to assist me in finding the necessary local help, while I figured out a way to get a girl aboard a flight to Leopoldville, especially one who might not be so keen on going. A couple of days later Konrad came running up to me with some news. He said that Lieutenant Colonel Kirk, the British military attaché, had been sniffing about, asking favours of Hoare. It seemed that further north there was still a whole load of British folk scattered about who needed rescuing. He said they were located across hundreds of square miles in Banalia and Bafwasende and that all British mercenaries were going to be detailed for the rescue. This put the wind up me because, after looking at the map, we saw the distances involved and so the time it would take, and, more importantly, it was right in the middle of the badlands. Bafwasende, in particular, was home to the Leopard People: the fiercest tribe in the Congo. I looked at

Konrad and shook my head. We knew we'd have to act fast. Whatever was to happen up there would take a while and, if we did have to square off with the Leopard lot, it would be a bastard of a fight, probably to the last man.

Now, when the Simbas first marched in on 4 August, the locals of Stanleyville had adorned themselves with greenery as a sign of their sympathy. Then, when the ANC came back with us, all the Congolese began sporting white headbands as a symbol of loyalty to them. Confusing? It didn't stop there. Nendaka, the ANC chief man, had established a huge holding area in one of the local stadiums and had begun what was to be known as the Stanleyville trials. I say trials; in reality a man was presented and if the crowd cheered, he lived; if it jeered, he was sent for the chop. It seemed that everyone was a perpetrator, a judge and a victim.

About an hour later I met up with three local lads who I'd managed to bribe into action. Two were from the ANC column that had smashed into town with us and the other was a local lad who'd been a Simba collaborator but whose life I'd paid a bribe for, in return for his services. He sported a white headband but still had a green one in his pocket just in case. The wind could change fast in this part of the world and I'd do well to know it. Still, what did I care? So we sat and had a smoke, until ten minutes later Konrad turned up with another three ANC boys who'd just arrived at the airfield. He thought we'd need them since we were probably heading into Mangobo, the native part of Stanleyville, where there was still a Simba resistance.

The timing of it was a difficult call to make. Either by day or by night my plan was full of perils and the more I thought about it the more I realised how stupid I was being. Essentially I was a mercenary hiring mercenaries, to do a job that was unnecessary, for a result that was uncertain. But no sooner had I entertained my doubts than we were packed up and ready to move, as Konrad's borrowed jeep had to be back before it was missed. Daytime it was.

At first we headed along the Boulevard Ryckmans and, like a two-car convoy on official business, we negotiated the friendly checkpoints and familiar roads until finally, as if it had dropped in pressure, the air changed and we felt all alone. I looked over my shoulder to see my turncoat guide rummaging around in his right pocket for what I knew he had in there. I got tense. This bastard could be leading us anywhere and how would I know it? He said he'd heard of the family and even claimed to have seen the girl. But I was starting to wonder. First he told me there was another place in the European part – after the address I first had had fallen through – where we'd probably find them but when I tried to ask him again, he denied having said it. Then, a minute later, he said that he had but had been told by someone who worked at the Hotel Victoria that they were back in Mangobo. Now I hated him and cursed my reliance on a bastard who I wouldn't even shit on for fun and who, only the previous day, was a condemned man made ready for slaughter. The first sight of that green band in his pocket and I was putting a bullet right through his fucking forehead.

I looked to my driver, the cool Konrad, his dark glasses over his motionless face, while his hair danced in the wind like the flag on an embassy car. He swivelled his gaze from side to side, hoping for the best but prepared for the worst, while now and then responding to directional taps on his shoulders from our Judas of a guide and inching us forward. 'I curse this place,' he said to me, without taking his eyes off the road. 'Now I crave the civilised . . . though maybe this isn't the true face of the people.' But then, shaking his head, he glanced at me. 'But I've seen nothing to convince me otherwise. The butchery and mutilation of men and women, military and civilian, is an ideology. There's absolutely no difference between the acts of the ANC and the atrocities of the rebels. Only the flags and uniforms are different. You know, today, when I went down to the airport to get this lot, I saw a prisoner whose eyes had been put out yesterday and was bayoneted today; now he's been left to bleed. And then,' he paused and gently lowered his head, 'the traditional way, they call it. The head porter from the Hotel Victoria: this morning they cut out his tongue in front of a jeering crowd. Then his ears, hands and feet were hacked off with razor-sharp pangas. Finally, and I couldn't believe this, a bamboo stake was driven up his rectum. I mean can you fucking believe that?'

I slowly shook my head but I could believe it. I'd seen worse, even committed it, though that memory would lurk only at the furthest and darkest realms of my humanity. *'C'est le Congo!'* I said. *'C'est le Congo!'*

'What?' his expression said.

But just then our attention was taken by two quick taps on the shoulder and a pointing arm that shot over us like a lightning bolt. *'La bas, monsieur, la bas!'* he cried and was out of the jeep and had disappeared before we'd stopped. I jumped in the back and shoved our ANC boy off the Browning, while Konrad pulled us up alongside the targeted house before jumping over and taking cover himself. We waited. Instead of bullets came three more locals, all insisting that we leave the jeeps and follow on foot. Two of the ANC boys began walking away with them, when out came a fourth boy, followed by a fifth. We'd long since lost the initiative. Now we were losing control.

I cocked the Browning to give them a scare – but nothing. Then I saw Konrad: he was literally having his elbow tugged by two of them, who now seemed to be getting aggressive and weren't taking no for an answer. I shouted to our ANC boys to get back to the jeep, which they did, and we all stood next to the motors watching the locals – around ten by now, mostly teenagers – gesturing us over in between gnarly shouts. I looked for our guide. He was now doubling back after seeing we weren't playing. I called him over. I turned to the ANC boy in our jeep and explained something to him very carefully to translate for me. The guide spoke English but now seemed to have forgotten it. I said that if the crowd didn't fuck off within the next ten seconds, I'd gun them down, starting with the guide. The ANC boy translated. But instead of the reaction I'd expected, the guide got angry, really fucking angry and started screaming at me like I'd just shagged his mother. 'Fuck this!' I said and before I knew it I was out of the jeep and had hooked the black bastard right across the jaw, which sent him staggering – and onto the ground. He hadn't expected that! Next thing his pals made a move but one step forward from Konrad, FN raised and his dark glasses glaring, and they backed off, then scattered like birds in a hurry. 'You little bastard!' I said to the guide man. 'What's your fucking game, eh?' And at that I thumped him again, before taking his two headbands, tying his hands and swinging him into the jeep for my ANC boys to use as a footstool. Now we were back to square one.

We started the engines and slowly began snaking away from the buildings. I had no idea what he was up to but it wasn't what I'd paid him for. We doubled back and I gave our situation some thought. There's a thin line between bravery and stupidity and this guide was surely trying to double-cross us in some way. All the money in the world would be worth fuck all if I was dead. So I stood my boys down and, on the route back, I made sure that we swung by the stadium to grab the footstool from the back and hand him over to the killing squad for some extra torture. It cost me ten francs to have him done right but I think it was money well spent.

After dropping the ANC boys at the airfield, Konrad started moaning again as we approached our billets near the

American Consulate. 'It's impossible to imagine a normal military unit,' he said, 'with no human feelings or at least no sense of what's right and wrong, like these people. War against an armed enemy is one thing but the senseless face-to-face killing of prisoners and civilians is the mark of animals, not people.'

I smiled. 'Lycanthropy, my friend. It's lycanthropy. Wait until you meet the Leopard Men of Bafwasende, then you'll see. You'll learn. These are . . .' I stopped. 'You know: *C'est le Congo.*'

'What do you mean?' he asked. But I didn't answer. You couldn't avoid its meaning. It was just a matter of time. Besides, on staring at the surrounding buildings, my thoughts suddenly carried me off. I suddenly had a thought, like when I found that ginger cat in the basement of the mission: I couldn't see it but it had always been there. She – the young girl – must be in our area; she must be hiding. I mean why the hell would she head to the shit-pit of Mangobo if she was able to stay in the centre? It just made no sense.

Later that evening I got word from Leopoldville that Rod was interested in the deal. But, like us, he was playing for time. His leg wasn't broken but his knee was badly twisted, which had rendered him unable to soldier. The worst of the swelling was down and so he was heading home in days, not weeks. On top of that I figured I might have only days myself, though luckily for me Hoare had to divert to Opala, just south-west of Stanleyville, to find the remnants of 54 Commando, who'd disappeared off the map just a couple of weeks previously.

The next day I heard all sorts of rumours of where she might have been hiding but, after chasing around shadows, none of them bore fruit. Then, the day after that, it was even worse. This time we ran into another bunch of crazy, drugged kids. All hopped up on their jungle juice and muti, they'd tried for the title but got well bashed. And so, several spent magazines later, we once again headed back empty-handed and now near empty-walleted. Things were getting desperate and that night all I could visualise was me, pushing my rock uphill like Sisyphus and then chasing down after it.

The next morning, though, was different. A kid who I'd never seen before came up to us and asked if I was looking for the Belgian girl. I wasn't looking for a Belgian but in desperation I said that I was. He told me about a family who, before August, had a foreign black girl staying with them. He said they lived near the Avenue Chaltin and he could take me there, for a price. I told him to come back later that evening and that he'd only get paid if I found her.

By the time he met me, I had only mustered one jeep and three ANC soldiers – and, of course, the ever-enthusiastic Konrad. This time we went straight for the house with little anticipation of anything coming of it. While hope springs eternal, neither of us had much faith in a kid whose balls couldn't even have dropped yet. But when we pulled up outside, all that soon changed. The house was cleaner – not in any way grand like a European's place but it was ordered and planned – and even though it had been violated during the months of occupation, it had been reclaimed from the madness in just those few short days. I jumped from the jeep and took a few steps closer. The gate was closed but unlocked, so I gently pushed it, cringing at the noise of its rusty mechanics. Through the curtains I saw light, then shadows moving. There seemed to be a few people around, so I turned to Konrad and gave him the thumbs up. Then I whispered to the ANC boys to speak Swahili for us, if needed. My French wasn't to be relied on, especially if shouting. I asked the kid, who was beside me, if he'd seen her here recently and, if so, who she lived with. He said he had and that he'd also seen Simbas coming to the house – some as often as three or four times a day. At that I thought that she'd obviously been a novelty for

1. Orange Grove Drive in the late 1950s: the house where we met A'luta

2. The Armée Nationale Congolaise (ANC) chopping away at the triple-canopy undergrowth on the long slog to Lisala, 1964

3. The Grey's Scouts patrolling on horseback, late 1976

4. Selous Scouts training at the Wafa Wafa camp on Lake Kariba

5. Terrorism stops here! A Selous Scout in action

6. Selous Scouts setting an ambush on an infiltration trail across the Zambezi and into Rhodesia from Mozambique, early 1978

7. 'Fire force' paratroopers, readying to board a
Douglas C-47 in support of Selous Scout operations
on the Rhodesia–Mozambique border in late 1978

8. Selous Scouts preparing for cross-border
operations into Mozambique in late 1978

9. Special forces in action: Selous Scouts with Rhodesian SAS helicopter support
return from an intense fire fight with ZANU/ZAPU guerrillas in late 1978

10. Zambezi hazards – unique to African water patrols – early 1979

11. Looking towards ZANU positions on the far side of the Zambezi, early 1979

12. Tank time: special forces after a week of heavy fighting against a Soviet-trained and equipped ZANU division, on the border with Mozambique, 1979

13. Rhodesian SAS returning after a long-range reconnaissance mission and two weeks of heavy contact

14. Under the radar: flying in to meet Italian Gladio agents at Camp Ruwa, a secret base in central Africa, for a live demonstration of Project Coast's research into peptide synthesis and its use in crowd control, late 1987

15. The landing strip at Camp Ruwa, 1987

16. A distant agent at Camp Ruwa before the drug trials, 1987

the rapists and so had probably got an arse like a wizard's sleeve – or worse. But in any case I'd near killed myself to find her so she'd better be bloody well grateful.

I crept up to the door and stopped. I motioned for Konrad on the Browning to cover us and the house, while I stuck one ANC boy up by the window and the other two beside me, ready to steam in. I was about to go for it but stopped short. How should this be done? Do I ring the bell? Excuse me, yes, we're here to take you to Europe. Or what if she was still getting shafted and her family were all dead? What then? What if the house was full of fucking Simbas? Fuck – what if? But that all went by the wayside when the ANC boy by the window took the butt of his rifle and smashed it in . . . fuck! So, like the drug squad in the morning, we piled through the fucking door as dogs barked, women screamed and men jumped about. Smack! I stuck my rifle right through some fat bastard's face as I trampled over him but tripped and careered right into an opening door, which I belted shut, trapping some kid and near slicing him in two. I readied myself and looked back, to see a shovel coming right at my face, which cracked me solid, sending me back against the door, where I once again crushed the damn kid. By now the whole fucking room was moving, as between my blurred vision, battle-hardened soldiers and determinedly aggressive women, the fight was on and no one was playing. Once again I'm standing up and now, grabbing a handful of long, black hair I pull it hard, once, twice, then three times, before it gives, snapping her head back and making her fall to the floor in pain, where I stamp in her face. In the corner three women are wrestling an ANC boy and one takes hold of his gun. Before I can do anything, another soldier runs his bayonet right through her, then drops down to clear his jammed rifle. I look around to get my bearings. I see a man's arse disappearing out the back door, while to my right someone lies bleeding in the corner. They're screaming, all of them, and aren't up for calming down. So I run to the huddle where the two ANC boys, now joined by the third, are about to rip the last two women to shreds. 'Stop!' I shout. 'Fucking stop!' Finally, after I throw one of them across the room like a Highland Games hammer and drop another to his knees, I get their attention. 'Right!' I say, puffing and panting. 'Fuck sake! Everybody just hold the fuck on!' I lean up and look about. There are bodies everywhere but not a young girl in sight. Next thing Konrad comes steaming through the door, thinking we've all had it.

'What the fuck?' he says, looking at the state of the place. 'What's going on?'

'Check for the girl, Konrad, quick. Look in the rooms. And you,' I shout to the ANC boy picking himself up from under the table, 'on that Browning!'

Konrad checks one room then the next, before finally wrenching the door away from the jammed-in kid and stepping over his broken body. He disappears, only to come stumbling back holding a teenage girl like he is manhandling a prisoner. It was her.

'Fuck me,' I said, holding out my hands to appease her. 'Konrad, not so hard, mate, take it easy. We're supposed to be saving her.'

He looked at me. He went to let go but she tried to leg it, so this time he picked her up and marched her out. 'Come on,' he said, banging her head off the door frame. 'Let's get out of this fucking place.'

I gestured to the boys and we left, while the women who could sat pleading before running after us as we tried to make our exit.

Back at the jeep we tried to get through to her. We spoke French, we spoke English, we tried Swahili and Swedish but she wasn't having it. She was hysterical, bitter and angry – and there was nothing else we could do. So, with no other option, we left the liberated house after five minutes in a state that the Simbas hadn't managed in five months and made a beeline back to our billets and the safehouse we'd earmarked on the off-chance that we'd get her.

With the ANC boys paid off, we stuck her in the far-away bedroom of a semi-demolished house. Thirty-six hours earlier it was home to the Simbas. Now it was ours and we'd chosen the furnishings. Blood and brain splatter ran along the walls like an organic emulsion, while the bricks, dust and debris teemed with life that was seldom seen but always heard. It wasn't much but we called it home. We sat her in the corner and tried to reason with her. I told her who we were and why we'd grabbed her, and that her dad had sent us and was now worried sick. This all seemed to calm her down but when I walked forward and took down her gag, she screamed like a maniac, then bit me when I went to stick it back on. I had to stop myself from slapping her. And by god it was difficult. I turned to Konrad. It wasn't that I valued his advice but sometimes an opinion can be handy. But nothing. Instead we stood there like a couple of clueless poofs who'd just been made fathers. I looked at my watch: it was now late evening. During the afternoon I'd learned of a flight out at 1100hrs the next day. I'd got friendly with one of the ANC officers at the airport and, after cementing our relationship with a whole gold coin – a small fortune – I could have whatever I asked for whenever it was possible.

I now realised that I'd made a prisoner of a prisoner and so began to get frustrated. It all seemed so unnecessary. I mean I'd managed the impossible but now, with the stone resting on top of the mountain, I began to see it slipping back down. She was mad, no doubt, and for whatever reason she had no interest in helping us, as whatever we did she was going to fight it. Getting a screaming girl aboard a plane was never going to be easy, but all the way to London? How the fuck were we going to do that?

The room was now dark and the moon shone through the glassless window and cast our shadows on the sinew-splashed walls behind us. Part of me wanted to kick her arse out of the seat and let her walk back to where we'd found her, while another part could so easily have killed her myself. But as the lure of fortunes in London was all but consuming, I had to keep pushing.

'Right, I've had it,' I said, leaning towards her but talking to Konrad. 'I've fucked about long enough here. This is our diamond and it's worth fuck all until we get it out of the mines and back to the buyer.' Then I leaned closer and whispered in her ear, 'We've come too far to be fucked about by you, do you hear? One way or another you'll be on that plane – and then back to London.'

And I turned to Konrad and led him out of the room. 'This is what we do. We tie her up, gag her and stick her in a coffin. Some of the ANC dead will be getting flown back to Leopoldville in the morning. We'll stick her in amongst them. Rod can get her at the other end. Fuck, if needs be we'll keep her in it, get her aboard a ship and let her out when we're at sea. If one of us has to quit to do this, so be it. In fact . . .' I said, grabbing hold of his arm. 'Listen, the money's too much to lose here. You do it, or me. One of us can head out on that flight with her and at Leopoldville we'll cross the bridge when it comes. Let's just get her out of here!'

Konrad thought about it, then thought some more, before . . . 'I'll go,' he said firmly. I smiled. That was fine by me; it was only to Leopoldville and I was in no hurry to miss the Colonel's mystery tour of the Leopard lands. So a few hours later, after having sourced ourselves a coffin, we bound her limbs before binding her to the base of the casket so she couldn't move or make any noise. I shoved a sock in her mouth and taped it shut, then grabbed hold of the lid and lined it up. She was utterly terrified but all I could see was a pile of money at the bottom of the casket. She shook her head from side to side and now, panicking like an ensnared animal, began nodding like she'd suddenly become sane and wanted to help us. But it was too late. Why gamble on trust when you can have certainty? So I slammed the lid shut and nailed it tight. I knew what that felt like – there are few things that come close. Along the side Konrad had driven several nails through the wood, before pulling them out to make holes for air. The flight would only take a few hours and she'd be out by teatime. What was a day? I explained to her the situation. She had hope. I'd had none. I did say that no matter what she heard, she should be quiet at all times and that if she did scream at all, at any point, we'd leave her in there. I also said that Konrad would be with her all of the way and that all she should do was go to sleep; the next face she'd see would be his in Leopoldville in just a few hours' time.

An hour later we had her lined up next to the war dead. Some were just in body-bags; others – especially the whites who were killed and who weren't being buried on site – were boxed and ready to go. As we made our way back to our hovel, I was completely exhausted. My mind and body were shattered from all of my extra-curricular activities and I was fantasising about my floor space within our derelict homestead. But that wasn't to be. Like a bee-sting on sunburn, no sooner had we parked up than a Brit who billeted one block over called me along to get saddled up. Hoare was back and we had no time to lose. At that I was pissed off but powerless and well knew that I'd have to ship out and leave Konrad alone. Still, I reassured myself, he was no fool and I could tell that he craved a good break. Like I said, he was a tough man but was new to barbarism. A few cold beers and a couple of Leopoldville hookers would help to sort him out. So I shook his hand and headed off, off to a fight with the Leopard Men – another story for another time.

Five hundred miles later I was back and once again stood outside that billet, but the building was bare. I asked some of the lads who were dotting about where Konrad was but they were new from Salisbury and so were waiting on the Colonel before getting their assignments. I'd been away for over two weeks and, with no access to the single-band radio transmitter, I'd been living in an information blackout. The trip had been long, arduous and traumatic but my mind had been elsewhere. Like a love-struck teenager, unable to rid myself of the image of my desire, I'd fantasised about my earner and the life I'd soon live because of it. Even when I'd been in the thick of it, the notion of it had stayed as a feeling if not as a thought.

But after a while, not being able to find Konrad was perplexing. He was my only access to information and without him my dream would all but disappear. I searched frantically, even missing a debrief that had just been ordered. So I jumped in a jeep and paid an ANC black to drive me up to the airport. I found my officer friend but he was in a meeting with one of our chiefs, Captain Mann – a white mercenary who was too close to Hoare for me to go blurting to. My officer mate looked out at me and I tried to analyse his expression: did it mean good or bad, or what? I was driving myself mad and now, caught between worry and anger, I went from pillar to post. But nothing. Everyone was new and I found it impossible to get answers. So I doubled back and, with a courage born of necessity, I made straight for my officer, who was now walking out with the captain, carrying files and area maps in large brown tubes. He saw me coming and so excused himself briefly to meet me halfway.

'Athol, Athol, my friend. How are you?' he said, extending a hand still some yards away.

'Good,' I said unconvincingly. 'Where's Konrad?'

'Yes,' he said, looking over his shoulder. 'Yes, Konrad,

please: there is a message for you in the radio room.'
And at that he summarily ended the conversation and
scurried back to the authority figure who stood watching
us disapprovingly. Two minutes later I was standing over a
radio clerk, watching him flick backwards through the files
with no sense of urgency. Licking his fingers, he searched
one way then the next, then read something unrelated to me
but of interest to him, while I breathed down his neck. I was
angry. I could feel my blood boiling. And, like waiting on test
results to see if I was dying, the tension was crippling.

I was about to cripple him when: 'Ah, here we are,' he
said, holding it up, oblivious to how near he was to death.
He handed me over a single slip of paper. It was a two-
week-old communication:

To AV from KP: Plane diverted to reinforce Paulis stop Was
grounded after fire stop Got separated stop Am assigned to
52 Commando stop All bodies buried with military honour
stop C'est le Congo stop

XIII

LONDON CALLING

'Fucking city boys!' he said, shuffling his chair to let the pint-carrying prick past, before wiping the drips off his shoulder like he was brushing away the flies.

'City what?' I said, shouting through the noise.

'City boys. Cunts from the banks and that – you know, the City of London. Posh cunts – think they're the business.'

I nodded and sat back. He was right but they were all cunts to me, so what was the difference? But then he got bumped again, which made me laugh, as another fat cunt brushed through while he was taking a sip and this time it went right over his shirt. I waited on the inevitable. But instead he just smiled and sat there. Seemed Billy, as I'm calling him, was in a 'letting go' stage of his life. Well, he'd just been banging on about ducks and watery backs for the last half-hour, while trying to be all Zen-like, so he had to leave it.

I knew Billy from the Guards. He was a hard man, no doubt, over 6 ft 3 in. and built like a beast, and it would take a brave man to deny it. I called him the Anglo-Glaswegian – well, he was a weegie who now lived in London – and,

like the yobs who leave jail as hardened criminals, the army
had taken a hammer to him and added some weight. So I
sat there watching him and was pretty impressed. The Billy
of old would have been rolling about, biting their ears off
and frothing at the mouth but instead he just sat there, as
if sitting in a temple.

'You all right, Gandhi?' I said to him, as he steadily went
red.

He looked up and I waited. 'Yeah,' he said, as finally the
pressure dropped, like air escaping from a balloon. 'See . . .
see how calm I am?' And at that he finished his pint and
used the edge of the tablecloth to dab down his shirt. In
fact Billy was all right. It might seem the wrong thing to
say, but war had made Billy behave better in the outside
world: more grounded and reasonable. At first I thought
he was just mimicking a junkie – in that if you're into
heroin, what good's a joint? What's a little knock in a pub
if you've fought in a war? But it wasn't that. Instead it was
the nature of violence itself, and his own ability to commit
it, that had been Billy's teacher. Like me Billy was now at
war with himself, and his choosing not to fight, when he
knew fine well that he could, was proving to be significantly
more satisfying. 'Abstinence rather than action,' he said to
me, trying be all monk-like.

'All right, all right,' I said, shaking my head and laughing.
'Let's see how long that lasts when you get knocked again.'
And at that I went to the bar.

London was, as it is now, a real melting pot. It's got the
lot: colour, creed and money – or a distinct lack of it for
many. Whereas other parts of the world can pacify your
need for riches, there's no place like London to remind you
that you're skint. And I was. That's why I'd called Billy. In
all my life I've only had one friend, Rod McLean, but Billy
was a definite contender. In many ways he was like me but,
though we shared the same ingredients, one part of the recipe

was off, resulting in two very different hotpots: while Billy was upfront, I was anything but.

Anyway, Africa had drained me and a couple of years on I was broke again in London. Besides, I was tired of running through the jungles and needed a break from the head fuck. So I called Billy – well, his old alchie mum – to see what he was up to and if he had any ideas for making a few quid. He did.

I got back to the table, not without kicking his chair for a laugh, which worked a treat as he turned around and, with even less Zen than David Carradine, motioned that he was going to hook me.

We were on the King's Road and the place was happening. I hated crowds, and hated all people, but like I was watching TV I felt remote enough to be in amongst it. In the far corner a band played their music, while the bar and floor, once busy, were now fully crowded. I liked the noise, not because of the music but because it covered the silent breaks between conversations that I found so impossible to deal with. Instead I'd hide behind cigarettes and take more sips than necessary to finish my pints, the pints then disappearing faster than they'd arrived. By seven o'clock I'd be drunk; by half-past I'd be reekin'.

I was now fixated. The City boys had gone from a sideshow to a spectacle. I watched their arrogance and it got to me. They were loud and acted young, although they were older than us – late 20s, early 30s. I saw how they were with the bar staff and with the people around them, Billy having moved himself round to avoid the consequences. He was talking to me about his plans and I was agreeing to them. But I wasn't listening – not a word – which annoyed him and so, like a bird who was being pacified while her bloke was trying to watch the telly, he complained that I wasn't paying attention to him. Anyway, they were buying wine, then spirits, then champagne and at one point Hugo, the biggest of them, threw a note at the barman's head when paying him. They laughed, while he was humiliated. Then he belched, loudly enough for me to hear it even though the music was on. I couldn't stop staring; I couldn't help thinking about him standing there with no skin on, or at least slicing him through with my blade. Then the smaller one, the ugliest of the five but the best dressed and with the trendiest haircut, began pointing. I followed his finger, until, less than five yards away through a parting in the crowd, I saw a female. She was young, about 20, and was stood there with a friend listening to the band and holding a drink. She was fat, really fat, and she knew it. She looked sheepish and uncomfortable. Hugo laughed and, like he was at a rugby match, began yelling. She saw him, she saw them all but, apart from shooting the odd glance, she stood behind her blushes and stared at the ground. I watched her. I watched closely. I watched how much care she'd taken before coming out. I saw how neatly she was dressed, how her colours matched, how her earrings and necklace coordinated with her bracelets and shoes. I saw her fingers and well-filed nails as she cupped her glass. They were perfectly painted. But she looked sad. I imagined her then, existing alone like me, in a body that imprisoned her, and in a state of such self-loathing that meant each day was a struggle to finish it. Sitting there, I became her. I imagined the sheer will it took for her to go out. I imagined the effort she made, the time it took, the thought put in. I imagined her fears. But I imagined her hopes too. I knew about opposites sharing the same space. Like me once she was putting herself out there, displaying all that was wrong and hoping for the best. Then I noticed them. They were standing up and rifling through their pockets, before throwing down their notes onto the wine-covered table. I strained to hear them but saw she was watching. And I got it. They were throwing a whip-round for whoever would shag her.

I felt a rage – a sickening rage. I'd seen a still painting and given it meaning. I watched the small one, the little ugly bastard, put up his hand, 'I'll do it!' he proclaimed, grabbing the money. I hated him the most. I hated him so much that his breathing offended me. I couldn't understand it. They cheered him like he was a stuntman who'd soon ride a bull. He was pathetic. In the male world he was far uglier than she was fat. How dare he not know his place? She wouldn't have gone with him if the cash was for her! Well, of course, in the end he shat it and put the money back. Seemed the wee man in big-man's boots was happy with an ego-stroking from his cock-heavy table. It must have been enough that his City-boy pals considered him capable of achieving the score, like getting a bye for a short putt at golf. Well, how fucking dare he! I turned back to see her but she was off. She might have been heading to another bar where these bastards weren't sitting but, in my mind, she was off home, buckled with a humiliation that would keep her in for a lifetime.

The band took a break and Billy started on again about money. I had next to fuck all and he had even less but he was saying that we'd sort it out the next day. But after a pause I stopped him ranting. 'Nah, mate,' I said, holding my hand up. 'I'm sorting it out now. Billy, get yourself to the door. I'll be out in a minute.' The wee man was off to the toilet. And so was I.

Hugo was still shouting, his audience was still laughing but the wee man was off on his own. The toilet was at the bottom of some stairs near the door. He stopped at the top, rummaged in his pockets for a smoke, which he found, and then, on the stairway, began looking for a light. 'Thanks,' he said, startled at the lit match I'd speedily held to his face. Then I looked deep into his privileged eyes in a way he'd never been stared at and followed him in. The toilet had a period-piece Armitage Shanks running the length of the right wall, while two cubicles – doors stopping a foot short of the floor – sat immediately on the left. He went into the first cubicle, while I walked to the urinal. There were three men in there: two pissing and one washing his hands. I took my dick out but I couldn't go. See I can't piss in front of people, so, standing there waiting on the others to go, I started to hate them too. I reached round my back and found my tool: a First World War German 'sawback blade' bayonet. I thought about doing them all but sense rather than drink got to me. Two left. Then I heard a rolling behind me, followed by the rustling of that tracing paper 'shit wipe' that takes layers off your arse. I looked to my left and one man was still there, so I glared at him and he looked at me looking at him, then fucked off with his long hair trailing. I was in!

I booted that door like I was escaping from a blaze. It fucked him – the door smashing his face in as I went in on top. With his pants near licking his ankles I leathered him from one side of the stall to the other, beating him like a heavy punchbag with no space to swing in. He tried to talk, he tried to scream but no sooner had he let out his first yell than I shattered his face with a footballer's head-butt, which belted him backwards. I grabbed his throat and, with my hands firmly round his trachea, I held him fast against the sidewall and, lifting his slacks with my foot, I took out his wallet. He tried to talk but I bent in close and began smelling his fear. I stuck his wallet in my pocket, then, with a fixed stare and a smile, I held my blade to his face. Now he knew where his place was! Still holding his gaze and filled with venom, I slammed the knife between his legs and tried to cut off his cock. But instead I missed it and splintered the panelling. So I shook it out and was about to try again when I heard laughing on the stairs. It was a voice that I recognised.

At that I readied myself, tucked in my blade and closed

the broken door behind me, leaving him for dead. 'Hugo, how's it going?' I lambasted, as he wandered in with his fat fucking face and stinking cigar. 'Nae bother, eh? Had a good night? You'll remember me, I promise!' And at that I tapped him on the cheek before making my way out.

When I got to the top, Billy was standing there like a doorman – in fact he was taking a couple of quid from some punter as an entrance fee. The fool twigged when I turned up but was told to get fucked – which, luckily, he did.

'Where you been?' Billy said to me impatiently.

I knew he was half-kidding and when I lifted out my new wallet, he soon settled down. 'I took it off that wee guy, that wee shit. C'mon!' I said, hailing a cab. 'Let's get out of here.'

In the cab I took out my find and rifled through it. It contained the best part of £12 – not bad for the day. About 50 yards up the street the cabbie stopped to whistle at a mate but I encouraged him to keep on moving. Hugo could get to fuck but the police could spoil the party and the night was still young. Twelve quid was hardly the down payment on a house, so we opted to arse the lot that night and worry about it the next morning.

Within the hour we'd gone from one bar to the next and now, propping ourselves up against a wall, we pondered our moves. 'Fancy a whore?' he said to me, now taking a slash in a doorway. I thought about it. Billy knew me but he didn't 'really' know me. Sex for me was an issue and it wouldn't help for him to know my truth. 'Come on!' he wheedled. 'Let's do a couple hookers. I know where to go – there's an area up there,' he said, indicating the direction with his head. 'It's not far. It's Soho. You know the place. Some of the birds are all right. I mean some are fucking stinking but there's a chance there's a few nice ones about. Come on

– fuck trying to score a couple of real ones, especially with you, you fucking weirdo. It's that or nothing.'

To be honest nothing was good. Thrashing that City boy was my kind of sex – and I'd had it. But he was off. And as I was staying with him near Brixton, south of the river, so was I.

Soho back then was right seedy, while now it's all poofs and could easily be Rome or Madrid in the summer. We'd barely hit Old Compton Street when a couple of munters approached us. 'Fancy a blowjob, gentlemen?' one of them said in her East End accent.

'Aye, I do – but not off you, ya pig!' barked Billy, which went down well.

She spat at him and had it not been for Billy the Zen and his raging horn for a decent bird he'd have punched her into next week. Instead we turned down one street and then the next. It was Saturday night and the place was busy. Then, after five minutes, we came to a door and went in. The staircase was rickety and falling to bits, and, as we passed by doors sealed shut, making them just more walls, I felt less than randy and more and more anxious. At the top we hit a door with a bell. And so, like two perverts, we stood there, waiting on them assessing us through a foggy glass peephole. The door opened and she was beastly. 'Is Darren there?' said Billy, thinking fast, to which a confused troll pig answered no. We left, laughing, and in ten steps we were in another entrance. The first encounter had persuaded my mind that things were all right. The place looked shit and the birds were worse but at least we'd be making it out, and so I relaxed and began to get into it. The next door, on the second floor this time, was opened by a madam. She was in good nick and friendly. But the living room looked like a bus station or dominoes night at the local.

'All right, love,' she said to Billy. 'We're busy tonight. The girl will be with you in an hour.'

I turned to Billy. 'The girl? As in the one and only girl?'

He laughed. Then, as we looked around, and at the men sitting patiently with their hard-ons, we decided to bail.

They say third time lucky and so did we, leaving the main area and heading down a side street or two to look for one more. 'Yes?' a woman yelled at the top of her voice as the door was flung open. 'You want in? Well come on then; in you come!' She was off her fucking head. 'No, don't sit there, sit here – yes, over here. Now what do you want? You want to see the girl? She'll be through in a minute. Now, take your jackets off. Come on!' And at that she disappeared, leaving us in shock. Like two chastised schoolkids, we sat on her sofa, awaiting our fate. So I went to light a smoke but she walked back in. 'No, no, no, I don't allow it. You can't smoke here!' So I put it out but was amazed. There was something about this woman. She was old – 50s – and had let herself go somewhat. But she must have looked shit hot in her own day. Now, dressed for the time, she walked her flat like a true madam, her long silk dress flowing around her, her hair neat and held up by a band that suited her. Two minutes later a girl came through. She was young, 18 at most, and attractive, with shoulder-length hair. She wasn't from London but somewhere up north – north of England, I thought.

'Now, who's first?' asked the madam.

I looked at Billy and shoved him forward. This was his gig; it was only right. But as he left, I felt I was the lucky one. I tried to make some polite conversation with the madam but she wasn't interested. I asked her for some water, as the booze was getting to me, but she didn't respond until I'd asked twice by raising my voice. Then I asked her if she was working – as in, was she up for a fuck. She said no – though she did answer that one first time.

The minutes were quick. Billy was quicker. No sooner had

I relaxed than he was out of there and now he was standing before me, grinning like a beast in a playground. 'That,' he said, 'was fucking mental!' And at that he slumped down beside me and made a grab for my water.

Now it was my turn. I stood up and made my way in. This wasn't the first time that I'd paid for it but it was certainly my first hooker in London. The room was darkened and the bed covers scabby. I could imagine how many bare arses had been there that day but before it bothered me I looked towards the wardrobe and saw a menu. Like a restaurant it had everything you could imagine, followed by a number. You name it, it was there. Then she came in – she was nice, no doubt – and told me to undress, which I did. So as I stood there naked, she fucked about in front of me, fiddling in a drawer. Then she asked what I wanted and demanded the money. At that I felt vulnerable, at the hands of a stupid wee girl, and it began to feel wrong. My demons were there, they were always there, but in that moment of absurdity – that I, the Congo Killer, was being intimidated like this – keeping a handle on things was proving to be difficult.

'Lie down,' she told me. So I did. Then, while I watched, she casually got undressed like she was in a fitting room. I hated it. I hated the fact that she acted like I wasn't even there. She might as well have said 'Come on and get stuck into me!'. The moment was without eroticism, without anything arousing. Then she sat next to me and began rubbing my back, which I hate, but while doing it she tried chatting like we were sharing a bus seat. She asked me where I was from, what I was doing in London, if I had been to Newcastle and, if so, where she should go. She asked me if I liked football. Fuck – she should have just asked about the mechanics of a combustion engine!

So at that point I stopped her. 'Wait the now!' I said, standing up and heading to my trousers with purpose. 'I've heard enough! I'm here to fuck – not to talk.' And at that I pulled out my wallet – well, wee man's wallet – and flung her the notes. It was a lot, best part of eight quid and a fair whack in those days. She paused and picked up the money. It was all I had. 'Right!' I said, taking control again. 'If you want all that – and there's more,' I lied, 'then you go get that fat cow in here with you.' She said something but I wasn't listening. Then in her nakedness she left and after two minutes came back in – with the madam. And the party was on.

At that I understood the true power of money. Sure I'd manipulated, tortured and maimed people into submission but this was the first time that I'd bought them. Everyone has their own price and that night in Soho it was exactly eight quid, or four quid apiece.

Within a minute I had the madam's big arse spread like butter, as she propped up the wall like it was a shakedown. Then, a moment after that, the little one, as cute as you like, was licking her arse like it was the last of the jam from the jar. I loved it. The power felt great and was truly addictive. The madam had been bossy, in control, if you like, as she had presented herself as above it all, and certainly beyond us. But now, for a few pieces of paper, she was bent over double, being defiled by a kid on the orders of me. I fucked one. I fucked the other. Then, as I sat wanking, I watched them fuck each other. The little one gagged – she wasn't into it – so I kept on, while getting off on her discomfort. Finally, and only when I said, I finished it off, by having them crawl around like dogs while I screamed out orders.

Pulling myself up, I stuck on my clothes and saw their disgust. They might have been professionals or seasoned campaigners but I'd broken their humanity for just eight pounds sterling. So, brushing my hair back, and without saying a word, I walked through to Billy, who was sitting there gobsmacked. 'What the fuck?' he said to me as I lit up my smoke. I said nothing other than 'let's go'. And so we meandered our way out and left the flat door swinging.

XIV

THE HIP OPERATION

Waking up at Billy's was always a dull one. For starters he lived in a semi with his mum, new dad, umpteen siblings – halves and quarters – and a multitude of pets: three dogs, two cats and a canary. The house was stinking and gave me allergic reactions. Each morning I'd wake up to the sound of his dad coughing his lungs out while farting away, then that same fucking joke, 'There's no safe fart over 40!', followed by him laughing to himself, still pished from his last bucket of vodka from the night before.

Nothing happened in the Billy household before the first fag of the morning. Sitting in silence, they'd stare at each other with fuck all to say till their nicotine levels were up to where they'd stay till nightfall and the last one before bed. His mum was nice but by Christ she was ugly. She was Glaswegian–Welsh and looked it. Her teeth were near gone and her jaw line collapsed, while her reddened skin was only broken by even redder blemishes and a crusty wart thing that grew bigger each day. That said, he loved his mum: she had a good heart and would walk over hot coals for him. His dad was a nice guy until his first drink, which was usually before lunch. Then he was a cunt and, like an old steamer, fancied himself as a heavy, though he was more of a 'jakie'. Still, this was no battered-kid story and, while his dad would spin a yarn or two, having two soldiers under his roof kept him from yarning the day away.

So, as usual, I woke up the next morning to his dad but fuck did it hit me: I'd spent it all! I was fucking pissed off. The problem wasn't what I'd used it for – the whore fest was amazing – but more about what else I could have done with the money. Worse than that, I didn't even have enough to buy my own fags for the first-of-the-morning ritual. Billy woke up to me cursing away and when I filled him in, he was cursing too. It might seem strange that we sat there arguing about money I'd stolen in the first place but there you have it – we were thieving bastards. I found the wallet and went through it again but no cash, only a couple of useless cards. After ten minutes Billy announced that we'd just have to get on with his idea, which he'd explain on the way.

Now being skint is one thing but to have absolutely no money to your name and, more so, not even to have the ability to raise it or see a day when it's coming is a very particular feeling. Mentally it's a state of hopelessness, or a worthlessness that saturates you like water. Even though you fight, it soaks you to the bone. Everyone you see is a target for your jealousy and the longer it goes on, the deeper the desperation gets.

We left that morning after having tea with unbuttered toast and, otherwise hungry, began walking to Charing Cross, the train and Tube station at the Trafalgar Square end of the Strand. When we got there, I knew exactly what he was planning. A good few years earlier, a month or so before Kenya, a couple of the guys had made a few quid by robbing gay men at the stations. It was known as 'rolling the poofs' and was seen as trouble-free and relatively easy for the following two reasons: firstly they were poofs and so less likely to fight, and secondly you could roll more than one in a day, because they'd never report it for fear of being outed, harassed or moved on by the police. So by two o'clock I was standing about, watching Billy. We'd tossed a coin and he'd drawn the first turn. He'd be the bait, then lure his victim away into the labyrinth of tunnels that connected the station entrances and cosh him – or, if his catch seemed rich, we'd go back to his house, where we'd screw it over and rob him blind.

But after a half-hour's cruising we'd got nothing. And as Billy walked about, looking guys up and down and getting fuck all, he was getting angry. We swapped around, because he obviously looked far too threatening. Now I was standing there when, after two minutes, a suited man came up next to me and started reading a paper. I looked at him, more like a mugger than a shagger, but lust, as I knew, could often be blinding. Then he asked me for the time, which I told him. Then he asked after my accent. I said South African–Scottish. He asked if I was going somewhere, to which I replied, 'With you.'

Cunt fumbled his paper as the burst of excitement near made him sick. 'Oh g-g-great!' he said, with a stammer in his voice. 'I know where we can go, as well.' And at that he ushered me to follow. So now I was off with some random man I'd just picked up.

He headed down the stairs and into the tunnels, and, when we walked around a bend, I glanced back to see Billy, who was sticking out like a fiend, stalking away. But then I felt a pull on my elbow and it was my man, now standing beside me and pointing to the toilets. And he was sorting out a plastic bag that he'd taken from his pocket. 'Don't worry,' he said soothingly. 'I've done this before. We can go in here but the doors on the toilets don't cover our legs. So if I sit down, you stand in this and I'll suck you off. That way, from the outside, it looks like a man on the toilet with some shopping between his legs.'

I looked at him – what?

'Don't worry,' he followed up, softly stroking my arm. 'It's safe and fun.'

Believe me, I wasn't worried. I was just trying to understand what the fuck he was talking about. But then I figured that getting him to a confined space with few people in it was just what I needed, so I followed him in past the attendant, who was on his way out.

Well, the toilets were stinking: that universal stench of stale piss mixed with bleach blocks that glow in the trough like septic sugar cubes. I hated it. So when I got into the cubical and he sat down, instead of my 'pork sword' to chew on, he got a 9 in. German sword, which I held to his eyeball, the tip just breaking the skin to let him feel his own blood. 'Now give me your wallet, your watch and that ring round your finger.' Well, he near passed out, so I removed the knife and shopped on him like I was picking fruit off a tree. Two minutes later I was heading to breakfast with Billy, with a tenner, a gold-plated watch, a chain I found under his collar and a solid gold pinky ring.

Two days later, though, we were back. Billy had sorted us out some work later that week and, while part of me was thinking about Africa and getting back to my life, I felt I owed it to my youth to stick around and play with the rest of them. The watch wasn't up to much and the pinky ring, which I found out was unique to aristocrats and the informed pretenders, was hallmarked with a crest and so only worth smelting. In any case we were low on cash and so, changing nothing but my shirt, I was once again standing at Charing Cross, looking for some action.

This time the fish weren't biting and, after an hour and a few stares from the station cops, we moved off for a pint. Four pints later we were back but, as I approached my perch,

I saw it was taken. Still, I thought, it could be a blessing and so I walked on over. He looked at me. He was near Billy's size and looked pretty fit – but a poof's a poof, so I didn't care. Then he looked away and lit a smoke, which threw the ball back at me. I didn't have anything to hide behind so I asked him for a smoke, which he reluctantly gave me. But then I felt lost. I had no idea about being the instigator so, after an awkward minute, which I truly hated, I asked him the time, then where his accent was from. It was from England, which made me look like an arse. Then I asked him where he was going. Well, that had all been good enough for me, so it must have been all right for him.

But now, five minutes in, and with Billy egging me on in the distance, I was starting to fret. Like a high-school loser asking out a bird, I said, 'Eh, do you, eh, do you fancy a walk?'

He looked at me and, with a haunting smile, said, 'All right. Let's go back to yours.'

'No,' I said, for obvious reasons. 'What about yours?'

'No, I can't,' he replied abruptly.

'Well,' I said, scratching my head, 'I know a place.' And at that I began taking him down to the toilets.

Now on the way down it all seemed off. I mean I can't say what's normal or not normal but the last guy seemed nervous, excited almost, whatever, but this guy was quiet and concentrated and never even looked at me. A moment later we'd got to the bog and I motioned him inside. I didn't have a bag or any of that so I fired straight in. But, though the floor space was empty, the cubicles were busy. So we stood there staring, and staring, and then staring some more, before my awkwardness got the better of me and I pretended to use the basin but instead turned round and thump! I bashed the bastard right in the jaw, before grabbing for my knife – but fuck! Instead of going down, he came right back at me, laying into me like he was drowning. I tried for my blade but he had me up against the sinks and wasn't backing off. So now we were punching and kicking and trying every fucking thing that was going – and then I saw him reaching and he pulled out a Stanley. Bastard! Now it was on. By this time the toilets had emptied, the users legging it, their shits still half-hanging. He swiped at my face, my neck, my hands and chest. He was frantic and, like a caged animal now facing its death, he had a strength that was overpowering. Then he turned me but, with the exit now behind him, he stayed to fight instead of bolting. Well, then it happened. Billy, from nowhere, flew through the door and near took the cunt's head off. He stumbled forward onto his knees but Billy flew over him, unable to stop, and slammed into the cubicles, demolishing the partitions. So I jumped on the bastard's back and he swung me about as I elbowed his head and tried cracking his skull. But, like a rodeo bull, he was jumping and while Billy was now smashing him, he was barging me up against a wall, which shattered its tiles all over the floor. Finally he dropped and spilled me with him. As I crashed to the floor, I saw Billy grabbing his wallet and trying for his watch. Then the two of us, as fucked as we were, give him one more boot for good measure before bolting like fuck – and away from the police.

Five minutes later we were past the Embankment and approaching Temple, on the banks of the Thames. We stopped and collapsed on a bench. We were fucked. 'What a guy,' said Billy, gasping for breath. 'What kind of fucking poof was he? A super poof?' I held out my hand and Billy threw me his wallet. 'Here,' he said. 'Let's hope it was worth it.'

I felt it. It was some fancy wallet made of sharkskin or something. 'We've scored here, eh?' I said, opening it. But damn, there was nothing. I flicked through the flaps: still nothing – absolutely fuck all. I was sick.

After a minute to take it all in, I chucked it back and began laughing out loud. 'Oh well,' I sighed. 'Just treat it as a training session, eh?'

'Aye, a workout that needs stitches!' said Billy, probing his now lumpy face, before looking at his new wallet. 'He's got cards in here, though! All right, John Harris [not his real name] – John "as fucking broke as we are" Harris – let's see what you've got.'

But then a silence, so I looked over to see him studying a card with a picture on it. 'What is it?' I said. 'What?'

He looked at me. Then he looked at the card and started laughing, though the pain kept jolting him. 'We,' he paused. 'We were trying to roll poofs, right? Well, my stupid friend, we just rolled a Para! Yup, we've just rolled John Harris of Her Majesty's Parachute Regiment.'

I looked at him. 'Fuck off!'

'Look!' He threw me his warrant card.

'So . . . we just rolled a man who was trying to roll us?'

'Yes, my brother!' Billy said, holding up his empty cash-holder. 'We just robbed a robber!' Bastard!

Two days later we were walking down Queensway towards a flat on Inverness Terrace. The poof-bashing was firmly arsed: apart from our mishap in targeting, there was no doubt that the London toilet company would be chasing us for a refit. This Bayswater flat was in one of those posh white stacks and was owned by a guy called Desmond that Billy had got talking to one night while out. Des, I was told, had a band. (I'm going to have to make up its name here, as well as Des's and its other members', to protect their worthless arses.) They were hardly the Beatles but, in the time before DJs, bands were it and could get pretty infamous without having to be on *Top of the Pops*. According to Billy he was from quite a well-to-do family and instead of his dad scoffing at him on leaving university, he'd actually supported him. The result was the musical marvels The Hip Operation.

The doorway was grand and the entrance was grander. But that's where it stopped. If I said 'squat', I'd be putting it lightly. Sure the building reeked of wealth, and so did Desmond, but he'd taken the bohemian lifestyle to heart. Instead of carpet he had exposed floorboards and fag ends. And instead of wallpaper he had old lead paint from the building's original construction and dark flaked layers from whoever else had lived there. Desmond greeted us like an all-welcoming vicar with long hippy hair. He stood there, a waif-like man with snake hips and Falmers – green velvet, at that – and while his shirt struggled to stay shut with its one done-up button, his collection of medallions swung like pendulums around his chicken-like neck. And I instantly wanted to snap it. His voice was posh and so was his manner as he introduced us to his fellow marauders. From one stupid name to the next, so he went, but I had long since stopped listening. In the corner lay three long-haired wasters – women, men, no difference. Without a grin or expression they sat dead with their eyes wide open. And while Des sat down, cooking up a fix, I steadily got the picture of why we were needed. The Hip Operation had been on the go for a year and were due to go touring the north – by that I mean north of England – with a couple of Scottish dates, if they could get them. Now they had a manager, a manager in the loosest of terms – really a junkie fuck who'd managed to book dates. From past experience of doing these gigs, though, and a fair amount of drug-induced paranoia, they wanted some protection. No big deal, Des said, but some of the clubs they'd play were rough and were, at times, less than happy to pay up, so a couple of heavies looking out for them wouldn't go amiss.

Well, that all sounded fine to me. I figured what they really wanted was a couple of roadies, helping them with their gear and deflecting the odd pint glass, as no doubt they were piss. Des said he'd pay us from his own money, so regardless of what happened we'd be taken care of. He said we'd get two hundred up front for the two weeks on the road and another hundred when we got back. On top of that, he said, the pubs might bung us a few quid if they had a good night and would definitely see us all right for drink.

So we agreed and the next day we stood to attention with our money in one hand and the keys to a Bedford Dormobile in the other. That, along with a Transit for the gear, would get the four band members, the manager and us around for the next fortnight. Well, it didn't take long to see that even bands have their politics. Up front in the Transit were Des and the manager, Derek, while we had the other three in the back of our Dormobile, stuffed in with the luggage. We promptly told them to shut it when they started to moan. I don't think they'd expected such caring security! Anyway, en route they were smoking and we were both drinking, and so the conversation got flowing. Turned out that Des was Peter the bass player's rival. And I mean rival. This might have been the flower-power era, and them the children of it, but they were ambitious and competitive – and it ran into everything. They competed for birds, for acclaim, for who took the front and for the direction of the band. By all accounts Peter was a good bass player but Des was a gifted lead guitarist. And they both knew it. Anyway, along the road to Newcastle we heard the lot but it soon got boring as they began sounding like fishwives. See Billy and me never talked about the past. I mean we'd have a laugh about Kenya or about being back in Britain but we never exchanged stories or dwelled on what was done. And although we both knew war, and in part missed it, for different reasons we refused to go into it. For me I was hiding myself. And for him, well, it was personal. But for both of us it meant a low tolerance and a distinct lack of patience for other people's prattling. That was a legacy that would soon define us.

I later knew a man who would take his Suzuki Hayabusa to over 200 mph before mulling over his problems. That was about perspective, as he claimed that only when his life could be measured in split seconds could he really appreciate the relativity of the issue. He was right. And so, as we drove, listening to their bitching, our enthusiasm for the whole idea began to fizzle out. Then Peter started talking about the club they were playing that night. 'Man,' he said, slurring his words. 'I hope you guys have brought your boxing gloves. This place is bad!'

'Yeah,' pipes up John the drummer. 'I remember this place last year. That's why Des wants you. The last two guys we had as security . . .' Then in the rear-view mirror I saw Peter kicking him. 'Yeah,' he went on, trying to come up with something else. 'Yeah, they did well but they couldn't make it this year.'

I looked at Billy, who'd now finished a bottle of cider. He piped up: 'What really happened?'

'Nah, nothing, man. Really, nothing happened. It's just it's a miners club, you know, and they can be pretty unforgiving.'

At that the soldier in Billy kicked in. We might have been heavies but we weren't stupid street tumblers. If there was a problem last year, and we were now going back to a working club with the same crowd, we needed to know about it. 'Right!' said Billy, now sounding more Glaswegian than usual – he did that when he got angry. 'You tell me now, or we'll stop the van and kick the fucking head off your shoulders!'

There was a pause. Then I saw a whole load of pushing and nodding, before, 'Eh, well,' said Peter. 'The last two guys got stabbed. Des does the gig because he owes the landlord money from a drug deal that fucked up.'

I looked at Billy, then back to them. 'Tell me about the drug deal.'

'Nah, wait, that's . . . that's in the past!' he replied, now trying to duck the whole thing.

Billy turned round. 'I'm not fucking about here. What's the deal?'

They said nothing, so, like an angry parent, I hit the breaks and leaned back to thump him.

'Stop – fuck – stop,' he moaned. 'That's how we do it. Derek sells. We do gigs and he sells – just to the landlords, mind, not to the punters. That's how we stay on the road and make our living.'

'What?' I asked. 'What are you selling – and how much?'

'Acid, weed, heroin – man, anything. I don't know how much. Derek and Des have it in the Transit.'

'It's usually a thousand,' the drummer pipes up. I looked at Billy. He looked at me. We needed to talk.

It was a service-station restroom where we held our war cabinet. And we'd been had – no doubt. We'd come along for the ride to keep our heads below the parapet but had instead been made into a couple of sandbags. That said, we were in no mood for leaving. There was money to be made and people to smash. Billy wanted to grab the gear and leave. I wanted to grab the money when they'd been paid and bolt with both. Either way we'd stick about and play it by ear. The minder idea was thus a faded memory. They could burn on stage and we wouldn't even piss on them.

No sooner had we got back in the van than our three kids started up again. 'Listen, though,' Peter said. 'It's a bad crowd at this one. Really. You're going to be at the stage all night, right? I mean, seriously, whatever you need to sort out with Derek is between you and him. These guys, these miners, are bad!'

'Don't you worry,' I said soothingly. 'We'll be real close, all night. Right, Billy?'

'Right, Athol.'

From the minute we hit this place, we could easily sense the tension. I mean this was the wrong band, for the wrong gig, in the worst place, at the wrong time. If Derek and Des were dealing, then why bother playing? Just turn up with the gear and fuck off. But no. For some reason they wanted to play here: the closest thing that England had to Addis Ababa.

I hated the place, really, but it was more: I hated the people. There were kids on pushbikes, little fucking tinkers who buzzed us like bees in a hive and hovered around as if we were the first 'white men' to visit. Then there were the older lads who turned up, their clothes ill fitting, their faces life beaten and who just sat there gobsmacked as if the circus was in town. And then there were the men: tough, sinewy bastards who trailed their knuckles, scratched their arses and evil-eyed us through the smoke of their endless 'rolly' fags. I hadn't even seen the women!

'Watch those Marshalls!' Derek barked at me as I manhandled the amps.

'I'm Athol,' I said to him. We hadn't been introduced.

'Yeah, whatever, Athol,' he said, dismissing me like a minion before pointing to where he wanted them. Then he walked straight past me like I wasn't even there and went on to his 'official state business'. I stopped dead. And as I sucked in the humiliation, nothing else mattered. That moment, that display of ignorance and arrogance mixed with an unshakable self-importance, was like a line of coke to my system. Billy saw me and smiled. He was starting to get me. 'Come on, then!' shouted an impatient Derek, his wide-boy accent drifting through the greying evening as he shuffled about in his snazzy suit. 'We haven't got all bloody night, you know!' We got moving.

The club was as you'd expect it. The light wood panelling ran from door to door, while the seats, tables and chairs were either bolted down or broken off, while extra seating lay scattered around: light corporation metals with orange plastic moulds, purposely stolen for the overflow evenings. The bar sold two types of whisky and one type of draught, and, as this night was special, they had imported rum, all the way from Manchester. Still, I wondered why these folk would buy drugs; they were workers, drinkers and brawlers, not fucking hippies and trippers. But then I looked through the double-barred windows and my question was answered: the buyers were the kids on the bikes. It wouldn't be long before they were selling their mum's jewellery for what the landlord was offering. A developing market.

Soon the setting sun gave way to the rising curtain. The band, knee-deep in worry, opened up with a couple of their own numbers until somebody shouted, 'Hey! Play something we know, ya bastards!' And at that they went with a tune that rallied the men and got the women tap-tapping their wrinkly stockinged feet to the beat before drinking the night away. Soon the booze, like the good times, was flowing.

Meanwhile, Billy and I were keeping our eyes wide open. We were here for the stash and that was that. As soon as we'd seen that the deal had been done, we'd be off – with the cash, the drugs, the whatever. And, not that it mattered, but if it did kick off, like they were adamant it would do, they'd still have a van to escape in.

At the top end of the bar Derek was holding court with a couple of locals. He was telling them 'wide cockney boy' stories and making them laugh. Not that they'd know it, but Pimlico's a far cry from the Bow and Derek was no East Ender. Behind us were the band, while in front was a sea of drinkers, with their potholed faces and NHS glasses. I looked at Billy and caught sight of Derek heading to the toilet or somewhere, so I motioned that he should follow

him. Ten minutes later he came back and pulled me over. He
wanted a word. I told him to wait for the break in the set.
So, while the band had a pint, we headed out to the van.

'I heard him talking,' Billy said to me, offering a smoke.

'Talking?'

'Arguing.'

'Who with?'

'I don't know but someone heavy, some local cunt that
was leaning on him.'

We sat there for a moment looking around. It was almost
summer but the night was chilly and the smoke filled the van,
blocking our view. I leaned in and wiped the windscreen. 'I
hate this fucking place. It's all wrong! They're watching us,
you know. Can you feel it?'

'Aye,' he nodded. 'I feel it, all right, like the jungle: the
thousands of eyes that are on you but you can't see them.
Those little tinker bastards. They're sure looking at us.'

'Anyway . . .'

'Yeah, and he said it's at home, in London – all of it.'

'All what?' I asked, still looking nervously into the
darkness.

'Drugs? Money? I don't know. But whatever it is, it's a
lot! He gave them something and said he'd get the rest.'

We sat for another minute before I tapped his arm. 'Come
on, we'd better get back in.' And at that we jumped out
and made for the uninviting door.

No doubt he had a whole load of something and we were
going to take it. I thought about how, like asking him to
come outside or taking him away later, when no one was
watching. But when we got back in, the band had already
started and the crowd were jumping, so we lit a smoke and
stood there watching. Derek was back at the bar, the men
were now snarling while the band, half-cut and in a world
of their own, jumped and grooved like it was a hot day in
Brighton. Next thing a wee bird who worked there came

up to us with a metal tray, a smile and two cold pints. That took our minds off the plotting – but just for a moment. I took a welcome sip and looked onto the stage but was bemused to see Peter, still playing, stepping across the wires to turn up his amp before strolling back. His bass was now louder and drowned out the other instruments. A moment later, and again still playing, Des walked over from his spot and, without looking, turned Peter's amp down and pushed his further up. I looked at Billy and nodded to the stage. At that Peter repeated his actions, still not communicating but walking over to turn his up and Des's down. Des, in turn, pushed it back down and shoved his up again. For the third time Peter made for his amp but this time, from nowhere, Des turned round and whack! He smashed his guitar right across Peter, sending him tumbling into the amps like a bowling ball hitting the skittles.

'Fuck me!' I screamed, as Peter picked himself up and, like a man possessed, took hold of a mike stand to run his mate through!

'What the fuck?' shouted Billy, as we looked at each other. The crowd had been into the music and now it was dead. Riled and angry, they began throwing everything from ashtrays to pint glasses, which smashed against the back wall. Next thing two punters rushed the stage and joined the fight. So I made to jump on but an arm stopped me. 'Now, you stupid bastard!' Billy screamed. 'Now's our chance!' And at that we turned round to see Derek getting pushed and shoved at the near end of the bar. We sprinted through the crowd and, like a human tidal wave, picked him up from under the anger and smashed him right through the club doors, out into the car park, before bundling him into the van.

'What? Stop! No, no!' he was screaming, trying to figure out what was happening through his state of shock. 'What about the band?'

'Fuck the band!' cried Billy, as I revved the engine of the Transit, trying desperately to find gear. The rear window shattered loudly as bricks and bottles hailed down on the Dormobile like it was a police van in a riot. 'C'mon, you cunt!' screamed Billy at me, as I was stalling the fucking thing, unable to shift it. 'C'mon!' Next thing the side sliding door got opened and Billy leaned back with my blade and started slashing away at the hands that were now making a grab for his collar. Finally the van shunted, then stalled, then moved again as the engine struggled and the back wheels skidded, running over a kid's bike as he barely managed to jump out of the way. 'Fuck you!' shouted Billy, with his head leaning out of the window. I looked in the rear-view mirror to see that the fight had spilled out of the club. Three bodies were now getting kicked to fuck as they lay there writhing.

'The band,' stuttered Derek. 'I'm not the only one needing saved. What should we do?' But we didn't say anything. Finally, after five minutes of driving, in which it became clear that we weren't going back, he got worried. 'Where are we going?' he asked. 'What, what the hell are you doing? Where are you taking me?' He made for the door beside Billy, but Billy took his head and put the bayonet to his face. 'We're going to get your money, you little bastard! And if not, I'm cutting your fucking eyes out! All right?' And for the first time in a long time we were blessed with a welcome silence.

It took an hour before it dawned on us that we'd better cover the broken window. Driving like that was a sure-fire way to get pulled over. And while we were doing that, we thought it better to keep our friend in the front with us, just in case. The only crime we'd committed so far was leaving a bunch of junkie fucks to get leathered. But if we did have this bastard tied up in the back and the law stopped us, then the stakes would be upped before we'd even touched base. Besides, the threat of pain is often more useful than its actual infliction and having him with us meant that we could really get to him. And so, for the next four hours, as we cut through the night of an English summer, Billy enjoyed his torment every time while I egged him on.

When we made London, the sun was fast approaching and Derek's pleas for life and claims of poverty had long since become annoying. He lived in Clapham North, which was only a mile away from Billy's. That made them neighbours, though no one was popping round for tea. We backed the van up and escorted him out and into his terraced housing.

'Not bad!' I said, as, walking in, we found ourselves in an Aladdin's cave. Indeed, Derek was no pauper. He had paintings and trinkets that ran the length of his living room and in some ways he reminded me of a man I'd once known in Rhodesia. I took a length of cord that I'd ripped from the curtains and tied him up tight until his hands went blue. Then, taking a psychedelic hanky that was pinned to the wall, I rammed his mouth shut.

Billy went to the toilet and now, being alone with him, I began to get feelings I'd thought were forgotten. In some ways the Congo had satiated my needs. I'd left like a heroin addict who had managed to cure himself with heroin – a junkie cured by junk, if you like. I was by no means 'better' but I had taken the human experience to its extremes and so craved the normal – if only for a while. But sitting there, admiring this man, this once-big boss man, who only yesterday had been shouting my orders and treating me like his minion, I began to pulse and in no time my wires, as crossed as they were, began tingling. I heard the flush go but then a moan and I felt relieved. Billy had obviously got the runs and wasn't quite finished. So I sat down on the floor and crossed my legs in front of Derek. I just smiled and stared, which made him uneasy. So, when I leaned in and began to inhale him, he made like he wanted to say something and I gently pulled on the rag.

'Under the sink. Under the sink. That's all I've got. It's all I've got – please.'

I stopped for a moment and thought. I figured I should take a look, so I crept my way over to the open-plan kitchen and opened up the cupboard. Inside were a brown paper bag and a whole load of money – a small fortune. But I put it back and walked towards the windows. The curtains were slightly open, allowing a beam of sunlight to penetrate the room and highlight the dust that gently danced around it. The morning was peaceful and the birds were all singing. It was all so calming and I put on the kettle to make the moment special. 'Shall we have some tea?'

Billy came back. He yawned, then began talking about how he could probably see his mum's from the roof. I looked at him and shook my head. The stupid bastard: we were here to steal, not for a social. 'Anyway, where's the money?' I called over to Derek in a shouted whisper as if I was shushing an animal without waking the household. He looked at me in total disbelief. 'What? What?' I said, holding my hand up to my ear. 'Where? I can't hear you.' It made him mad and as he became more and more tormented his eyes welled up. 'Right, Billy, let's turn the place over. You check the rooms; I'll do in here.' So Billy took the place apart while I made the tea. 'Sugar?' I shouted.

'Please,' came a distant voice between the rummaging.

'You do live alone?' I asked Derek. He didn't answer. At that Billy came back.

'Anything?' he asked me, the sweat dripping off him. I handed him his tea and a biscuit from a packet that I'd found unopened.

'Nah. Fuck all here,' I said, which made Derek wriggle on the floor.

'What's he trying to say?' Billy asked me.

'I don't know.' Though, of course, I did. 'Do me a favour, Billy, would you? He's got a garden outside. Give it the once over. Crooks often plant their shit outside.'

Once again we were alone.

There comes a moment in all prisoners' minds when they realise the true point of their detention. Derek had always thought, as he should have, that all I was after was the money. Sure, that's why I was there but it wasn't what I was interested in. In later life I worked with the detained, who had nothing to offer but the breaking of their bodies. Yet within that they found comfort, assuming that our actions were directed towards extracting some sort of information that we wanted from them. But they were wrong. Often enough their breaking was never a means to an end but the actual point of the exercise. Breaking bodies for torture's sake, you see, breaks spirits and, unlike death or torture for truth, done right it has an almost spiritual dimension begging to be explored. For the subject, then, it's that point of realisation that nothing you do and nothing you have can make the slightest bit of difference, as it's the action and not the outcome that is the point of their confinement. Such an epiphany, then, leads to a very dark and lonely place – which at the same time is Eden for every technician.

At that Billy came back through the door all dirtied and sweaty and this time went straight for Derek and kicked him hard. He winced with pain but his eyes never left mine. I was the true source of his anguish, while he was the fruit of my temptation. 'It's all right, Billy,' I said, holding my hand up. 'I know how to do this.'

XV

THE TRUTH HURTS

The grass is always greener. This is a human misconception that only hindsight can reveal. Every man needs a purpose, a cause, a crusade to believe in, the hope of some imagined reward or a better life. That's why the world's in such a mess. I mean it's all bullshit. Religion, politics, the way things are done: it's a pack of nonsense with next to no truth or relevance. People walk this earth – they have done since the monkeys fell out of the trees – but we're not the apex; we're just part of the journey. Some day we'll have moved on – that's a fact – and like the difference between the lines on a football or rugby pitch, the only thing we'll change is the game. The grass will always be green and the earth will still turn around. But so what? The human condition – the form I so hate – is blind, short-sighted and limited. How can an evolving earth be explained by the static story of the Bible, written by men who thought the earth was flat, or an ever-changing society be confined to an authoritarian ideology? But we do subscribe to such things and by Christ we're ready to die for them. In all we're just dogs chasing our tails and I am no different.

Ambition can be as much a fuel as it is an agent of paralysis. No matter what I did, I could never be content. Money came and money went, while hopes that were realised were soon shattered by their own revealed emptiness. I near ripped that poor bastard to bits. I walked out with a pile of money and sorted out Billy with his share later, after I'd had my fun. I also obtained the details of a real heist up north, back in Newcastle, where I put a team together and, with the help of Rod McLean, stole a small fortune. This was not without its dramas but I believe Rod has already told the story in *Cut-Throat*.

I believed in nothing; now I believe in less. But back then, when the '60s became the '70s and I found myself right back where I'd started, in Rhodesia, it didn't take me long before the struggle around me became my struggle within. How and why I fell into it, though, needs a quick grounding, again so you'll know what I'm on about. As I soon learned . . .

Britain had established the Central African Federation in 1953, which included Southern Rhodesia (Zimbabwe), Northern Rhodesia (Zambia) and Nyasaland (Malawi). After the African National Congress (ANC – not to be confused with those other useless bastards from the Congo) was banned in early 1959, Joshua Nkomo fled to England to escape imprisonment. When he returned, he formed another organisation that was swiftly outlawed before forming the Zimbabwe African People's Union (ZAPU). ZAPU was in turn banned in 1962 and in 1963 Robert Mugabe created a splinter group from it called the Zimbabwe African National Union (ZANU). Both ZANU and ZAPU launched guerrilla offensives against the Rhodesian government during the 1960s. Now, in 1963, Britain dissolved the federation and Southern Rhodesia became known as just Rhodesia, which led to, on 11 November 1965, Prime Minister Ian Smith signing a Unilateral Declaration of Independence from the

UK. I find it amusing to know that the only other country to have declared its independence from the UK illegally was the USA. But anyway, here's a quick glimpse of what the future would hold for Rhodesia . . .

On 2 March 1970 Ian Smith's government gave up on trying to gain official acceptance from the UK and declared Rhodesia a republic, though it was not internationally recognised. The following year its government had black representation. That said, by December 1972 fighting would erupt again between Rhodesian troops and the ZANU/ZAPU guerrillas, which, apart from a brief lull, would become a full-on insurgency that would last until September 1979. Although the Rhodesian army would win the battles, the politicians would lose us the war, so on 4 March 1980 Robert Mugabe, the ZANU leader, would become prime minister, and on 18 April Britain would recognise the country's independence as a republic within the Commonwealth and Rhodesia would officially change its name to Zimbabwe. But I was oblivious to all of that, of course, and even if someone had been able to tell me, I wouldn't have been able to accept it.

All through my life I've carried an emptiness that sane men can't know. The answer to who I was as a man would always depend on the people I was with at any given time, the real answer still being a lifetime away from being realised. Early '70s Rhodesia treated me well. I had the house, the car, the money and the life – but by God I was bored. Comfort, it seemed, was best enjoyed as an aspiration and not as an achievement. And so in the vacuum of boredom it wasn't long before my idle hands craved the Devil's work. I signed up again and never looked back.

For the first time I was actually fighting for something I believed in. You see, I was never a true Brit, and I was obviously never a Congolese coon, but I was a white Rhodie and my country was calling me. Answering that call gave me a purpose, something beyond sating my needs, and the taste of that fight was a very different animal indeed. What it was and why it has since defined me is simple.

Africa is the most racist continent in the world. But whites only play a tiny part of it. White Rhodesians were, on the whole, not racists and always maintained that an educated black man would ultimately think and vote like an educated white. Education, then, and not segregation, was the way to a brighter future. But back then I couldn't see it. For me an unwell black might eventually go to the hospital but even an educated one would visit the witch doctor first. It's impossible to overestimate an African's belief in the power of myth. And while the opportunity of emancipation has existed for a century, the average black African is still unemployed, has five or six kids and shares *everything* with his relatives, including his wife.

He is not, then, inherently interested in politics, I figured. All politics in Africa are tribal, while political ideas, religion and colour were just new concepts and divisions he'd never understand. Parties are organised along tribal lines and not through ideologies. If two tribes are enemies – and they always are – and one fights for the rebels, then the other will either fight for the whites or form their own rebel group to fight the first tribe. In the days of old the English were masters of 'divide and rule', something the Portuguese would follow in Angola, when the three Marxist groups reported each other's movements to their colonial masters for years.

All African countries are thus fictitious, created by drawing lines on a map with a total disregard for tribal boundaries, loyalties or hatreds. The European colonisers cut tribes in half with borders they could never see, while expecting them to be respectful of boundaries they could never know – in all, a no-hoper from the start. But, that said, we whites can't shoulder the blame for all of Africa's ills.

Many of the blacks, even in the '70s, had never seen a

car, a watch, a water pump, the first floor of a house or a toilet and so had to be taught to think in an entirely new way: for instance, the Shona language had no words for or relating to time, while others used one word to describe a variety of objects. The locals therefore had no need for intellectuals, only basic skills. And with no tradition of private property it was little wonder that places such as the Kamina airbase, which I saw decimated in the Congo, had become a ruin. Black Africa in general became an obvious seedbed for global communism, with 'one-party government', the perfume-covered word for a dictatorship, slipped comfortably on top. Apart from the property issue, only a draconian hard man could hold a country together whose electorate had no concept of their flag or no need to vote – a concept Bush in Iraq would have done well to learn about.

Mozambique, for example – our border country and access to the sea – had two main tribes: the Makua and the Makonde. One lived on both sides of the Tanzanian border and made up the main forces of Frelimo, while the other made up 60 per cent of the Portuguese Army. When independence came, Frelimo took power, dragged the country down into hell and, in true Orwellian *Animal Farm* style, became worse than their colonial predecessors, thus giving rise to their struggle with Renamo – a group I'd later come to know well and supply arms to.

Now, like so many others in my country, we sat watching as our beloved Rhodesia drifted the very same way, with the two main terrorist groups following this pattern. It was useless, then, I thought, to wait for education to detribalise the masses. Tribalism to Africans is as fundamental as nation, language and religion are to us. The only detribalised Africans in the world are the descendants of the New World slaves – uprooted by force, deliberately mixed, taught an alien language, dumped on the other side of the world for two centuries, outnumbered and educated by whites. And before you cry 'racist', believe me, back then, to us in the 1970s, the world around us was a threatening menace that was rapidly closing in. What would you have done? Sat back and let it happen to the land you were born in? If you need any further convincing of how we saw our impending fate, a quick glance at the African map and its black-liberation 'success stories' of the time should at least give you a taste of how we saw things going.

In Uganda a quarter of a million blacks were killed in Britain's former model colony. People were forced by the army to line up and kill each other in turn; made to eat fried pieces cut from their own bodies; monkey meat became the signature dish at the finest hotels; whole groups were ethnically cleansed; stadiums stopped holding sports and began facilitating beheadings; and the government ministers chopped off penises with swords before feeding their political opponents to crocodiles.

In Nigeria a two-year civil war killed a million, with thirty thousand slaughtered on day one alone. Locals were lured out of the jungle with Red Cross trucks and butchered; prisoners of war were shot; children were nailed to huts and burned to death or left to starve; wild animals were deliberately infected with rabies; and all criminal offences carried the added spectacle of a public execution.

In the Central African Republic there was legalised mutilation for all criminal offences; overcrowding was solved by beating the prisoners to death; and compulsory tribal initiation rites were written into law by their witch-doctor president, leading to the country's foremost citizens – intellectuals and all – being forced to crawl through ant-hills naked.

In Rwanda 100,000 Tutsis were killed by Hutus, though, as we now know, that was a mere aperitif to the slaughter that would soon follow. In Burundi 100,000 Hutus were then killed by Tutsis. Their bodies were taken away in army trucks and dumped in the jungle.

In Equatorial Guinea – a place I'd later do business in – there was the re-legalisation of slavery and the exile of the entire literate population. In Senegal, a fictitious invasion by Portuguese soldiers gave the pretext for boiling political adversaries in oil. And in Zanzibar almost the entire Arab population was murdered after a few were caught drunk during Ramadan.

In Zambia, former Northern Rhodesia, the powers that be had wasted no time in nationalising all the land, abolishing churches, mission schools and so on, while in Mozambique, next door, wives and daughters were raped, sons kidnapped and ears, lips and noses cut off *'pour encourager les autres'*. Beyond that, in the mother of all ironies, all private homes and farms were taken and run into the ground, to the point where they then had to ask us to feed them.

In Angola the National Front for the Liberation of Angola (FNLA) began a 13-year struggle, infiltrating from the Congo and committing some of the most infamous atrocities in Africa: the dismemberments by buzz-saw. The Portuguese, the poorest nation in Europe, tried to fight the entire communist world by proxy. European settlers who built the first modern cities in western Africa were then forced to leave their lands after 500 years of heritage and sweat, with a suitcase and a stack of money that couldn't be exchanged with anyone.

In Ghana, Kwame Nkrumah, although dead, had left his 'cult of personality' legacy, which still goes strong today. Dissenters were, of course, jailed or killed or both. And in Kenya, as I well knew, the Mau-Mau terrorist Jomo Kenyatta tortured and maimed, while wrecking the country's agriculture and dividing up European farms into uneconomical plots for the Kikuyu, Kenya's largest ethnic group.

In the Congo, well, enough already said about that bastard

of a place, as mass rape, cannibalism and torture were, for many, national sports.

And I could go on and on. The list is as long as the continent is dark. And then there was us – somehow the bad guys. Rhodesia: the place where, although not perfect, whites still waited their turn behind blacks in the queues, where you could drink with the locals and them with you, and you could marry inter-racially or take any job if you wanted. But no – to the outside world, buckling under the weight of their own perceived guilt, this was unacceptable. Instead we should capitulate to the anarchy and backward barbarity of the above. Well fuck that! Not if we could help it.

Arriving at Wafa Wafa training camp on the shores of Lake Kariba was like being born again. It was a defining moment – my New Testament, if you like. I knew a few guys from my past who were already in the regiment but while others had opted for an easier time in other parts of the country, as far as I was concerned this was the only unit I wanted to be part of. They were the Rhodesian Army's Selous Scouts – ruthless and the best.

The regiment was a combat-reconnaissance force whose mission was to infiltrate the black population and pinpoint rebel groups. Only the best of the best would fill its ranks and only 15 per cent of those who signed up emerged with the right to wear the coveted brown beret. Trained to operate in small undercover teams capable of working without supplies for weeks and of passing themselves off as rebels, each man had to be a self-sustaining loner – in the bush, a mental conquest beyond anything physical.

The selection process was utterly horrible – said to be tougher than the SAS course – and was the only thing ever to have broken me. Training troops for a standing army was one thing, I soon saw, but training them for a nation's survival was quite another. And it started before we even got there. With 25 km to go before reaching our training barracks, we were booted out of the bus and told to run the rest through the bush until we reached a few straw huts and fuck all else. This would be our barracks. When we got there, there was no food and none would be issued. Instead came 48 hours of exhaustion, starvation and an antagonism that could have startled the SS and sent them packing. By the end of day two forty-five out of my original sixty-three had dropped out.

The basic course was 17 days long. From first light we were beasted before taking stressful and dangerous combat drills that went on and on with no end in sight. The day ended with an assault course that could rattle the dead, as heights and nerve-breaking manoeuvres were as constant as the drop was real. Then came night training.

I'd read about accounts in the concentration camps where they talked about a specific type of hunger – it's a hunger that free men can't ever know. But after five days without rations I knew it. Or so I thought, as I was forced to forage off the land and eat from under the rocks. On the third day a dead baboon was hung up and left to rot in the blazing sun. The stench was appalling, as it festered with maggots and insects and all. Two days later it was cut down and, to our horror, was gutted and cooked to become our evening meal. We ate it like vultures, tearing at it like hounds upon a fox. But I soon found out that this perverse ritual had a more practical meaning. Rotten meat is in fact edible if thoroughly boiled, though if reheated a deadly botulism can form. Scouts on a reconnaissance mission, where supply was impossible, could survive on a rotting carcass – something often found in the bush. It tasted so bad that the flavour still haunts some men. Though I've since enjoyed worse.

The last three days of basic training were an endurance 'march or die' hell. By this time we were truly knackered and had to carry weapons, ammunition and a pack loaded with 30 kg of rock over a distance of 100 km. The rocks, I soon saw, were painted, so they couldn't be chucked during the march and replaced nearer the end. The final 12 km was a speed test that had to be completed in two and a half hours – an almost impossible task given the ground we were covering and heat that sucked every last bit of moisture from us, leaving us half-mad, like saltwater-drunk sailors who'd been drifting for days.

Major Ron Reid-Daly, the crazy who set this outfit up, had learned his trade with the British SAS in Malaya during the anti-communist war, after originally leaving Salisbury in 1950 for England. The man was a leader to some but to all others a legend. He was once quoted as saying: 'I reckon in most armies today I simply wouldn't be allowed to put these poor bastards through the kind of selection course we give them. They'd think I was trying to kill the men who volunteer to join us. I agree, there is something of the prison-camp attitude towards our men under selection and training. We take them to the very threshold of tolerance mentally – and it's here that most of them crack. You can take almost any fit man and train him to a high standard of physical ability but you can't give a man what he hasn't already got inside him.'

Wafa Wafa, then, roughly translated from Shona, means 'Those who die, die; those who stay behind, stay behind.' Not much of a choice there. The few of us who did make it, and who fitted the bill, were given a week's rest before being taken to a 'special camp', only to begin the 'dark phase'.

It's somewhat funny but when I arrived there – an exact replica of a rebel hideaway – I could have been forgiven for thinking that, beyond our ruthless savagery and capacity for endurance, there wasn't much else we could be taught to cement our killing power. In fact I was wrong. We were expected to be able to actually disguise ourselves as rebels. If we were to be as effective as was needed, we'd need to look, act, talk and shit like the enemy. The mind is capable of some startling achievements when sufficiently determined. Given the will and the time, we can land on the moon and send a mission to Mars – and turn a 6-ft white man into a 5-ft African. And so the 'pseudo' groups were born.

Blacking up with burnt cork and make-up, while wearing stupid floppy hats and beards, could do well to hide our European features. But it was more. It was the subtlety of observation and the trials and errors by which most things get solved, not to mention the sheer balls of posing as a stone while being a rock. The 'dark phase', in essence, was about losing us and becoming them.

Of course there were the uniforms and weapons, and the operational tactics that we'd bought, tortured and killed for as the course had continued alongside our duties. But what clinched the deal was our attitudes. We broke with habits like cleaning, shaving, smoking, drinking and keeping regular times – a mindset unique to the developed world. We changed the way we ate and what we cooked, even down to the ritual slaughtering of animals, where we'd bleed a goat's neck before strangling it to death – a pointless enterprise to all but the faithful. And although only a blind rebel would be convinced by us close up, it was knowing how and when to use our own black soldiers that would make the difference between us and them.

Rhodesia needed every man for the fight and no sooner had the sheen been dusted from the cap badges than we were formed into 'sticks' and sent packing. A stick was our standard formation. It consisted of two or more white officers and up to thirty blacks, each one a Selous Scout, to be secretly dropped together at night near a suspect position, from where we'd make the rest on foot through hostile and difficult terrain. Once we were in position, a well-hidden observation post would be established, where we'd become part of the landscape. With no resupplies at all we'd live undetected, to track and take the fight to the enemy without them ever knowing we were there.

At first, using intelligence originally from South African Special Branch units, we'd send the black Scouts, posing as rebels, to recce the villages, while we stayed at the observation posts, only to appear at night. After an assessment we'd then move back into the villages to try to get our Scouts in with the local contact-man. The contact-men were kingpins in the insurgency struggle, because they introduced and integrated the rebels into the local population while accommodating them with food and information. Once our Scout group had been accepted by the contact-man, we'd arrange specific meetings with other local guerrilla groups, though that was easier said than done. You see, they might have been villagers but they were never village idiots. Most contacts were inherently suspicious, especially given our unannounced arrivals. Twice my stick had to go to extreme lengths to substantiate our stories: once me taking a beating off my black soldiers as I pretended to be their prisoner; another time them shooting an inch above my head to fake my death from a distance. I even knew of a mate of mine, Tony Woodward, who staged an entire mock night attack on a white farmhouse, complete with fake bodies and animal blood seeping out underneath white death sheets – a convincing scene, if ever there was one. And they bought it. Most attempts, then, were successful, while those that weren't were usually chalked down to one of the black Scouts being a turncoat and giving the stick away.

Once a rebel band was set up, we'd have them done in. Now, as tempting as it was, the last thing we could do was take them out ourselves. The attack squads were always within our area but never on our doorstep. And by placing the rebels under the firepower of other, non-Scout units, we could hope to exist as rebels and set more up for another day. The real killing, then, was done by helicopter-borne 'fire forces', consisting of a helicopter gunship, three troop-carrying helicopters and an American-built Douglas C-47 Dakota filled with paras, who'd arrive in our place to the surprise of many.

That's not to say that we weren't involved in the thick of it. Most of our combat, outwith our recce capacity, was cross-border. And of that there was plenty. In Mozambique and so on we'd track guerrilla units for weeks on end, searching for signs of enemy activities, especially in the morning or early evening, when the sun's slanting rays highlighted even the slightest sign of movement, paying particular attention to disturbed vegetation, sole footprints, bird movements (often a giveaway), blood and excrement and so on. The bush is a map if you know how to read it. These pushes were no doubt the hardest of our duties, as we struggled to survive off rats, snakes, baboon meat and various animals' eyes, while often having to drink water from the carcasses of dead animals – a yellowish liquid that doesn't bear describing.

As a direct result, though, we'd led columns of armoured cars and troop carriers on cross-border raids, right into Botswana and in particular Mozambique, culminating in our finest hour – and my last moment. In August 1976, seventy-two of us in three Ferret armoured cars and ten Unimog trucks drove sixty miles over the border to Nyadzonya/Pungwe and, disguised as Frelimo fighters – the Mozambique 'government' – we entered the camp and drove around their parade ground before shooting the hell out of 5,000 guerrillas who never knew what had hit them. Over 1,000 dropped where they stood – a huge kill – while hundreds more would follow before we doubled back, with prisoners – 20-odd ZANLA insurgent officers – and blew up the Pungwe Bridge to prevent any pursuing behind us. Although not one of us was killed, six were injured, me being one of them. It wasn't serious and was my own fucking fault, given I was a bit too eager in the turkey shoot – or stupid, as the case may be. A piece of fragmentation lodged in my thigh, which then became infected because I was too stubborn to take medical advice and rest up. The next thing was that my knee joint had swollen with poison and I was fucked. I couldn't believe it.

XVI

THE CHICKEN RUN

I suppose it was akin to a Premiership footballer sustaining a season-ending injury. Not the end of the world but in a profession where the clock ticks a season is like comparing dog years to human ones – a whole lot more. I could lie and say that I took it all in my stride, or hobble, but I didn't. I was gutted and moped around like a bird on the rag. That was until Colonel Williamson came knocking. A stern-looking man and a relic from the Empire, he spent little time getting to the point. Had I heard of the chicken run, he asked me. I had. It referred to the mass emigration of whites fleeing the country in fear of the growing success, popularity and numbers of the rebels. Then, after a pause, he looked straight into my self-pitying eyes and said, 'That he which hath no stomach to this fight, let him depart. For he today that sheds his blood with me shall be my brother. And gentlemen in England now a-bed shall think themselves accursed they were not here.' It was Shakespeare and the quote was in high circulation at the time, considering the number of people fleeing.

In later years I'd come to know the full extent of our

manpower leakage – and it was staggering. Ultimately, by 1978, there were only 260,000 whites in Rhodesia amongst a black population of around 7 million and, as the insurgency progressed, white emigration far outpaced immigration. In fact since Britain had dissolved the federation in 1963 until the end in 1979, some 180,000 whites had entered the country but 200,000 had left, the worst year coming in 1978 when a net loss of 13,000 was calculated. Under the 1957 Defence Act, as I already knew, young whites had to commit to six weeks of territorial training in the Rhodesia Regiment, followed by an enlistment in the reserves. But by 1966 the basic term of national service had increased to 245 days, only to be upped to a full year by 1972. And this time they included the goffles – the coloureds and the Asians – who numbered around 37,000. Soon all the stops were being pulled out but no matter what way the limited resources were configured – such as six weeks on, six weeks off – economic disruption was beginning to cripple us through the back door. Eventually, by January 1978, new immigrants could only defer their service for six months, as opposed to the previous allowance of two years, which was hardly a major selling point for getting people in and was probably, for many, the beginning of the end. But as I stood there in my doorway, still two years before, the answer to our troubles was as clear as the day was long: mercenaries.

At this point there were around 1,600 hired guns in Rhodesia, who served in every element of the security apparatus, including the SAS, Selous Scouts, the Rhodesian Light Infantry, the unique-for-the-time Grey's Scouts, who patrolled effectively on horseback, and even, as I mentioned earlier, the British South African Police Special Branch, who alone were responsible for the accumulation of some spectacular intelligence results. As the mid-'70s came, the guerrillas grew more and more murderous. Joshua Nkomo was able to infiltrate the country from neighbouring Zambia, while Robert Mugabe's guerrillas were based in Mozambique, where he'd taken up residence after being imprisoned for ten years. The pressure of this, like market forces, would soon dictate government policy.

Until then little official recruiting had gone on outside the country. The British, Canadians, French, Australians, Germans, Greeks, Scandinavians and Dutch who had heard the calling had done so through word of mouth or a specific invitation. Indeed the Rhodesian Government Information Office would advise soldiers on the enlistment processes but would do little to help them get to the training centres. Those successfully taken did have their fares refunded but, by definition and from my own experience of the Congo, shelling out cash up front was an unnecessary obstacle that many couldn't be enticed to hurdle.

That, though, was all about to change. Out of necessity Ian Smith's government began to recruit professionals from all over the Western world. At first articles, then adverts, were placed in *Soldier of Fortune* magazine, which attracted a fair few Yanks fresh from Nam. Then, when Major Robert Brown, the magazine's publisher, finally came to Salisbury to meet Colonel Lamprecht, the head of our recruiting section in 1977, things developed even further. Others such as myself with mercenary connections from the Congo were sent back overseas to our respective countries in an effort to press-gang, persuade, whatever, the best of the best that this was a cause worth fighting for. But it wouldn't be easy, especially for me. You see, Rhodesia was a country that was technically a British colony in open revolt against the British Crown but, unlike the Indians or the rest, we hardly saw ourselves as traitors. In fact, unlike the Boers of South Africa, we were as British as a suburb in Surrey – and proud of it. But that didn't alter the fundamental point: that when I arrived back in London in 1977, I was attempting to siphon the best warriors from the motherland to join a fight that would only sustain the existence of a dependent regime gone rogue. But, from a flat in Museum Street in London, and with the help of an old companion, I seemed to manage it.

The basic pay, although better than the British Army, was far from great – around £40 a week – though, as we cast the net wider and attracted more Americans, it would rise to between $500 and $2,000 a month, while the contracts went from two years to three. Looking back, I'd like to say that most men joined for the lifestyle, the *esprit de corps* and the excitement. Shit, I'd even like to say that others signed up just out of downright racism. But I can't. Money motivates, while comradeship only sustains. And of all those who I waved onto the good ship Rhodesia, none had cross-questioned me over whose bullets they'd be ducking, only how much they'd be getting paid to do so.

That's not to say that I didn't slightly manipulate the danger picture to make the outlook much more favourable. 'The terrorists,' I'd say, 'are not freedom fighters and so the Rhodesian Army is a relatively safe place to be, unless you happen to step on a landmine, run into an ambush or catch up with the bastards you're actively chasing. In fact the cowardly guerrillas stay away from soldiers, because soldiers carry guns and shoot back. The purpose of terrorism is to discourage civilian cooperation with an established government – our government. What's not safe is to be an unarmed farmer or black villager in a terrorist-infested zone. Such a poor soul is likely to be told, "We're coming back next week. Don't tell the soldiers which way we went. And when we do come back, we'll have all of your maize and two of your daughters."' The story usually worked. Easy money, they thought!

That said, the mercenary experience these guys would have was significantly different from the one I'd had in the Congo. Instead of bands of reckless marauders, just as capable of savagery as good, these lads were joining a well-structured and disciplined army of professionals and were signed up under the same conditions, other than a few quid more, as the regulars. Many of the men I recruited would soon find themselves gravitating toward the special forces, which in part was due to a certain air of mysticism but primarily was due to the calibre of recruit that those like myself were able to put forward.

Although they did us proud, it was all for nothing. After holding our fingers in the dam for so long, the weight of faux African unity, coupled with crippling Western sanctions on Rhodesia, born out of ignorance, simply became too much to thrive in. Anarchy, tribal conflict and poverty had instead rendered our 'First World quality of life' dream just that: a dream. And, as a result, all of the races would suffer.

No matter how many battles we won, it was an impossible task. And like Sisyphus from the underworld, rolling his stone up the steep hill, so the intensive bush war against Marxist terrorism was doomed to failure. Not only that but it diverted time and resources from a multitude of social programmes that could have accelerated true equity, without ever having needed the savagery, much of which was directed against peaceful and defenceless black civilians by their own freedom fighters. The overt complicity of some Western nations in this campaign of ZAPU/ZANU terrorist violence, in the name of black-majority rule, brought about the eventual collapse of Rhodesia in 1980.

This was in spite of the fact that Rhodesia had been able to progress to an elected majority-rule government in 1979. The elections that brought this government to power were witnessed by international observers, including a high-profile team from Britain, and were declared as free and fair. The result was that old Rhodesia evolved into the new nation of 'Zimbabwe Rhodesia', with Abel Tendekayi Muzorewa as prime minister of a coalition, and adopted a new flag. But the West, still labouring under the guilt of its colonial past, and with a need to appease the Organisation of African Unity, which by now was mostly composed of despotic and corrupt dictatorships, seemingly refused to recognise the new black-majority government.

Put in an impossible situation, the new government was forced into a conference with the terrorist ZAPU/ZANU leaders in London, where pressure was applied to hold fresh elections that were to include those organisations. The fraudulent elections took place in 1980, accompanied by massive intimidation of the population. This proved to be the beginning of the end for democracy in Rhodesia and the concept of free and fair thus disappeared under the maniacal regime of Robert Mugabe. Those who could left the country.

As for those of us in arms the special forces continued to fight and function up to and during the elections of February 1980. We had been told that a few of the 'heavier' members of the top brass had been planning a coup to pre-empt Mugabe's installation as prime minister (Operation Quartz) but it came to nothing. The white units – or the special forces, composed of the Rhodesian Light Infantry, the Selous Scouts and the SAS – were dissolved, while most of the mercenaries removed themselves from the danger of nationalist reprisals, many heading into South Africa in the hope of immediate enrolment in their Defence Force.

Now the relationship between Rhodesia and the South Africans wasn't all that you'd think. While sympathetic to the white-minority government, South Africa continued to withdraw vital economic and military support all through the 1970s and, as well as placing limits on fuel and the munitions it supplied, it never even accorded us diplomatic recognition. Some say that this was because of Prime Minister John Vorster's policy of 'Detente' – the thawing of tense relationships with the black African states – part of which involved sacrificing Rhodesia to buy more time for his country. Others, including myself, saw it in relation to the embittered history between the British-dominated Rhodesia and the Afrikaner-dominated South Africa.

First was the fact that the founder of Rhodesia had tried to overthrow the South African government but, more so, it was the small matter of the Boer war, when in particular the Boers, Afrikaans-speaking whites, released British prisoners unharmed and allowed them to walk back to their lines barefoot, while the British instead invented concentration camps 50 years before the Nazis and left 25,000 of their women and children to die of hunger and disease. That said, sense eventually got the better of the South Africans and no one was passing up the chance to incorporate some of the finest military units ever turned out. Whatever role South Africa played, the outcome was to be a Zimbabwe/Rhodesia that now decays ever more by the day under the cancer of Mugabe, whose legacy of violence and oppression on my home country will be everlasting. And we were the bad guys? *C'est le Congo!*

XVII

GLADIO

I held my breath as the footsteps got closer. Then, as the keys jingled before being inserted into the lock, I removed the safety and leaned in even closer. The opulent smell of class and the scent of the aged furniture wafted through the grandiose apartment with ease, assisted by the breeze from the open shutters that rattled in the night somewhere beyond me in the darkness. I heard talking, which startled me. He was meant to be alone; I was sure of it. Being grabbed for a calculated risk was one thing but getting jail for pressing on for the sake of it when the risk unexpectedly increased was of no use to anyone. I wiped my brow. Rome in the summer was stifling and, unlike back home, air conditioning wasn't a given. 'Come on,' I kept saying to myself over and over again. I wanted this over and done with. But he didn't enter.

His voice was soft and the way he laughed on the other side of the door made me picture his face, based on the one photograph I'd seen of him. That was now two weeks ago and the pressure was on. But I wasn't going to let it get the better of me. I'd take as long as I needed. I'd watched him from a distance, then from up close. I'd looked at his story: who he worked with, where he socialised, even who he shagged – and that was a pile of riding! I'd taken all the info I was given and verified it for myself. I trusted no one. I never had and never would, especially not now. The lock then turned and the door made to move but again he stopped. It was a neighbour, I thought. With only one flat per landing in the three-storey block, the man on top had doubled back to spraff some more.

Now the door opened and the light from the ancient staircase cut the darkness and threw his shadow over the medieval tapestry that hung on the wall behind me. My pistol had a suppressor, so the noise wouldn't be deafening, but with the extra body nosing about on the stairs I'd have to let him walk past me before making my move. And that made things messy – drifting from the plan. But still he didn't come in. Instead the door closed again with a clunk, which startled me. It was made of steel, concealed beneath wooden panels, with a H-frame locking device and six heavy safe bolts that acted like mortises. I'd seen these before and they were near impossible to get through. Even the keys were difficult to copy – with each side being unique, an imprint was useless. But these security measures were all insignificant to me; I had the original and was given it by . . .

Convincing the careful that you're the real deal – a genuine state-sponsored nutter – would sometimes take an act of insanity. And Dino Sacriponte, as I'm calling him, the gatekeeper in Rome to a world that South Africa was desperate to penetrate, was asking for no less. All my pseudo-group partner and I had to do was to murder his son.

Now I heard the keys dropping on the other side of the door and hitting the stone floor. But the voices had stopped so I knew it was on. I adjusted my position and, like an athlete limbering up, gave my limbs a shake and stretched my neck muscles. Then, with a flick of the wrist, the door sprang open, before he took one step, then two, then flung his keys onto the counter . . . and bang! No – it jammed! The fucking gun jammed. And so, in the dark and with fuck all else in the way of weapons, I lunged across the space to try to pistol-whip him. But I couldn't. With the silencer on the end it might as well have been a wizard's wand, as he ducked, then screamed like a bitch and made for the door. So I blindly grappled with him. I took hold of his shirt, then his belt, and now, behind him like I was trying to mount him, I yanked his head back and coshed him a fucker. He was crying and yelling, and I was sure we'd be heard, so I got on his back properly and tried choking him out. But bastard! I felt this burning in my eyes and, as I struggled to breathe and he struggled to his feet, I realised that he'd maced me. Fuck it hurt, as it stunned me, knocked me back and sent me sprawling to the floor. But as he made for the door, still screaming away in fear, I dived at his feet and we tangled again. I couldn't let him go or it would all be over! He kicked down on my face, my neck and my face again. He knew that he was fighting for his life and that I was no thief. But by now I was raging so I sank my teeth into his calf muscle and bit down like I was trying to tear it off. That doubled him over so I smashed him repeatedly, connecting with hard, then soft, then hard again, as each time he became less and less active. Then silence. But I knew he was pretending so I leaned in and, through his suit trousers, I bit on his balls like a frenzied animal. That woke him up! I thumped him again but this time, putting my hands round his neck, I began squeezing the life out of him, one pulse at a time. I didn't let go and, caught in the moment, I began losing myself.

I'd never had the privilege of killing like that before and, of all my macabre actions, that one gave me the greatest and most sustained pleasure, as the more pressure I put on his neck, the more sexually aroused I became. He scratched and scraped as I felt the last dying pulse of his system and the last beat of his heart. Now he was dead. They say death is the loneliest point of living, in that it's the only place we venture into alone. But right there, in that act, I'd gone with him, right until the brink, to where the doors closed and he left me standing. Now, like a spurned lover, I lay over him, panting and jealous. I flipped him over and took his wallet. But before going through it, I untucked my shirt and with a corner I tried wiping my eyes. But the sting made seeing impossible so I made for the kitchen to run some water. It took me a minute to gather my senses. I'd just fought, won and killed on nothing but sheer will and necessity. But now I was drained when I needed to be alert and thinking.

I staggered back through to his body and was tempted to lie down beside him or switch on the lights. Instead I opted for a lamp that sat in a cloak cupboard just yards from the entrance. I saw that the flat had a small toilet with a crocodile-head trophy in it, sticking out of the wall. They'd shoved a toilet roll in its mouth to use as a holder, which made me mad. I admired strength and hated to see it disrespected or diminished. I looked in a mirror and saw I'd been scratched. So I went back to the body, which lay face down, and in the shadows held up his hands. I'd need them.

I fumbled around blindly for my pistol. It had fallen during the struggle and had landed, as things usually do, in some impossible place a half-mile from where I'd dropped it. At the full reach of my fingers under a two-seater sofa I began massaging the metal and coaxing it into my grasp. But just when I got it, I heard a noise, so I jumped into the cloakroom and turned off the light. I waited. The pistol was an Italian-made Beretta 92. Sacriponte had given me one to do the job and insisted that I used it. I don't know why – it might have been an attempt to frame somebody else for the killing, or whatever – but to me just possessing it could tie me into other crimes unknown. I wasn't that stupid. So I'd chucked it into the River Tiber and only partly honoured his by getting my own one, which wasn't easy, given that they'd only made 5,000 of them, back in 1975.

I narrowed my eyes in the darkness but decided that the noise was nothing. I was on edge, no doubt. Outside in our Renault 4 was my wing-man, a certain ex-Congo mercenary called Konrad. Our paths had crossed again in Pretoria three years beforehand. Any trouble outside and he would have come in blasting or shouting or something. But nothing. So I crept back out and now, with a sense of urgency, I legged it back to the kitchen and looked for something to chop off his hands with. He had my flesh under his nails and I wasn't leaving without them. The best tool I could find was some turkey cutters, which would have to do. Thirty seconds later I was kneeling beside him and, like a gentle mother clipping her boy's toenails, I began snipping off the tops of his fingers one by one and carefully placing them into a polythene bag that I'd sourced from under the kitchen sink. Two minutes later I was done.

Now it will seem strange but it was only after I'd wrestled, bit, throttled and snipped that I finally bothered to look at his face. His hair was right and so was his build, and fuck, even his aftershave was the same horse piss as I'd smelled just two days previously in the Via Veneto nightclub I'd seen him in. But at that very moment, just a second before I was going to stick the proper lights on, I heard the door go behind me, giving me just enough time to jump around and reach for my pistol. As soon as I saw that it wasn't Konrad or Sacriponte, I fired: twice in the chest and once to the head. He dropped. I'd just shot my target, while at my feet lay his lover. I'd fucked it!

I'd been told to leave him there. So I did. I bolted over his corpse, kicking his legs away from the front door and slamming it shut. Two breaths later I'd cut across the gravel quadrangle, through the entrance archway and was speeding off into the night, with Konrad at the wheel. 'What took you so long?' he complained. 'You weren't up to your usual, were you?'

I shook my head while slamming the dashboard in an effort to convey the urgency of the situation to him. 'There was two of them. I thought he was talking to a neighbour but it was his fucking boyfriend. He must have sent him into the flat while getting shit out of the car, or somewhere. I don't know.'

'So?'

'So I went for him first by mistake, and . . . and the fucking pistol jammed. Bloody Italians. They can't make shit unless they're eating it! Come on!' I shouted again. 'We're in Rome. Traffic lights are only a suggestion. Move it!' And at that we disappeared back to our own part of the centre: a small penthouse apartment in the endearingly named Jewish Ghetto. I filled him in on the full story and went to bed.

The next morning I woke up to the sound of church bells and took my coffee and breakfast smoke on our rooftop terrace, which we accessed from a spiral staircase in the corner of our living room. Konrad was already up and out, as he started every morning with a run through Villa Borghese, a stunning public park not so far away from our flat. I, on the other hand, always took it easy when I could. 'Take your rest while you can' was a bush motto I'd found difficult to shed.

They say Rome is the Eternal City and it is. But it's only in moments like these that you appreciate it. Sitting in amongst history, in the heartland of Italian Judaism, so labelled after Pope Paul IV ordered the city's 8,000 Jews to move there in 1556, I saw the sun rise over the timeless spires and the Vatican, while the mopeds below me busily buzzed through the streets, leaving me in a thin layer of calm to indulge my latest memory. The heat of the morning glow and the cool air that breezed over me were almost cleansing, while in the distance, and coming closer like falling dominoes, came the bells for the faithful, ringing with tradition, though competing with secularism. Rome, like the rest of the progressive world, was smacking modernity head on – and losing. I fixed my sunglasses and opened the newspaper. I scanned through its pages, one way, then the next, but nothing. *La Repubblica* had no mention about a double murder in Rome, though on page three, in a column that I nearly missed, were a few words about the son of an Italian industrialist who'd been killed in a boating accident near Porto Ercole, an Italian Riviera resort some miles north of Rome. The second paper I had, *Il Messaggero*, speculated suicide, as the body was still missing. I wondered whether this might have been a cover-up, especially given how quickly it had got into print.

Sacriponte was some guy. He was a staunch anti-communist worth millions – hundreds of them. And he had really done the rounds, as each achievement only pushed him to the start of the next – a self-imposed purgatory with no end in sight. He had dealings in India, Southern Africa, the United States and all through Europe, and was a fixer and an accommodator. While politicians would come and go, Sacriponte was for ever – our slogan in jest but in reality we meant it. You see, Sacriponte was an ideologue, a one-man institution who was part of a shadowy phenomenon known only to the few who controlled the many, and was our wormhole to power, cutting through the bullshit 'space' of Western-world diplomacy. And I'd just killed his son.

I'd killed him as a favour to his father and had done so because he was gay. Simply speaking, Sacriponte preferred to have him dead than to have the world knowing that his second born was a homo. I should say no more.

Now, why Sacriponte senior was so important to us is

what I'll get to but why this insanity was relevant to our acceptance by him is simple. He knew who we were and why we'd come to him, but for him to 'trust' us, namely acknowledge the existence of his world and let us into it, he needed something to hold over us – over me. The killing of his son, in this respect, was a request that I least expected, but it put him in the clear for the crime while still allowing him to have control of the evidence. Like the Selous Scouts those years before this was a pseudo operation and he needed convincing. So who were we? We were Section 6.

Myself and a small team of others had all gone the same distance to get there – apart from Konrad, who'd made his own way in through the back door. After Rhodesia we'd got into the RECCEs, the South African special-forces unit, and had ultimately ended up in 32 Battalion, or 'Os Terriveis', 'The Terrible Ones', as we were known, serving in Namibia and Angola. But, only a few years in, the situation in South Africa was steadily changing. A new skills set was needed and we fell right into it.

There comes a time, I suppose – and this can relate to anything in a person's life – when you're suddenly confronted with the fact that what you're faced with isn't what you've been projecting onto the circumstances but a reality you've chosen to ignore. 'John Barlow', for example, was a guy I'd known in Pretoria. While working together, I'd listen to his endless stories about his wife – ex-wife – and how each day she found some new problem to moan about. These problems were not of his doing but a creation of her madness. No matter what he said, or for how long he explained things, the next day they'd wake up as if it had all been forgotten. I even remember him looking at me one day with bewilderment on his face as he told us that the Sunday before she'd screamed at him for not spending enough time with the kids but, as he was about to leave for the cinema with them, she threw the car keys at his head while yelling about how he couldn't wait to get out of the house and away from her. Then, when he got back, she moaned at him because she said he was having trouble dealing with his anger and letting things go. I'd never been in a relationship but I was now married to my cause. And it occurred to me that she was just like the situation we were dealing with, that in an ideal world this stupid fucking woman would see reason and understand that what she was doing was illogical and not based on facts, while all the time her problems were illusions because the foundations on which she'd built them were in themselves wrong in the first place. Each time he entered her circular arguments, he hoped that by appeasing her she'd change and that with every two-hour, all-consuming discussion she'd finally 'get it' and be the woman he thought he knew and wanted her to be. But it was hopeless. To me South Africa, like Rhodesia, would never be the country we believed it to be and were so desperate to cling on to. The rest of the world had determined that we, the white few, were simply in the wrong and that, even though we screamed at the top of our voices and even though the country, if let go, was destined to fall into the suffering and anarchy that had befallen the rest of the continent, we did not deserve to be heard, because of an ignorant preconception that made those judging us the very bigots that we were in fact supposed to be ourselves. In that realisation the question cannot then be how do we fight for the deckchairs on the sinking *Titanic* but how do we manage our escape after acknowledging the inevitable. This, however, takes foresight, brains and above all balls, as it means facing the truth while acknowledging our own weakness. Perhaps for this virtue alone history will see fit to redeem us.

And the game started early. Before the eventual state of emergency in 1985 and the infamous 12 August 1986 meeting chaired by Prime Minister Botha where 'the gloves came off', the new mantra became the 'counter-revolutionary strategy'. Unlike before this wouldn't be aimed at solidifying white-minority rule in South Africa but would be more about 'managing' the process of reform over the long term and, most importantly, at our own pace and not at the behest of any nationalist movement or the international community of ignorance. For this the process was placed firmly in the hands of our military and intelligence communities.

One of our primary tools was that of targeted assassination, as opposed to the wholesale murder of revolutionaries. Only a few weeks would have been necessary to kill everyone in the ANC but, like in Argentina, it would only have bought us another few years. Nor was it like Project Phoenix by the US in Vietnam, where simply cutting the heads off the opposition's leaders would do. Instead it was a selective removal of opponents at the times of our choosing, especially where the courts system was inadequate or, if overseas, unworkable. For this purpose three branches within the South African security apparatus were born, all stemming from one very dangerous tree: Project Barnacle.

Barnacle was established at some point during 1979 when the then head of special forces, Major General Loots, and Major Neil, my old commander with the Selous Scouts, were summoned by the minister of defence, General Magnus Malan, to Pretoria. Malan wanted to put together a new breed of coverts, one that would run adjacent to special forces but function as a long-range reconnaissance capability, similar to the Selous Scouts, which would utilise the lessons they'd learned in Rhodesia. At this time Rhodesia still had some life in it but, as the writing was on the wall, the South African special forces soon recognised the potential for an influx of expertise should they want it. And they did.

The task of Barnacle was the usual special-forces mandate:

identify guerrilla infiltration routes, find and fuck their training camps, then direct air strikes onto their heads. But its function soon expanded. At first it was known as the Section for Pseudo Operations, then D40, before being named as Barnacle after a random selection of registered code words necessitated it. Konrad had been with it since the start.

From the get go it operated a series of front companies, each one masking its true function. First it was NKJM Estates, which fell short since its operatives knew fuck all about property and the four-metre high, half-metre thick walls with attack dogs were hardly the makings of a welcoming business. This then changed to NKJM Security Consultants, which worked, until paperwork – hardly the speciality of ruthless warriors – got in their way. Finally, and with Konrad hanging on for dear life, it became President Security Consultants (Pty) Ltd, with its head office in Verwoerdburg.

Initially operations were limited to deep-penetration recces but after a gradual hardening of the necessary stomachs the directives were soon altered and solidified in a 'Top Secret' memo of 9 January 1981 from Major General Fritz Loots, with the wording:

Purpose:
The management of ultra-sensitive operations

Function:
1. Elimination
2. Ambuscades against individuals of strategic importance
3. 'Operativeness' as instructed in super-sensitive operations
4. Gathering of combat information regarding the above-mentioned operations
5. Gathering of information as assigned in cases where other sources could not be utilised

6. The conducting of certain special security tasks, such
   as observation of sources/agents and performance
   of certain special tasks, such as observations of 'at
   random' security experiments as instructed for special
   forces

On 18 February this was furthered with one more classified directive, specific to the elimination of 'enemies of the state' and 'super-sensitive' covert operations, in particular the killing of those within our own service, where it was sometimes deemed necessary. I wish I could say more just now, but there are two families in particular who didn't have a dad home for Christmas thanks to Konrad.

From Barnacle came A Section (foreign), commanded by Major Craig Williamson, as head of the G1 Branch of the security police, who left his position at the very end of 1985 supposedly to go into business, though in reality to establish Longreach (Pty) Ltd, a company registered in the UK but very much part of the Department for Covert Collections (DCC). With Williamson as chairman, this front company aimed to influence businessmen in favour of the apartheid government and as such wasted no time in undercutting the ANC's credibility through its own brand of political warfare. The operations it undertook were all constructed to prevent people knowing they were involved with a foreign government. The skill was to steer its subcontractors without ever controlling them – a neat trick that takes some practice. An example of this was the International Freedom Foundation (IFF), which was ostensibly a conservative think tank based in Washington DC but in reality was part of an elaborate South African military intelligence operation, code-named Operation Babushka, tailored to combat apartheid sanctions and gather US support for Jonas Savimbi and his UNITA movement in Angola. Other projects were less clandestine but equally interesting, such as the anti-communist film *Red Scorpion*, which was filmed in South African-occupied Namibia and in part funded by Military Intelligence. And then there was us, Section 6.

Still a year before the Civil Cooperation Bureau (CCB) came to fruition – the third arm, which I'll later get to – a group of us were assembled in a smoky meeting room on the Speskop special-forces base, just outside Pretoria. 'B.M.' was a kingpin in our apparatus: a Second World War veteran who should have long since retired but seemed determined to fossilise before realising his age, while those around him seemed even more determined to keep him, as replacing him was deemed to be impossible. We'd even joked that when he died, they'd have him stuffed or kept on ice till the science was right for bringing him back. I thought then, after knowing this no-nonsense man, that he'd waste no time in spelling out what we'd soon be up to. But he didn't. Instead he just stood there, like he was counting heads on a school trip, and said nothing. So I looked round the room and, though I recognised a few of the lads from the RECCE circuit and one woman, the rest were all but a mystery, though that would soon be dispelled when I began to realise what we all had in common. The first similarity was that we were all from covert forces of some description. The second was that in all of us I could see a self-styled insanity that seemed to expand when like meets like. Lastly, and more importantly, we all shared a European heritage and so, no doubt, a passport.

B.M. cleared his throat and, with a piece of chalk, began jotting down notes on what was simply an old school blackboard. Then he looked at each and every one of us, coughed again and said, 'Right, it's basically this: we need you to work in Europe. You'll be away for some years and it could get tricky. If you get caught, you could be on your own, while if you don't and you do make it, you'll all come back as secret heroes and probably never have to work again. Now who's in?' And at that he was met with silence. We waited, then waited some more, and, if only to break the silence, Konrad put his hand up. 'Erm, can we know what we're doing?'

B.M. shrugged his shoulders, paused, then firmly shook his head. 'No, my lad. That's the one thing. I can't say what you'll be getting into unless you sign up for it first.'

We all looked at each other and smirked. The man was mad. Never in my time had I known something to be bought before the customer had seen what it was.

'You can't tell us? Not a thing?' said some Welsh guy who sounded like he was only months off the boat from the valleys.

'Sorry, not a damn thing. We've looked into all of you, a lot, believe me. And we know none of you are married, have kids or seem particularly settled. You've all got extensive backgrounds. Some are impeccable,' and at that he looked at several of us. 'And now we'd like to give you a unique opportunity to continue serving.'

'Under who?' asked some other guy I'd never met. But again B.M. said nothing and at that he left the room to give us some time to get thinking.

The minutes passed but the time went slowly. Some talked openly; others just sat there and stared. It all seemed like some scam you'd get at a Las Vegas convention hall, where they'd turn the heating up when selling you timeshares in the Bahamas. Finally, after I'd finished my second smoke, he bowled back in. 'So?' The only person to leave was the girl, which pissed him off. Girls like her were hard to come by but I'm guessing she had a biological clock that needed satisfying before any more gallivanting could be done. With a disapproving look on his face he waited for her to shuffle her way out. Then, after an unnecessarily long pause, as if to make a point, he carried on. But only with the admin.

Two minutes later we sat with a pen in one hand and a contract in the other that committed us entirely but still gave nothing away. And at that I truly got it. Whatever we'd be doing, wherever we'd be going, we'd be crossing the wire and, in doing so, all of our actions would be unconditionally deniable, should it all go wrong. And it could. There are guys in prison to this day, in Europe, who got grabbed on government jobs but who took it on the chin as a private venture. I'm thinking of one right now who, until recently, was rotting away in a UK jail.

Once the papers were signed, we eagerly faced forward to see the prize we'd gambled on, which was still hiding behind 'Bully'. 'Right,' he said. 'Operation Gladio. We want in.'

My jaw hit the dirt.

Now what you have to realise is that for the South African government the issue relevant to the period we were in wasn't simply about black versus white but was also about right versus left. The world was truly gripped by a cold war, where the two big power blocks slugged it out in a multitude of skirmishes all over the globe. And Africa, like Asia, was a playing field no different. It just so happened that all of the black nationalist movements, as I've already said, gained their ideologies, training and even support through weapons and funding from the Soviets. This meant that, for many, apartheid South Africa was never in a race war but in the same struggle as the rest of the free world, only the communists we were fighting weren't red, they were black. For this, then, certain ulterior agendas of ours were temporarily forgiven, overlooked, whatever, while alliances were sought after in unlikely places and under very dubious circumstances.

Loosely known in Europe as Operation Stay Behind, the idea of Gladio was to build an alliance of clandestine networks of anti-communist guerrillas who'd fight to the death behind the lines in the event of a Soviet invasion and subsequent takeover. The plan was later codified under the umbrella of the Clandestine Coordinating Committee of the Supreme Headquarters Allied Powers Europe (SHAPE), the military arm of NATO.

The concept first arose in Britain as early as 1940, when France first fell. Numerous arms caches were buried for later use by a special-forces ski battalion of the Scots Guards. After the war new units were created throughout Europe and set to face off against the Russians.

Although the UK version was simply known as Stay Behind, those in the rest of Europe all went under differing names. In France the unit was called 'Glaive', named after a gladiatorial sword, while in Austria the unit was named 'Schwert', meaning the same. In Turkey the unit was called 'Red Sheepskin' and in Greece just 'Sheepskin'. Sweden's unit was called 'Sveaborg', while in Switzerland it went by the title P26. Other groups, such as those in Belgium, Portugal, Germany, Holland, Luxembourg and Denmark, all went nameless, to our knowledge, while in Italy it was known as 'Operation Gladio'.

That said, all wasn't as simple as it might have seemed. As time went by and the atomic age hung the balance of humanity by a horsehair, the purpose of the super-secret 'stay behinds' as resistance groups in the event of a Warsaw Pact invasion became somewhat murky. For one, how any Russians would take over the radiation desert Europe would have become after a nuclear war stemming from a full-on invasion is questionable. In all reality by the time any Soviet tank would have reached the sunny shores of St Tropez, there would have been no more Kremlin to give them their orders, or Pentagon, Government Communications Headquarters (GCHQ) or NATO, for that matter, to fight them. The truth, then, was that these secret structures soon became involved in combating the dangers of 'internal subversion' – something we knew a shit-load about – and so aimed their readiness at anything from countering demonstrations and influencing opinions to the full-on planning of a *coup d'état* as a potential last resort.

Italy, as an example, always had a large communist party, and in some areas of the north you could be forgiven for thinking you'd just driven into Stalingrad, from the sheer number of red flags suspended from the trees. As a result the CIA established Gladio in 1956, its name again deriving from the short stabbing sword used by Roman legionnaires in their more imperial times. The Gladio network was operated by the Italian secret service and initially funded by the CIA, recruiting and training some 600 people on the island of Sardinia, though by the time we were sniffing about, we figured some 15,000 had ultimately been processed through the network.

Now, depending on who you listen to, the account of certain events after 1972 can somewhat vary. That year the Italian communist party had polled 27 per cent in their election – a massive amount given that Italy was a NATO country supposedly 'at war' with global communism. But when it increased to 35 per cent just four years later, something had to be done, lest Italy was lost via the back door and the communists invited Stalin down for spaghetti.

The 'strategy of tension' was consequently developed, which included a string of murders and terror attacks that were attributed to the far right during the 1970s and '80s. These actions were meant to control and manipulate public opinion using propaganda, fear, disinformation, psychological warfare, terrorism and 'false flag' actions – operations made to appear as if carried out by another entity. The agents used in these cases were backed up by the intelligence services, NATO, the stay behinds and, of course, Gladio, who, due to their clandestine nature, were largely unmonitored by civilian agencies and so able to pursue their own right-wing, anti-communist agenda.

Now there's no doubt that Gladio units were up to no good. I can verify that for certain. But to what extent they bombed and maimed indiscriminately – such as the 1980 Bologna Station bombing, where 85 people were butchered – is certainly debatable. The aim of such actions, some say, was to make the public believe there was already a communist insurgency and cry out for a more authoritarian government. But we never saw it that way. For one there was no need for it, as apart from it being unnecessary, mass slaughter always focuses attention in places where you might not otherwise welcome it. No – Gladio agents were into killing but, like us, it only applied to a select grouping of targets and only where the courts or other means were failing or unable to secure the desired outcome.

For South Africa contacts within these groups were to prove both essential and necessary as time went by, as we'd use them for money and arms, supplies and support – especially when the world hit South Africa with its 'crippling' sanctions and knee-jerk embargoes. But for us it was more. As B.M. had gone to great lengths to explain, our function – especially mine and my team sent to Italy – would be to befriend, not infiltrate, as that would be counterproductive, and form working alliances with not only those who had the ears of the powerful but those who were in fact the shadow governments themselves, waiting in the wings, poised to take over should history see fit. And in Italy that meant Propaganda Due, or 'P2'.

If the Gladio network was thus the armed force, the secret Masonic lodge P2 was the elitist 'shadow government' whose function was to direct it. Staunch with right-wing ideology, and in some cases far-right sympathies, P2 was headed by the 'puppet-master', real name Licio Gelli. During the war he'd been a member of Mussolini's blackshirts, before acting as the liaison officer to Hermann Goering's SS division. By 1974, then, P2 membership comprised the leading elites of Italian military, political and economic life, including cabinet ministers, MPs, the army chiefs of staff, intelligence chiefs, senior military officers, as well as many top diplomats, bankers, media moguls and industrialists.

Now we'd known of this for some time – a beneficial by-product of being a country where many expatriates would come for a fresh start after a lengthy period of debauchery. But it was only after 1974, when Gelli met with the former NATO supreme commander Alexander Haig in secret, that we began to get an idea of how this ultra-covert network might be of benefit to us. At the US Embassy in Rome, Gelli received top-level American blessing for continued financial support for the Gladio–P2 network and its plan for the 'internal subversion' of Italian political life.

Now in June 1982 a banker called Roberto Calvi was found hanging underneath London's Blackfriars Bridge with his hands tied behind his back and bricks shoved into his coat pockets in what appeared to many, and certainly to me, a Masonic slaying. The location was itself symbolic, with the bridge sitting on the edge of the Masonically named Square Mile, which connects the City of London financial district to the rest of the capital. Calvi's privately owned bank, Banco Ambrosiano, had a huge black hole in its balance sheet amounting to over a billion or so dollars – money that was later found in the accounts of the Vatican Bank, earning him the nickname of 'God's Banker'. Now all of this is, for the moment, another story. Suffice it to say that, in the investigations, P2 came into the public eye, as Licio Gelli was one of those suspected of ordering his murder. In searching Gelli's home, the Italian police discovered a list of over 600 names with evidence that linked them to P2.

Gelli would ultimately stand trial for fraud and, later, murder, for the collapse of Banco Ambrosiano and the death of God's Banker (he was convicted of the former and the latter is still ongoing). But by this time his role as a 'state within the state' had already been publicly exposed. That said, while P2 took the heat, Gladio as a network remained perfectly intact, thus leaving us with an opportunity not only to work within it but, like never before, to influence its actions. And so, sitting that evening in our dark, smoky room in the Speskop special-forces base, that's exactly what we were intended to do.

Now the reason my jaw was the first to hit the floor when B.M. mentioned Gladio was that, unlike the rest of the guys around me, I'd already heard of the stay-behind groups and, to a certain degree, had worked with one of them when I'd been recruiting mercenaries for Rhodesia. The network varied, though, in its purpose and its goals, depending on which European country it was operating within. Britain's stay behinds, for instance, were tasked to combat a specific internal threat, which was the attempted takeover of civil government by militant left-wing groups. The UK network was thus operated by Britain's intelligence services and selected members of the armed forces. In a very real sense MI5 operated a civil army, with trained operatives, and infiltrated them into whichever left-wing group they saw fit.

Certain elements of the criminal world were also part of the stay-behind force. These underworld members were loyal to the right-wing cause and, importantly, should senior figures deem an outright *coup d'état* necessary in the event of a militant Labour win at election, they were well outside of government control. Such people included, as an example, my old friend Rod McLean – a leading member of the UK's stay-behind army and an interesting story in his own right. You see, ex-soldiers, and in particular mercenaries, from the post-colonial wars were ideal candidates for the stay behinds. As a whole they were well trained and motivated but more importantly they were adventurers who appreciated a few quid and could always be trusted to keep their mouths shut while being duty-bound to the Crown. It was because of this thirst for fresh adventure and bounty that a lot of us from the 'old days', namely from working in the Congo, Rhodesia and West Africa, kept up relations, even though we'd gravitated towards our own specific intelligence services, security forces or related industries. We therefore still had a hand in the clandestine community of politics and ideas circulating both within and without our individual countries, and our chatter was often encouraged by our agencies. When overt cooperation was deemed to be risky, we formed one of the many informal channels of communication exploited by the respective intelligence services.

Sacriponte, then, was to be our way into this world. As part of his large economic portfolio he was heavily into the arms trade would later help us to buy and source all sorts, from small arms to larger systems, and was no stranger to delivering whatever was needed to certain places that even a mechanised army would have second thoughts over going to. Sacriponte was also on the original list that the Italian police discovered but, due to a certain amount of foresight, had ensured that his details were coded and so had escaped almost all of the heat, leaving him in a unique position and us, as I've said, with a golden opportunity.

Now, back to that morning on the rooftop terrace in Rome. I heard the door go below. Clutching my .357 Magnum hand cannon, which was never far from my side, I jolted out of my reverie and popped a head down the stairs. It was Konrad coming back from his run. I negotiated the cast-iron spiral staircase and, like a lord of the manor in my kitsch silk dressing gown, Kimono Dragon rippling on the back, I made for the kitchen to grab the last of the coffee. Konrad was mad.

The cupboards were clattered around in and their doors slammed. Then the washing basket received a boot like the last kick of the game at Wembley. I had to ask. 'Anything wrong?' I said sarcastically.

'Bastards!' he said. 'I'm out of here.' And he flung me a printout. It was from Pretoria. 'Yeah, we're to move things up. I'm off to Stockholm. You're going to Sardinia.'

'Sardinia?' I said. But I looked at the paper and saw that he was just having a laugh. In fact it made no mention of me, only that he had to be in Stockholm by the end of the week. I didn't know why, nor why he seemed so outraged at the idea. I mean Rome was a great gig but Stockholm was no poor second prize. Besides, we were supposed to be on the move and had already spent too long as a unit in one place. I sat down and watched him storming around. Then, as he opened the fridge to take the glass of water that he always poured out before running, so he'd have a cold one to gulp down on his return, I saw him jump back.

'What the fuck is wrong with you?' he bellowed.

At first I had no idea what he was talking about but I soon realised. In the fridge, as the freezer was fucked, sat a bag of human fingertips. He was squirming. Konrad knew me better than most by now but perhaps the gaps that still lay in his knowledge of me were beginning to narrow. 'Sorry,' I said. But I didn't mean it.

'That's fucking stupid!' he moaned on. 'Get rid of them.' Then he looked at me like a scolding bird as I sat there grinning. 'Now!'

But to me he was being just that: an annoying girl. He was pissed off that he had to head up to Sweden and, as he was anal about cleanliness, was no doubt bothered about the fingers being next to his mortadella. So, not wanting to sound feeble, he chose to channel his anxiety into a rant about keeping incriminating evidence rather than face his own truth. But he needn't have bothered. I knew it all too well. I knew that these fingers – fingers with prints and with my flesh still under the nails – were as good as a signed confession and an assault in a police station. But I couldn't help myself. You see, I'd recently developed a fascination for trophy collecting. I found that keeping something of my prey, of my victim, was like walking away with a lover's jumper or scarf, still heavily scented in their perfume or body odour. I remember seeing a guy in Namibia always carrying his wife's hairband into battle, tucked into a sealed plastic bag and hidden away in his pocket. He'd smell it incessantly and was well touchy with anyone who remarked that he should have taken her knickers – that way we could all have a sniff. To me, then, these fingers, their shape, their discoloration, the fact that I owned them, were all tokens of love and, as bad as that is, that was my sexuality – no different. I walked forward and reluctantly grabbed the bag. The night before I'd lain on my bed and tried to wear them like thimbles. I'd felt consumed and fascinated and so had pushed my tips into his – a messy business but a sensation I'd enjoyed, so much so that I'd brought myself off while still wearing them. For Konrad and the sake of peace, though, I flushed them. I then had to restrain myself from killing Konrad because of it – a feeling I often had to battle with, as close company bothered me.

That afternoon we went to meet Sacriponte. I had orders from Pretoria that a Joseph Mkhatshwa had recently arrived in Rome and was meeting with a local communist group some time that week. This happened a lot and was part of the ANC's strategy for drumming up sympathy and assistance. Often it was down to other agents to monitor them: bug, observe, interact with them through infiltration, whatever. Most of the time it was left to Williamson and his Longreach tentacles, or a derivative of either. But this time our target wasn't only fund-raising but was directly seeking arms from the Eastern bloc to fight our boys in Mozambique. And this bastard in particular had personally tortured four of our RECCEs to death. We knew who he was meeting with but I can't give the outfit's name, because it still exists and would dearly love to sue as its heyday has long since passed.

It was a hard-hitting entity at the time, though, and had all the right connections to get what it wanted within weeks rather than months. It was very dangerous and not to be underestimated.

I met Sacriponte at his apartment. This place was a palace and, with each room larger than the combined space of any flat I've ever lived in, was more of a heritage centre than a living space. That was money, I thought, but for the moment I left my jealousy at the door. The man was a great entertainer, so much so that every evening he hosted a dinner where the who's who of Italian, European and often American power-wielders would grace his dining table. His elegance and etiquette were legendary, as was his reputation for bedding the ladies. And believe me this guy could ride! If I was a normal chap as opposed to the weirdo who wanked wearing a dead man's fingertips then he'd be the guy I'd want to be like. But anyway, I sat down and gave him the details of who I was looking for and why we wanted him. Honesty was the best plan with Sacriponte, because we all knew he'd double-check everything that came his way. Within five minutes he'd found me the name and address of the person our target was staying with and, after a couple of espressos, had found the place where they were supposed to be meeting later that week. And at that I left.

The spy game, I soon saw, was like the soldier life in that it can have weeks of madness followed by days of calm. And in the calm periods you don't quite know what to do with yourself. After the meeting I sat and had a coffee in one of the tourist rip-off bars next to the Spanish Steps and steadily smoked my way through a half-pack of Camels. I watched the way people were going about their business and began to fixate on how different life would have been if only I'd had it in me to normalise myself. But even the thought of fitting in made me sweat with anxiety. Like in the West End in London, with all the life, the lights, the

Nice!!

action and the birds, everyone seemed to be having more fun than me, going somewhere better, and doing something more interesting, while I sat there lonely, watching all the men looking far richer, happier and more contented than I was. And that pissed me off.

See my problem was always simple: with half of me struggling to fight off insanity and the other trying to keep my animalistic instincts at bay, I could never feel settled. By anyone's definition I was off my fucking head, no doubt. The things I'd done and the actions I'd taken were enough to have me sectioned. But then there was the stuff that was beyond the pale, like eating flesh with the dogs, whose mere existence was proof of my point. Schizophrenia or lycanthropy? I would never truly know. But I did know that my halves weren't separate, as one state would so easily influence the other – a circular hypocrisy that would often make my head hurt and force me to do harm. Luckily for a stranger, though, that day duty saved me. I looked at my watch and saw it was time.

I walked over to a phone box, fumbled in my pocket for a small brass *getoni* and called in to Konrad. These were the days before cellphones and our radios were strictly for using in jobs. When he answered, he seemed to have calmed down a bit and told me that Sacriponte wanted to see me again that day, with him in tow this time, and that he'd meet us in a Chinese restaurant next to Porta Pia, a landmark beside the British Embassy in Rome. So I swung by in a cab and picked up Konrad, and within half an hour we'd cut our way through the stationary traffic that is Rome and now sat facing Sacriponte and another man, who as yet I'd never met, while Konrad had been asked to keep a lookout outside. The man was American.

He never said who he was working for and I knew not to make the mistake of assuming that every Yank worked for the CIA. There were a lot of bullshitters out there, some bad, some great, and as a golden rule no one was to be trusted. Sacriponte said that we had a golden opportunity. He said that the group Mkhatshwa was meeting was top of their hit list. Like I said before, this group was good, proved by the fact that 20 years on, and 15 after the fall of the curtain, it's still banging on about the same old shit, waiting to say I told you so when the grand experiment of capitalism fails. Anyway, I was told that the meeting was taking place the next day and that the street was Via Isodoro Del Lungo, a suburban street right on the outskirts of Rome. They suggested – well, Sacriponte did, while the American chewed his prawn crackers – that we take the whole lot out with one shot. It surprised me that he was saying this, especially in front of a man who was a stranger to me. He knew that meant it was impossible for me to say anything and so incriminate myself. And I didn't. I sat there staring until finally the Yank stood up and announced he was off to buy some smokes at the tobacconist's around the corner. I moved tables. Sacriponte laughed but he'd have moved restaurants, never mind tables, if I'd pulled a stunt like that on him. Then he looked me in the eyes and said, 'Let's bomb them!'

If I never said 'get fucked', then I certainly felt it. My orders were to do someone in, not to blow up half of suburbia. Since 12 March 1982 and the bombing of the ANC offices in London, the whole explosives idea had been put on hold. There were numerous reasons for this, one being that the necessary explosives and triggers had come through the South African diplomatic pouch, an unchecked bag that every government sends to its embassies, which had left a trail back to Pretoria. As time would progress, this obstacle would diminish when the necessary party goods could be sourced locally but for the moment such acts were strictly off the menu. So, cutting a long story short, I ended the meeting with a handshake and went to see Konrad armed with an address and a bucket of intentions. As I stepped through the doorway, the Yank happened to be walking back in. He smiled but I looked right through him. I crossed the single-lane road of the Nomentana, a long Roman artery that had single taxi and bus lanes on either side of the main road, and met Konrad, who was still standing outside trying not to look suspicious. I laughed when I saw him and suggested that he might as well cut two holes in a newspaper to peer through, as he was attempting to hide behind a thin tree-trunk half his size.

Just as we were about to leave, I heard a voice from the restaurant and turned to find Sacriponte calling me back over. Within a few strides I was next to him and he told me to get Konrad as well. There was no problem with that, so I called him over. But he just stood there and wouldn't move. I looked at him, then at Sacriponte, who looked confused. 'Come on!' I shouted again. But he stayed firm. I ran back across. 'What's the deal, mate?' I said inquisitively. But he said nothing. He just looked at me, unsure of himself, almost like he'd seen a ghost. 'You all right?' I asked, standing waiting on a response.

'Yeah, yeah, I'm . . . well . . . no worries. I just feel a bit sick, you know? I think I had one of those fingers in my breakfast,' he tried to joke, though something wasn't right. Giving him the benefit of the doubt I walked back towards the restaurant. 'Listen,' I said to Sacriponte. 'He's not feeling so well. We had a bad pizza last night. What was it?'

'Is no problem, my friend,' he replied. 'I just wanted you to meet John. He's a good man to know. I should have told you before that he was here – or at least discussed our business without him. For that I am sorry. But we can do this another day.'

I smiled and looked at my reflection in his sunglasses. 'Of course,' I said and thought all was forgiven. You see,

Sacriponte had that thing: it was a sincerity that radiated out of him. Even though he could be trying to sell your own kidneys back to you, you felt special with him, as from the small fry to the big fish, when he spoke to you, you were in the limelight. And so I left him and thought nothing more of it – for the moment.

That evening I met a covert from Longreach. They were busy trying to figure out a way to monitor some anti-apartheid conference that was being held that week. For me it was more of a courtesy call to a guy I knew well from Os Terriveis, and at the end of it I'd left in a van bought specially for a job they'd planned but never carried out.

The next morning Konrad and I were sitting 30 yards outside Mkhatshwa's hideaway, waiting with bated breath and scoffing down a bag of cream cakes.

Now here's the deal. Contrary to what you see in the movies, killing as a profession is a very messy business that often relies on luck and balls more than meticulous planning for certain success. The deed in itself is hard enough to plan for, as, full of variables, it often gets aborted when some cunt gets in the way or the subject doesn't show up. The idea of some super-sniper in an urban environment shooting away from a distance before making a smooth getaway is a complete myth. For fun, if you want, pick a random place – a doorway, a parked car, a shop – and then try choosing a shooting spot. It's enough to fuck up your plans that one door is locked, a window is bolted or a group of kids are hanging out, not to mention the impossibility of getting in and out without being seen, especially when the crack of a rifle has shattered the neighbourhood. In the end it's something very difficult to train for as no two jobs are alike. For one, you've only got a window of opportunity in which to do the job – and in that window your target might well be exposed but be in amongst other people, who will somehow be determined to get in your way or chase after you when you've fired your shot. And secondly, unless you're a suicide killer who doesn't need an escape route, familiarising yourself with your environment is a far cry from knowing it and, as a rule of thumb, those who know it win.

So although we were only on a recce at half-eight in the morning, planning for a job we had nearly two days to take care of, when I happened to glance in my wing mirror to see our target's big black arse walking towards us, my instincts took over. Before knowing it, I'd jumped out of the van, punched him solid up against the hedge-topped wall and, with nothing but my fist in his mouth to keep him from shouting, Konrad slid the side door open and we bundled him in.

The noise from the back was obvious. I mean any passing fool could have realised what was happening. And to make matters worse there was no passage between the back and the front unless you got out and walked around, so there was no safe way out while he was still conscious. Luckily the guy was ageing but, as he was no stranger to confrontation and now realised he was in a fight for his life, he began putting up an alarming resistance. Konrad smashed him time and time again, while I did my best to choke him out using his own jacket lapel to cut off his air supply. Finally he flopped and was incapacitated just enough for me to take off my belt and tie his hands, before creeping out the back door, half-expecting to see a crowd of well-stunned spectators. Luckily there were none but that wasn't to say there hadn't been any before who were now panicking at home, speed-dialling the police for assistance. So I jumped in the front and put my foot down, half-hearing the two in the back tumbling over as I sped the wrong way up a one-way street. Taking a left then a right, then realising that the van was a giant giveaway whose description was probably out, I spotted a market some 50 yards away, where every cunt and his dog had pulled up in their vans to do business.

By the time I'd picked our spot, 20 yards behind the vans that lined either side of a houseless avenue, the fruit and veg sellers and the butchers and fishwives were too busy to notice their new arrival. And so, some yards in front of a small gypsy camp that sat on derelict ground, I glanced about, before jumping out and into the back.

My hand was bleeding from where the bastard had bitten me and I was sure I'd chipped my elbow in the struggle, as both pain and nausea rocketed through my body. But, like a randy man on the stairs of a brothel, the prospect of what lay before me was more of a painkiller than any morphine fix.

It will seem unusual, then, that on an average street, on an average morning one winter's day in suburbia, a tiny part of a far-away war was fought out with such bloodthirsty aggression. I looked at Konrad, who was now sat on top of him and reaching for his 9 mm. But I stopped him. He shook his head, because he knew what was coming. 'No fucking way, man! I'm not having any of your shit here. It's too public.' And, believe it or not, his hand actually jerked the pistol up towards me, before he checked his impulse and brought it back down. I looked at him and for the first time started to see something in him that I couldn't yet label.

'Out the fucking way!' I said dismissively. I'd had enough of his acting up. Whatever way this bastard was getting it, it was going to be done now, so what fucking difference did it make if I took something for myself? 'Get in the front,' I said. 'Make like you're doing paperwork or something. I'll just be a minute.' He glared at me again but chose not to protest and so jumped out and into the driver's seat.

The man was pissing me off and the whole being-sent-to-

Sweden excuse was well wearing thin. We might have been a two-man team in a 'civilian' outfit but I still had command and he'd better start respecting it. I looked at my feet and saw a black body now beginning to stir. I removed my shoe and pulled off my sock. I rolled it up, stuffed it in his mouth all the way down his throat, then slipped my footwear back on. I looked around me, as once again I was all dressed up with nowhere to go. I figured a van must have a toolbox – but no. Then I thought of the spare wheel, which would presumably come with a wrench or a jack. But after fucking about for a minute I saw they'd been removed to create a space to store something that had never ended up being placed there. I scratched my head and began to concede that I'd just have to strangle the bastard, as time was getting on and I knew it was reckless to be still sitting here a good 20 minutes after snatching him. But then I saw it, and could have missed it had he not rolled over to choke, which forced phlegm to come spewing out of his nose. It was a can – a can of expanding foam Polyfilla – and at once I knew how it had got there.

In the old days before electronic alarm systems, most domestic alarms only triggered a bell that was boxed and placed on a street-facing wall some way off the ground in an inaccessible position. Of course these boxes – which often had the logo of the alarm company branded across them – had to have vents in the side, otherwise the noise couldn't be heard. It was soon found, though, that if you sprayed the foam through the vents, it would expand and solidify and so stop the bell from ringing. That was probably what they had stowed it in the van for but they had never got round to using it. I would, though.

I pushed him onto his side and, with a bit of a struggle, undid his belt and manhandled his trousers down to his knees. He looked up all dazed and confused, and for certain thought I was just going to shag him. I looked down at his black ass and floppy willy, which dangled down over his fat, flabby thigh. And I hated him. Not because of who he was or what he was doing. And not because he was a hero to those who wanted the last of African civilisation tossed into the cesspit with the rest of it. But because of how he now looked: so feeble and weak. In fact he was completely fucking useless and to my disgust was clearly relieved by the belief that his arse was only getting shagged and so offered it up by almost cocking it in the air. It's strange to think how weak some men are. So I shook my head. 'No, Comrade Mkhatshwa,' I whispered. 'No such luck. You are getting it but it's not me that's going up your ass.' And at that I stuffed the nozzle firmly in place and near emptied half a can of expanding, solidifying foam right into his rectum. Amazing! He squirmed one way then the next, then his belly grew like a pregnant woman as his organs and tubes began stretching, before popping, one by one. And there was this look of total bewilderment all over his face, more of shock than of pain. So I sat there transfixed, panting like I was fucking him. And then I was calm. He didn't die straight away; he lived. He lived for minutes, even though his entire insides were nothing but a mass of solidified foam. It was nothing short of a wonder. Finally, when he took on the death rattle and I knew he was near, I lay down beside him, determined that he would carry my face into hell, like our boys had no doubt carried his. He did.

Moments later I was sitting in the driver's seat after shoving Konrad aside and negotiating the van around the gypos, nearly running over a three-legged dog in the process. I made for a place that Sacriponte had told us to take stuff to in a hurry. It was a Mafia chop shop in an area I'm not going to mention. Half an hour later we were there and the van and its contents were all but a faded memory. Hailing a cab, we took it to Stazione Termini, the main train station, then walked across to Piazza della Republica, before taking another one over the river to the area of Trastevere, which in Roman dialect literally means 'across the Tiber'. Finally, after a few circular jaunts around its medieval side streets to make sure we were alone, we hotfooted it back to our flat in the Jewish Ghetto and a well-deserved cigarette.

XVIII

FELLING A PALME

It was just as well that Konrad had to leave early the next morning for Stockholm, otherwise the black cock in the fridge would have really made him flip. It was my trophy and I wanted it close. I was glad to see the back of him, not just because of the adolescent attitude he'd been developing but because I was in full satiation mode and witnesses diluted the thrill, like the thought of your granny when you're just about to ejaculate.

But I couldn't help but question what I was turning into. Like most people I was a work in progress. What was of interest one day was old news the next and some of my actions made me proud, while others made me ashamed or, more often, indifferent. I am, then, a hypocrite, full of opinions that change with my mood. I scold the African black man but often behave worse – worse because, unlike him, I know better. Instead I rely on my skin colour to justify my high ground. Because others of my race are right, strong, clever and ingenious, then so am I. But I'm not. The snake that I once thought I was, who was blameless by virtue of birth, had now begun to desert me, leaving in its vacuum my doubt. And doubt – or self-doubt – is fear. To the normal mind being wrong and admitting it to yourself is far more significant than being right in the first place. But to mine, whose certainties were what got me by, being wrong was an earth-shattering occasion.

Towards Christmas in 1985 I'd never been so busy while feeling so unsure of myself. I found that I couldn't cope with it. If this was my midlife crisis, then it had come at the worst time in an impossible place, as working in Europe was a very different experience from working elsewhere. Much later, in 2001, I went to Mexico on some business. On occasions my mind played tricks on me and, for a second, from the vegetation and the climate, I believed I was back in France, along the south coast, or in Portofino on the Italian Riviera. But behind the hedges and the Inca silhouettes lay triple-layered concertina wire and more guards patrolling the enclave than there were white folks living there. Only then, when the reality of Mexico slapped me square in the face, would I be jolted back from their intended smokescreen and the Third World reality would bite me in the ass. Europe, then, like the US, is a mindset as much as a place. It is characterised by a sense of order and propriety, things work, people take notice and, one way or another, they usually have a sense of right from wrong. You can't just bribe or buy your way past the usual checks of society. You can't beat your way past its obstacles or murder an obstruction. In fact the West, to the likes of me, is a very claustrophobic place and, like a wild animal having to adapt to its cage, it frustrated me in a way that was not easily reconciled.

That said, it can work both ways: a European mindset can be a liability in a more lawless environment. I remember one night, on that same Mexican visit, when I was sitting in a local bar outside the seaside enclave in the town of Playa del Carmen. I was there to meet a man who was a drug trafficker – for now another story – and so had taken a few days extra to savour the atmosphere before heading back home. Anyway, the bar was only a block or so from the main tourist street, certainly not in a bad area, by any means, but there was a definite change in atmosphere that put you on your guard – or should have done. Sitting on stools, less than five yards away, were three young white folk: two guys and a girl in their late twenties. Two were a couple and, from what I was hearing, they were there for a week, while the other man was their scuba instructor, who they'd chanced across while out for the evening. After drinking there for an hour, all seemed well, albeit with the girl unsteady on her stool and just managing to avoid falling flat on her face on a fair few occasions. At one point, though, she stood and walked up some stairs to a first-floor toilet. Now the bar was empty apart from me, them, two bar girls and a Mexican guy who was up at the bar smoking a cigar. The floor above was completely deserted, apart from a one-person toilet at the far end, only ten yards from the stairs. I knew this because I'd been up there just half an hour before. But Christ, what happened then startled even me.

The diver guy said to the boyfriend – a man twice his size who could easily have snapped him in two – that the girl might not find the toilet and so he'd nip up and make sure. I watched him go up the stairs, then disappear. After 15 seconds the boyfriend obviously realised something was up, bolted up the stairs and into the bathroom to find that the diver man had shoved his bird up against the sink and was less than two seconds away from raping her. For some reason this little shit found it acceptable – not in terms of right or wrong, as I'm no man to judge – but acceptable to go up there in full view and commit an act that to many is grounds for a killing, knowing that less than 30 seconds later the boyfriend would no doubt be up there behind him. I mean come on! The man, then, must have been acting on impulses that carried no aspect of reason. The boyfriend, fortunately, was clear headed enough to get himself and his girlfriend out of the situation. Instead of taking his head off and being faced with doing time in a Mexican prison, he put his efforts into extricating himself and his foolishly drunken girlfriend from a perilous environment. The waitresses said nothing. The man at the bar hardly put his cigar down, while the 'beast' tried and failed to get the boyfriend alone with him, beckoning him outside and away from his girlfriend.

The point I'm making, though, is why did the boyfriend allow the man to go up the stairs in the first place? Perhaps sometimes, whether we admit it or not, we like to be liked. We want to seem liberal – a man who is trusting. The boyfriend made a bad call. He preferred not to insult the guy by treating him as a threat, even though there is no clear-cut manner in which you can predict a man's intentions. That doesn't mean you should live your life seeing everyone as a threat – that's an existence of pure paranoia – but it is a question of degree. The guy put his girlfriend at risk by indulging the stranger. It's easy, then, looking back as I am, to see threat where once there was trust but after a long life on the dark side, I can say this: people might change, act oddly or be unpredictable but certain actions have obvious outcomes and so it's to these, and not the people themselves, that we must react. When Konrad started acting up, I knew there was a problem. I knew it was better to offend him than to suffer the consequences of whatever horse shit was affecting him. Still, as I would later ask myself, how do you cope when your circular room reveals a dark corner?

Two days after I killed Mkhatshwa I went to Sacriponte but found he was in India until after the new year and so my plot had thickened. I wanted to meet that American guy from the Chinese restaurant. Konrad was avoiding him for whatever reason. Perhaps he'd learned the lesson too: better to offend and be sure than to be polite and regret it.

By now all sorts of money and arms were being pumped into South Africa, Mozambique, Namibia and Angola through the Gladio networks, while all kinds of knowledge and expertise were flowing from us into their systems. This was now the primary purpose of our much coveted relationship. And if Williamson and Longreach were the overt coverts, then we were the left hand that the right never knew was beside it.

When Speskop was constructed, five laboratories were readied specifically for the use of our own special forces, which were engaged on a newly developing chemical- and biological-warfare programme under the charge of Dr Wouter Basson called Project Coast. The seeds of Coast had originally been planted in the late 1970s when our guys were being threatened with chemical agents by the Soviet-backed Cubans in Angola, resulting in a chemical defence and vaccination-research programme being rushed into service. Basson, meanwhile, spent many a week at the behest of covert-friendly Western governments playing catch-up and became the head of Project Coast in 1983. From 1985 onwards, through a series of front companies, he was facilitating Western scientists to work in secret at the newly built research facility. Soon, then, Coast was leading where once it had followed.

Basson saw that there were three types of chemical weapon: lethal, incapacitants and irritants. For sure those countries concerned with waves of Russian arms sweeping across the Rhine saw little use for irritants or happy gas. But to those of us who saw a threat from within, such a knowledge base could prove invaluable if we only kept probing.

Of particular interest to Gladio was Project Coast's extensive research into peptide synthesis, where the aim was to disperse mind-altering drugs to a given population without them ever knowing it. In some ways this was the holy grail of weaponry for us, given the possibility that a civil disturbance could simply be drugged into submission. Under Project Baxil this ambition would be nurtured, while in later years recommendations of ideal drug combinations were given to a technical work group for potential trial.

Although Europe and the West were officially fighting a war on drugs, their very governments were hypocritically researching the best way to spray their dissenting mobs' mouths shut. According to our live research – and believe me when I say that our lab rats weren't rodents – Ecstasy could nullify a threat by inducing euphoria while Mandrax – a drug of choice for the time – could numb their raging emotions. Benzodiazepines (BZ), meanwhile, altered perception and caused hallucinations with mood swings, while cocaine mixed with BZ would lower aggression, thus diluting the need to throw stones on the streets. But beyond that it was so much more, as, given an inch, Coast took up a yard. In terms of what we were up to back home in South Africa, you name it and we tried it. We tried to make pills that changed your race, made your dick fall off and your hair fall out. We mixed chemicals with water, with food, with soap. We stuck paraoxin on clothing, in cigarettes and beer. Christ, even baby milk was laced with Aldicarb. We induced cancer, transmitted anthrax and cultivated HIV. Indeed it was a crazy time with crazy people and nothing was ever off limits. And, just as we had our guinea pigs, we were the guinea pigs for Gladio, whose scientists monitored our research. We tried and erred in ways that even the worst of their worst wouldn't have stomached. And for that they loved us. All we had to do was to keep them informed.

Now comes the tough bit. Just after the new year of 1985–6, I was called back to Pretoria. We'd been in Europe for six months solid and, although we'd been moving about, we were still centred around our safehouse in the Jewish Ghetto. I'd by now passed three new team members into

Gladio, who were far better at administration than I ever was, while I remained focused on more 'terminal issues', or the planning thereof. That said, the black dick that now lay neglected in my newly fixed freezer was the last trophy I'd been able to get hold of. Twice I'd been given a target only to have it pulled at the last minute, once from above and the second time by circumstances beyond our control. But back in Pretoria the winds were changing. For the first time I could feel a pressure in our structures that I hadn't felt before. People were now talking about when and not if, some even casting their eyes on jobs in Canada and the likes, which really pissed me off. Others, worse still, spoke about a civil war, should black-majority rule ever happen.

Section 6, meanwhile, had succeeded in achieving its objectives. In a short time we'd befriended and joined forces with Europe's best-kept secret and now counted them as an ally, while many of Europe's governments only paid lip service to condemning us. But then there was Sweden. It will seem odd that a country at the top of the world should seem so preoccupied by our small patch at the bottom. It held no concerns in our land, through history or people, and had no interests in the region where our exploits could threaten them. Yet Sweden was the first Western power to give direct aid to the liberation movements and was by far the most generous, while also being the most persistent in demanding our toppling.

Pretoria, though, was encouraged by the overt policy of 'constructive engagement' conducted by the USA and the Conservative government in Britain, along with West Germany's objections to any meaningful sanctions. For the time being it felt enabled to fend off the scourge of communism and to keep its front-line states, such as Mozambique, on the back foot. In 1984 Mozambique was obliged to sign the Nkomati Accord, promising to cease hostile actions against the country. It signed this because of the success our military was having against its terrorist bases and infrastructure but it moaned to the rest of the world that its people were the victims of a cruel and repressive regime.

As the front-line states seemed to be weakening, while our internal forces were getting stronger, Sweden saw a need to lend greater political and material assistance to both, especially to South Africa's United Democratic Front (UDF) and the Independent Trade Unions. That help amounted to more than $300 million in 1986 alone for the enemy at our gates, while Sweden soon, as a result of its government's policies, became the principal backer of our insurgency within. Why?

Olof Palme, the Swedish prime minister, was a controversial political figure on both the international and the domestic scene. His outspoken criticism of the Vietnam War and the USA, his campaigning against nuclear weapons, his criticism of Franco and Fascist Spain and his support for the Palestine Liberation Organization (PLO), who were busy blowing stuff up at the time, all ensured that his office was as unpopular abroad as he was at home, especially among Sweden's right-wingers, some even accusing him of being pro-Soviet and not safeguarding Sweden's own interests.

When Palme returned to power in 1982 for his second stint at the helm, Zimbabwe had become independent but Pretoria had increased its security attacks against neighbouring countries that were housing our terrorists. And for some reason that really made him mad.

At the 'Foreign Ministers of the Nordic and Front-line States' meeting, which Sweden organised in June 1984, and the meeting in September of the 'Socialist International', with those states and the liberation movements of which Palme was the driving force, the cause of liberating South Africa from apartheid was said to have been significantly advanced, both through increased national sanctions and by strengthening the 'Nordic Programme of Action'.

Indeed in his last speech, of February 1986, he was quoted as saying: 'This system [apartheid] cannot, would not, be able to survive if it were not in various ways supported or accepted or tolerated by the rest of the world. And so the rest of the world is directly implicated in the continuation of this system.'

It seemed illogical then that a foreign power could drive, fund and infiltrate by proxy the takeover of a foreign and sovereign state without anyone taking any action. At a fundamental level this inaction was akin to an acceptance of guilt. But bullshit, I thought, and saw red every time even we in Section 6 were not taking action. Williamson may well have felt comfortable monitoring what-was-what-with-who at these conferences but to what avail? I mean what was the fucking point? If you're not going to do anything about it, then just read the transcripts or wait for the press release. I mean I knew that we could never invade Sweden – a military response was out of the question – and it was because we were not the barbarian troglodytes that they had portrayed us as that we weren't rounding up random Swedes and interning them in a Namibian desert camp. But their actions combined with our lack of response was unsustainable and I thought that, of all the groups, Section 6 was best suited to deal with it.

Soon, though, I'd feel that I'd jumped the gun on my scorning. I was told by B.M. after several requests to see him that things were happening and that Konrad and a few others were already in Stockholm making amends. But two days later I found out that this was about helping Longreach to counter anti-apartheid propaganda, so I soon went back on my self-appointed warpath – but to nowhere. My orders were orders and if I wanted a place at the South African table, then I'd bloody well do as I was told.

By mid-January, then, I was back in Rome and, alone in my Jewish penthouse flat, I sat sipping a whisky and smoking a Cuban – a new-found habit that I pursued for the image more than the taste. The next day I'd be meeting Sacriponte and I'd have several questions to ask him.

In fact when I saw him, the usually mild-mannered 'aristocrat' was nothing short of a raging bull. This took me aback, as he hadn't shown emotion even when having his own son murdered. It didn't take me long to see, then, that whatever was bothering him amounted to an 'all or nothing' deal and, though he was a man with his fingers in many pies, this episode was set to near break him. It was strange, then, when what was on the tip of my tongue was also the first word to come off of his: 'Palme'. Sacriponte wanted to shut him up. At that I felt my stomach go and was very alone.

Now when first you look through a window, you see things within a frame. It's like those demonstrations in the Middle East you see on TV, when you might think that thousands of people are spontaneously getting together and demonstrating their support or praise for something or other but what you don't see, unless the camera pans out, are the hundreds of coaches parked up or the bearded bastards with sticks, beating them into compliance. What I'm saying is that in later life it became obvious that, although my team had made contact with Gladio, we were far from being the only ones in there. The South African security set-up was expert in letting you believe you were doing something for one thing when in reality you were doing it for another. Sacriponte, I found, was an apple from the same tree – a master manipulator if you like, just like them. And with his own direct line to the powers behind me, I soon became less of a king and more of a pawn. If I didn't know it then, I soon would. But back then I was convinced that what I was doing was my duty to my country: hitting back at our enemies while playing my part in quelling European militancy and staving off communism. And in most ways I was, but . . . well, I'll get to that.

Now here's the deal. Planning to do in some average guy in Western Europe is in itself difficult. But planning to hit someone special, most of all an important figure, is just plain crazy. Apart from the how and where, and the security around him, you've got to think about the fallout. I mean what would the result be and whose head would it fall on? Besides, in some cases it's better to have the devil you know than the one you don't.

Making it look like an accident would be out of the question. Sacriponte referred to us trying something like this, which made me suggest that he should stick to his dinner parties. An accident might well work in the internal politics of an African country – for instance Mugabe and the army-truck routine, which was a constant source of amusement to us, given that every Monday the papers announced some opponent of his was killed after colliding with an armoured personnel carrier – but that was Africa. No, if an assassination was to be done, then either someone was going to die doing it – and we were never Muslims – or it would need planning, someone on the inside and a bucketful of luck.

Whatever the deal was, a week later I was in Stockholm. In fact there were a few of us there, because, as ever, an anti-apartheid conference was going on, where the who's who of criminal and militant rebellion were being paraded around like heroic victims. Those included Oliver Tambo, Thabo Mbeki and Abdul Minty, all of the ANC, as well as others from the UDF and the South-West Africa People's Organisation (SWAPO). I met back up with Konrad then, who was working with two other guys. One was a policeman and a staunch right-winger who had regularly visited South Africa to train – I'll call him K.P. – while the other was a Swedish secret-service officer who I'd always disliked. He was a bit older but admittedly useful; he'd been working for us in Section 6 for some time now. I'll call him D.B.

Because of the conference that was happening that week and the nature of its subject, right-wing tensions were high, while security was tight. I'd mentioned to Konrad what Sacriponte had wanted to be done and it came as no surprise to me that he'd been mulling it over with the two men I've just mentioned. Feelings had been running high about Palme for some time and in those circles they mostly saw it as only a matter of time. They were right.

At 8.35 p.m. on 28 February 1986 the Palmes left their Vasterlanggatan old-town residence for a subway train to the Grand cinema. There they met their son Marten and his girlfriend before settling down to watch a left-wing production called *The Mozart Brothers*. At 11.00 p.m. the film ended and by 11.15 p.m. the four of them were standing outside in the sub-zero temperatures of an icy Friday evening. After parting company with their son, the Palmes then walked down the Sveavagen road, crossing over towards a paint shop known as Dekorima. A man in a long dark coat, who'd been lurking about for some minutes, greeted them, before pulling out a pistol and, with two shots, gunned Olof Palme down. The man then calmly put his weapon away and ran up the Tunnelgatan – a flight of 89 steps – never to be seen again.

The killing, of course, has never been solved and, apart from a police investigation into who actually did it and why, nobody has ever been able to answer the most burning question of all: why would Palme, on such a cold evening, at that time on a Friday night, decide to walk home – a mile and a half – with his wife? And secondly, if so, why would he choose such a circuitous route (a detour through Stockholm's rowdy nightspots such as Sergel's Torg and the Haymarket) and even then be on the wrong side of the street to take it? Was this a set-up? A chance killing by a random maniac? Or some sort of combination of the two?

Over the years I've watched as one theory has replaced the

next. From Kurdish separatists and synchronised assassins to that poor patsy Christer Pettersson, a local drug addict, who did some time for it before finally being acquitted. In fact the case, in my view, has equalled the killing of Kennedy and has since been termed as the crime of the century. For years now I've carried the truth like another trophy to put in my fridge and, like a lottery win, have basked in it each day, when the memory that it really did happen hits me again. Anyway, it's not for me to get into the insanity of the aftermath. What I can state are the facts of what happened in those few fateful hours. I should point out that I'm doing this not because I need to but because, when the time comes to categorically prove what I'm saying, I'll be fulfilling my whole purpose in telling this story in the first place. But that's for the end.

It's difficult, then, to set about planning to murder a prime minister. You need to know where he'll be at what time and then study the ins and outs of the area at different times of the day, so as to plan your escape with differing amounts of people in the way. If you're just a lone nut, such as a suicide bomber, the out is less important but when you're secretly acting on behalf of a government, getting away with it means everything. I've since heard that Palme, like Sweden as a whole, had prided himself on his openness and accessibility, to the extent that people like him could walk freely around without needing an escort. In part this was true, but just because he'd walked some 13 times to work without a bodyguard and had been watched having dinner alone with his wife in the weeks beforehand it didn't mean that it would be an easy job to pull off. Even sniffing about would have got your collar felt, as a huge part of VIP protection is counter-surveillance. In fact we made a previous attempt on his life and failed by a whisker while the conference was on. Believe it or not, a small bolt on a door to the hotel lobby was the difference between his life and death and only three days previously Konrad and I were almost caught lurking about outside his house.

Konrad, then, wanted to involve another man. He was another right-winger, who was also a Nazi and part of Sweden's stay behinds. But I said no. I knew who the guy was – an idiot – and without pulling my punches being a neo-Nazi by definition makes you a fool. The past is the past; this was the present. In fact, at this stage, I started to have doubts about the job as a whole. Five in the gang was four too many, as in an ideal world – if you're, say, killing for sport – the best way to get away with it is to act alone and to choose your victim at random, otherwise it's easy for the dots to be joined. I called it all off for the time being. I felt that, had our orders come direct from Pretoria, then by duty we'd take the risks that the job would throw at us, but the fact they came by proxy from Sacriponte, so we could never be sure of their authority, and that he was insisting on the job's urgency, had made me wonder. After all geopolitics move slowly, while only business and finance place a significance on the hour hand!

That's not to say that the game was off. By now we'd drawn up quite a system. Each man in the team had his job and, while we might not kill the PM right there and then, our work had still made it an option for the future. Instead we'd now focus on hitting him hard through another means: his son. We knew he had kids and that taking one out would be crippling. I understand that, on reading this, you'll surely debate its logic but at the time and in the company we were keeping it all made perfectly good sense. There was, of course, a difference in the two threats that they respectively posed to apartheid but Marten, their second son, a 23-year-old out-and-about young lad, presented himself a damn sight more than his father ever did. Thanks to D.B. it didn't take long for us to find him and, after a couple of days, we were pretty much set to whack him. The plan was simple: walk over, at night, in somewhere less than busy, and shoot the bastard dead. It had to be done this way to make our point: a specific killing, deliberate, 'professional' and without emotion. The dots would be joined but proof would be hard to come by.

And so back to that cold night in February. K.P. was working his shift, while Konrad was following Marten. I was staying in a safehouse belonging to a Swede who knew D.B. from the secret training camp they were at in Rydsford. He thought we were with Longreach. D.B. had popped round to the house to talk about what their bugs had picked up from Thabo Mbeki's hotel room. Now the safehouse was on a parallel street to Adolf Fredriks Kyrkogata and so was within a stone's throw of the Grand cinema. The doorbell went and, after the usual checks, I opened it to Konrad, who was panting away like he'd been chased by a gang of schoolkids. I took him in and no sooner had he seen we were alone than he said, 'You're not going to believe this. Guess who's round the corner?'

I joked, 'The Pope?'

'Palme. Father Palme. And I think he's alone. I mean without an escort.' We near dropped our coffee as D.B. had a quick glance through the window. 'He's at the cinema around the corner with Lisbet [his wife].'

D.B. looked back at me. 'So?' he said. 'Here's our chance.'

I thought about it. 'All right,' I said. 'Let's have a look.'

In fact by the time we got round there, the Palmes had just finished buying their tickets, after joining the back of the queue to await their turn. And at that moment we knew we were on.

When we'd been planning for Marten, we'd devised a standard night-time, three-man procedure. The gunman, Konrad, would park the first car, hired with false papers, in the area and keep a set of keys with him, while D.B. would sit one block over in the second – he'd be the escape driver and carry a police radio. Both knew the city and spoke the language. I would stand back and cover the area by foot, before leaving in Konrad's car once he'd made it to D.B. The whole idea meant that no matter what happened he'd have choices in his escape route, while all the time he'd be shadowed by me. We'd practised the idea a few times at walking pace, not wanting to be running along the streets as fully grown men, and found it both flexible and suited to the Stockholm streets, especially when in contact with each other by two-way radios. We decided the plan would work just as well for his father, with a few small adjustments to fit the circumstances.

Now there's a reason why the public can't let the famous dead lie. And in part it's a symptom of the modern age. The gods have come down from the mountain and have been replaced by celebrities, who, although rich and powerful, are nevertheless just human. Except the media serves to make them gods again, reproducing their images until they seem larger than life, more vivid and alive than ourselves. They live a hyperreal life and so, to us minions, they must suffer a hyperreal death. Elvis is alive, Bruce Lee's body just exploded and Lady Diana was the victim of an MI6 plot. Well I say piss! In fact the famous and mighty can be lured to their deaths in the same everyday ways as the rest of us. And what I'm about to say is proof positive of that.

D.B. knew Palme from the old days. The whole basis of the Palme mystery rests on why he walked to where he was murdered. Surely he must have been trapped or tricked, while looking for secret documents relating to alien landings? Well, perhaps in general he was but that's not where he was off to that evening. You see, Palme was a secret-service man himself and, although he hadn't seen him in two years, he knew D.B. well enough to consider him an old friend. But it was more. They first got close in their youth and so would perhaps have shared adventures together that were less than family orientated. In any event D.B. bought a ticket and, as he was last in, had found himself at the back in the dark. At a certain point, then, Palme left for the toilet, where D.B. 'just happened' to be. As they recognised each other instantly, they laughed and joked for less than a minute, until D.B. said that he was here with a young woman, who happened to live just two minutes away. If he wanted, the Palmes could wait five minutes after the show and he'd give them a lift back home in his car. That way they could catch up and have a laugh, sort of thing. He'd rather Lisbet didn't see his girlfriend, though, since she was still in her early 20s, so he'd walk her home first. He told Palme that his car was parked on the Sveavagen, just outside the paint shop. I can only speculate that Palme, like most married men, would vicariously live a wilder life through others less settled. But of course I can't say. What I do know is that he agreed to the lift. And so, while the movie played, we set ourselves up. D.B. lingered until the last moment, double-checking that Palme's bodyguards were not around. At 11.00 p.m. precisely he picked Konrad up to swap jackets and hats, then drove his red Volkswagen into position, facing east on David Bagares Gata. Konrad jumped out and meandered his way back, along the street and down the Tunnelgatan stairs. He arrived in the kill zone at exactly 11.15 p.m.

I, meanwhile, watched the other people leave, followed by the Palmes, who then waited for a further two minutes before parting company with their son, Marten. Then they walked to where they thought they were getting a lift. Our radio procedure was simple: we would only talk if there was a problem. My radio remained silent, so I followed them some 20 yards, then speeded up slightly as they began crossing the road. The ground was frozen and the air was chilly, and snow crunched under my feet when I stepped off the kerb between two parked cars. From a distance I could see Konrad standing in the doorway and watching me. Olof gestured at him, thinking it was D.B. acknowledging him, but it was Konrad nodding at me. The Palmes were now in a trap and there was no way out.

I stopped. I could say that my heart was racing but only through the intensity of my focus, as my mind was deadly still. Finally they got to within a few yards of each other when Palme must have realised it wasn't D.B. and attempted to keep on walking. But Konrad went with him for those few steps. Then, as I stood there in that pocket of anticipation, I saw them struggle as Konrad put an arm around Palme while using the other to pull out his weapon: a .357 Magnum. He fired two shots: one into him and the other, reaching slightly forward, into her. He turned, looked back at me, then sprinted up the stairs. Palme was left lying in a pool of his own blood and within a moment was dead.

They say practice makes perfect but on the hop it's a different story. I watched the ensuing commotion from the corner and saw that Konrad had not killed Lisbet, as she was flapping about in a panic. There's nothing like a campaigning widow to rally support, so doing her in as well as Palme was a must. But he'd fucked it. I had to get out of there and out of the country. I doubled back and casually walked to the safehouse, where I packed my bits and pieces together in what the Americans know as a 'bug-out bag' and drove off in the car that Konrad had parked up beforehand.

Throughout the weeks of planning the one thing that had stayed firm was the route and means of escape. When something like this happens, you've got to assume that a) you've been seen, so there's a description of you in circulation, b) that the police are actively looking for you, and c) that sooner or later some bastard's going to be kicking in your door after you've been grassed up for clemency. For these reasons the best option is to flee immediately. Now airports and ferry terminals have both got their drawbacks. For a start when you're there, you're stuck, while all the time you're beholden to someone else's scheduling and, with every border cop desperate to make a name for themselves, you've got to be a black, disabled, homosexual single-parent war widow not to get a pull. In the case of Sweden we knew we'd only have a small window of opportunity to clear out of the city centre – the hardest part of all. And as long as we weren't on the road an hour or so after the hit, we knew we could probably avoid the police in the initial aftermath.

Our meeting point was thus on the road to Nykoping, just south of Stockholm, at D.B.'s weekend house. It took me over two hours to get there but when I did, I saw that both D.B. and Konrad had been there a while. You'd think that after all the excitement the boys would be buzzing but both were nearly asleep when I banged on the door. I shook their hands and shared a drink but before long D.B. went to bed and Konrad and I sat in silence and waited till morning.

Well, not quite. You see, at the end of the day, I trusted no one – not even those with whom I'd just been involved. We'd always agreed that, whatever happened, our escape from the country would be from the harbour, a marina now some 15 miles away. In fact D.B. had a boat and had planned to sail us both to Turku, where we'd catch a flight out through Helsinki. But that was never going to happen. Before the sun came up, I kicked Konrad's legs to check he was still sleeping, before I gently manoeuvred myself into D.B.'s bedroom.

A Swedish-designed building is often inspiring and the skylight above his fat, festering head was frosted beneath the bright winter stars. He snored, choked, coughed a bit, then snored some more. In the dim starlight I watched my shadowy arms grasp hold of his neck and begin to steadily squeeze. I loved it. D.B. was scum. I hated his face, his stories, the way he looked and what he said. I tolerated him because I had to but beyond that he was a traitor and so died as a spy, without quarter. It took just minutes to wring the last beat of his heart out of him but I lay there with him after I'd finished. The dead can't leave me, nor stray in their attention. As the sun began to rise, I dozed off with my lover but only for an hour, just enough to get my head back together.

I went through to the kitchen and grabbed a coffee and a smoke, before rifling his larder for the tools of my trade. Serration is the key. It's difficult for some people to imagine dissecting a body. But I enjoyed it. I enjoyed its make-up and the revelation of what lay under the flesh. In the bath his eyes stayed open, which I loved, as he watched me disembowel him and wrap his intestines around his head. I became fascinated with artistic compositions such as this, where parts were juxtaposed contrary to the possibilities of nature. I stood up when his legs were off and, after propping them up against the white-tiled wall like two crutches, I wiped the blood off my face and walked to the radio. I turned it on and understood nothing, so I flicked the dial until I found the BBC World Service. Sweden was in mourning. I was mid-cutting. By the time I heard Big Ben's chimes and the words 'This is London' I was halfway through his neck. I kept the head until last, as I found him to be too beautiful to disfigure. If I'd hated him in life, in death he was my love. I walked back through to the kitchen and saw that Konrad was stirring. Then, as I fumbled around in a cupboard near the far-end window, I felt that somebody was behind me. I turned round and saw him stagger backwards.

Now it will seem strange that a murderer can be spooked by a murderer. I mean Konrad had just made world history but in spite of that he stood there gobsmacked. I found what I was looking for and walked back towards him. He reached for his waistband but his gun had been chucked. I walked right past him and back to my work in progress, only saying, without turning to look at him, 'He was a danger, mate.' I bent double and scooped the last of the sinew into the polythene rubbish bags.

He said nothing, until, after plucking up the courage, he mumbled, 'What about the boat? How the fuck are we getting out of here?'

I smiled and looked up. 'Not this way, mate, not this way!' And at that I beckoned him over to take a warm black bag out to the car, which nearly made him gag. It was then that I caught sight of myself in the mirror and it stopped me in my tracks. The bags were dropped as I stood there transfixed. I looked hard, before taking one step closer, followed by one closer still. I couldn't recognise myself. It was as if a stranger had borrowed my body. What I saw made me feel dizzy, like my soul was struggling to take hold of my flesh. I was red, all red, from head to toe, and my hair was matted. With congealed blood, bile and excrement all over me, I looked a menace and for the first time I saw it. But it was more than that. I opened my mouth. My teeth were blood red, while between them lay tiny strips of torn human flesh. I couldn't remember eating him. Now I was a witness to myself like never before, like a man on drugs who looks in a mirror: distorted, displaced and without human affinity. I looked at Konrad to see that he'd been talking right at me but I couldn't have repeated a word. So I spoke without hearing, as if in a dream world, fighting in jelly, where blows do nothing. My face was like rubber and my lips now hung numb.

I told him, I think, that something had come up and there'd been a change of plan. He looked blankly at me and now, as the seconds began ticking, he became suspicious that somehow I was a turncoat and was now after him. Well I was, but not how he was thinking.

I'd thought about killing Konrad but having him alive was worth more than the risk of having him dead. I don't want to state the obvious but death is so very final! Anyway, I said that Finland was off and Norway was on. But nothing more. He got pissed off but that was his problem, though I could easily see what was bothering him. He'd pulled the trigger and D.B. had ferried him away but what had I done? Well, apart from just having killed Konrad's safety net, not very much. Now his escape options had gone and I held all the cards. So I stood there a while longer, before taking off my clothes and, in my pants, like all those years before, rectifying my operating theatre, by washing down the bathtub, the walls and then the floor. Forensics weren't going to be a big issue for me – it's not like I was staying around for the reaction of somebody missing him – but sense is sense and there's no need to give your enemies the present of fire. I searched his drawers and found some clothes from his slimmer days that were now outdated. I only needed them until I'd got rid of his body, though, and then I'd put on my own from my bug-out bag.

Then I heard it again and I knew we had to get going: 'This is London, the time is . . . and here is the news . . .' On hearing the broadcast, Konrad's knees wobbled and a look came over his face that I'd only ever seen that first time in the Congo. 'That's right!' I jeered. 'You just bashed the prime minister!' He was silent.

We readied the last of the house and, with Konrad in my Volvo and me in the VW with the body, we headed back north, passing a police roadblock since set up for those coming south. Now, what I didn't say just there is that, straight after I jumped into the VW and got it moving, I felt something slide to my feet when I braked at the first turning. It was a weapon. I looked down and recognised it as Konrad's. Two rounds were missing from the chamber and it stank of powder so it had definitely been fired. I felt enraged – so much so that I wanted to put D.B.'s body back together so I could knock fuck out of him again. I imagined that Konrad would have tossed it to D.B., assuming that D.B. would chuck it over a bridge or in some place en route, given that this was his turf and so would know the best spots to lose it. But he didn't! The .357 is the key: find the gun and the case is closed. Why had the dirty bastard chosen to keep it? To set us up? To cover his own back if it all went wrong? To collect a reward that right now stands at nearly five million dollars? Whatever. I wouldn't know. But half an hour later and off the beaten track we slung the body-bags into the ocean, having made holes in them to help feed the fishes, while torching the car and beating it out of there.

Stockholm, though, was alive. I mean there was a buzz in the city like carnival time in Rio. People were out, off work and flabbergasted. Nobody could believe that Palme had been killed. I had Konrad change the hire car – one Volvo for the next. He was nice and polite and so gave no reason for alarm. The VW was hired as well, though by D.B. under a false name. It now had fuck all to do with us. I checked into a hotel near the airport and at 8.00 p.m. my true escape route was due to arrive – an old friend to whom I'd paid a stack of cash beforehand to rescue me.

If you look at any particular eventuality, say the numbers on a roulette wheel, you'll see that of those 37 numbers, all represent luck. Nothing beyond chance can affect them. But imagine that ten of the numbers are related to those who operate around you, while five are directly within your control. To be a professional is thus to control and determine these, while accepting that the rest may not come up in your favour. I'd known for long enough that an urgent escape would be needed and one that didn't utilise the normal ports of exit. My friend had consequently sailed a yacht to Risor in Norway. He'd then flown back from Oslo – the capital, just further north – to his home country and waited for word. From a call box en route to D.B.'s weekend house the night before I'd called to say come and he'd taken the first flight in. A week and a half later, when the focus was firmly on the investigation, we negotiated our way to the Norwegian border and, as three homosexual ornithologists, left the country and landed in . . . well, not quite yet.

See here's the deal. The police fucked up the investigation – no doubt. It was somehow just bungled, either through all the cock-ups at the beginning, which were numerous, or by hitting and giving up at various dead ends, where certain people's stubbornness got in the way – to what ends I can't say. We had one good man on the inside – that's it – and he wasn't even with us when the job got done. It took us over six months to make contact with him again and by that time his fellow officers were away hunting some Kurdish folk who doubled up as goat herders at the weekend. Anyway, what I gave you above is the exact story of what happened that night – minus that which would qualify this as a textbook or a piece of journalism. I have just one more important thing to add. Of the two others involved who are still with us today – K.P. and Konrad – one is a loyal and remarkable man, while the other, as will soon become perfectly clear, is a dirty ratfink bastard, a Judas of the highest order, who has been out of my reach for the last ten years. I have hunted him to the ends of the earth but have not been able to find the rock under which that piece of vermin is now living, as remarkably his cover, his so-called insurance, is not the shadows but the gaze of the public and their all-seeing eye. This man, in essence, is nothing more than a cold-blooded killer but has become a well-enough-known figure to fear a crushing fall from grace.

I am now at the end of my life and in some ways am sustained by the need to have just one hour with my dearly deposed friend. But I should now accept that, in my lifetime at least, he has evaded me. What I want him to know and understand, though, is that, although I am about to die, my quest for revenge will most certainly not die with me.

XIX

GREAT ZIMBABWE

'You've got to attack civilians,' he said to me, not looking
up from his pizza. 'The people – women, children, the
innocents who consider themselves to be far removed from
the political game – cannot be allowed to affect your life
from their armchairs.' I looked at him and agreed. I was
more concerned, though, with meeting that dumb Yank
again, as by now I knew who he was and wanted him to
help us. But Sacriponte went on: 'The reason we did it was
quite simple: to force the public into feeling a greater need
for security. You can't ask for something you don't know
that you need.' Then he stopped, wiped his mouth with a
pristine pressed napkin and summoned a waiter. '*Un poco
piú vino, per favore.*'

The sun was high but not yet hot and while he confessed
to the 1980 Bologna bombing, which took me aback, he
casually sipped wine, one glass at a time. This was an early
lunch at the Foreign Ministry club on the Tiber. Simply
known as '*Il Circolo*', the circle, it commanded spectacular
views of the river and the surrounding greenery. If I'd only
known better, I'd have been more impressed by the who's

who of Italian life that passed before us, acknowledging Sacriponte without ever stopping. Like the elephant in the room, people knew about him but no one would mention it. And I knew about that.

I'd officially returned to Rome to tie up some loose ends, though in fact I was here of my own accord, as I'd recently become obsessed with something I'd heard by chance but couldn't believe as fact. Nobody in Pretoria had spoken of Palme. Like Sacriponte, passing himself off amongst the elite of Rome, so I wandered the corridors of power back home while people winked, whispered, but never stopped by. B.M., when I first sat in his office, ranted for half an hour and never said a word about it. I'd never been after a medal but, by Christ, a handshake would have been nice. But nothing.

Konrad then came into the room and sat down. He was late and B.M. dressed him down, which made Konrad mad. You're supposed to respect the rank and not the man, but B.M. was more of a relic and would often get caught up in his own self-importance. In any case this bad air seemed to consume the assassin, as, unlike me, he'd expected a hero's welcome with a brass band and ribbons. B.M. instead said that new things were happening and that within the next few months we'd be getting reassigned, if we wanted it, or, as he'd once promised, we could be paid off and so enjoy an early retirement. Konrad, thinking stuff over, opted for a pay-off. And now, realising that his actions amounted to a self-imposed prison sentence within the borders of his own country, he began haggling over the price. At that I left.

The next day, though, I was hauled back in and spent three hours with B.M. and another two high rankers, basically building up a picture of Gladio and the powers that controlled it. Still there was no mention of Palme and when I brought it up they treated it like some distant crime that no one was thinking of. But then B.M. let it slip. You see, information flows from different sources and is then pasted together by the people who care. The CIA were our closet allies; either up front or by proxy they were the bank-roller controllers of all that was Western. B.M. wanted to know my relations with the CIA in Italy, which I gave. But after I'd finished, he looked at me like I was holding back and said, 'And that's it?'

'Yeah, that's the lot.' And I meant it, especially given that my presentation came with documents and photographs.

'What about John Miller [not his real name]?' he said abruptly. My heart thumped.

'Who?' I asked.

'Miller. Konrad told us about the CIA man, Miller, who you'd met with Sacriponte outside the British Embassy.'

At that moment I knew something was up. I'd never said to Konrad that the Yank's name was Miller – not even at the time. Fuck, I didn't even know his surname, only John, and I definitely didn't say anything to Konrad, who was behaving like a teenager at a school dance. But, to cut a long story short, I let it go and by the end of the month was happily back in Rome closing down the two front companies that we were working with.

Il Circolo, then, is an elegant setting in the heart of the city. The small winding road that leads off the rat run soon opens up to hidden parkland where clay tennis courts and diplomats' wives both sun themselves and hide, in between the well-watered foliage. Taking a right, and along a hundred-yard path, you'll come to the main area, with a swimming pool at its centre and the main complex to your right. Sacriponte had been playing tennis that morning and, when the wine arrived, he made his excuses to leave, citing that he'd left something up the stairs on the changing-room counter. No sooner had he gone than Miller appeared and sat down.

He congratulated me on chopping the Swedish Beechwood,

which surprised me somewhat, then began to talk shop. But no sooner had he started than I began to realise what was happening. I'd been had. Sometimes you can be so convinced of something that suggestion alone is enough to spur you into action, like bashing some guy because someone's told you he's been talking to your bird – an action deemed rational when your Viagras have gone missing. Sacriponte, then, had suggested that I take Palme out and no doubt Pretoria had known all about it. But it was never really an order, only part of our readily accepted mandate. Sacriponte, I then found out, had not removed a political rival and the spectre of communism but a business competitor within the world of capitalism – simple as that. Now it's not for me to speculate on why but it was something to do with an arms deal, a big one worth billions. Palme was eager to stop it and Sacriponte for it to go through. And for that Palme was whacked – assassinated by people who thought they were serving their country but in fact were serving one man's greed. But anyway. Ten minutes later Sacriponte came back and I had to fight against my urge to ram a bread-stick through his eyeball. I felt like standing up and screaming the truth from the top of the towers, or threatening him, blackmailing him, whatever. But I didn't. My mind was distracted when Miller said, 'Where's Konrad? I've not seen him for years.'

'What?' I said, holding back every bit of fury I was feeling. 'How do you know Konrad?'

He laughed, then shook his head, figuring I was joking with him. 'I've known him since the Congo in the '60s. We made a load of dollars together. Didn't you hear about that?'

'About what?' I asked, feeling my stomach tremble.

'That girl. What was her name? That African girl in Paulis. He turned up on a flight with some African girl from Stanleyville who he wanted shipped out to London.'

'He did what?'

'Yeah,' he continued. 'I was the station officer at the time and he came up to me, after being pointed in my direction by one of the local Congolese leaders.' He looked up, then lit a cigar while trying to remember his name. 'Some big brute of a man: Ced . . . Cedric. Anyway, he'd approached him, or the other way round, and they ended up in front of me, because I was the only one who could get them out of there. And I did – though it's probably been the most unusual request I've ever fulfilled.' Then he innocently looked at Sacriponte, whose attention had been taken by the Argentine ambassador's stunningly beautiful trophy wife. 'Can you believe it? She was some African chief's daughter. Very rich, they were, very rich. All I had to do was to fly her back to London and arrange to collect the money. The easiest 50,000 I've ever had to sweat for.'

I was silent. If the Congo was truly the place to be neck high in shit and still have the dirt kicked in your eyes, then within that lunch I had just had it proven. I had raped and pillaged my way across the badlands of Africa in search of my jungle prize, only to have been Judased by the man who I'd least expected it from. And, worse still, it had taken me 20 years to know it, during which time I'd fought with him, lived with him, saved him and suffered with him.

From experience I know that being buried alive carries an unusual by-product. Beyond the terror there's a sense of helplessness that seldom comes with other predicaments. In Vlakplaas, a South African secret-police training centre, I'd learned that torture by a technician is a battle of wills and that, even though a subject's body is broken, until death there is always a possibility of survival. This pocket of hope, and the small battles along the way, are like life rings for a suffering soul to cling on to. I've been on both sides of the concept and so am well qualified to say so. But at that moment, even though I sat in the open opulence of *Il Circolo*, I felt the coffin lid close and saw myself screaming.

I didn't sleep until I was back in Pretoria. I'd hastily completed my business on autopilot and now, tearing around, spent my days looking for Konrad. I couldn't find him and instead, like I'd done with Hugh all those years before, indulged myself in a constantly playing fantasy of what I'd do when I found him. But for me, though, time alone was crippling, while time off was dangerous, and as the red mist became the air around me I found it difficult to rely on those controls that I'd spent a lifetime developing. I knew he was here – he had to be – but Africa's a big place to get lost in, especially for someone with a golden handshake and the misplaced loyalty of the people around him, and he no doubt would have heard through the grapevine that I was coming after him.

A week later I was finally towards the tipping point of my scales when I got a call from B.M., which saved me. When Major General Joep Joubert took command of the special forces in November 1985, replacing General Kat Liebenberg, he recognised the need to reshape Barnacle. He was later quoted as saying in his application for amnesty from the Truth and Reconciliation Commission:

> In the mid to late 1980s one of the major goals of national-security policy and strategy was to bring the revolutionary organisation and mobilisation by the revolutionary movements, particularly the ANC, to a halt. By this time it was also clear that the ANC was not going to be stopped by normal conventional methods and that revolutionary methods would have to be used.
>
> As the institution for external operations special forces would also have to intensify its external operations, since the necessity for unconventional and revolutionary action was already clear. It was also clear that clandestine and covert

operations would have to take place internally, for which special-forces members would be used.

It was more or less then that the name CCB was adopted as a replacement for D40 or Barnacle. The revolutionary and covert nature of the plan, amongst other things, involved:

One: That ANC leaders and people who substantially contributed to the struggle would be eliminated.

Two: That ANC facilities and support services would be destroyed.

Three: That activists, sympathisers, fighters and people who supported them would also be eliminated.

The CCB would thus be a civilian strike force and operate in total secrecy. By April, then, the Civil Cooperation Bureau, or in Afrikaans the Burgerlike Samewerkings Buro (BSB), came into action. Each of the nine regional sections was run by a regional manager, much the same as Barnacle had been structured. There was a tenth section but that was for internal operations and so ran with a slightly different structure to the rest of us:

Region 1 – Botswana.

Region 2 – Mozambique and Swaziland.

Region 3 – Lesotho.

Region 4 – Angola, Zambia and Tanzania.

Region 5 – UK and Europe.

Region 6 – South Africa.

Region 7 – Zimbabwe.

Region 8 – South-West Africa/Namibia.

Region 9 – Non-geographical but used to supply intelligence to the other regions.

Region 10 – Non-geographical but used to supply finance and administration.

Tasked, then, with 'monitoring certain external opponents of the regime with a view to their possible extinction', our mandate could hardly have been clearer. If Section 6 had before slipped under the radar with Longreach while attempting to forge alliances for its dirty work, so the CCB was a no-holds-barred attempt at a unilateral answer and made no apologies for doing so. As with Project Barnacle, units attempted to build up their own networks in order to reduce their reliance on other sections, resulting in the establishment of front companies and organisations. Our units were never accountable to the local or regional security structures, only to the central chains of the special forces, and so had considerable latitude when it came to target selection and operations. All of these actions were hallmarks of covert units designed to operate independently of oversight, accountability and, ultimately, even command.

Beyond that, though, the organisation was seen as a long-term project, needing at least ten years to come to fruition. The goal was to create a network of underground companies that acted as legitimate businesses as well as being fronts for intelligence gatherers and target selection. Businessmen and prominent leaders in their respective communities would be integrated into our service, making them part and parcel of our 'inner' and 'outer' circles. The inners consisted of 'overt members', who were full-time employees of the South African Defence Force (SADF), while the outer band was made up from 'coverts', who, in theory anyway, had no idea who their handlers were working for. That meant that three distinct categories of coverts were used: those who thought they were connected to the regime in some way but were unsure as to which part, those who had no idea at all and, thirdly, international criminals, who were best suited to this kind of work. Planning was, of course, carried out by us, the overts, while the operational parts were often contracted out to the coverts, especially when it came to assassinations. That's not to say that we overts did not carry out assassinations too.

Soon, then, hit squads drawn from mercenaries, the security wings of the extreme right and veterans like me, of South Africa's 32 Battalion, were tendered and put to work, resulting in, to name but a few: the attempted murder of Godfrey Motsepe, the ANC representative in Brussels, on 4 February 1988; the death of Dulcie September, the ANC representative in Paris, on 29 March 1988, involving my close friend the late Dirk K. Stoffberg, who, as an arms dealer and head of Z-Squad Incorporated, a consortium of highly trained assassins, paid two former Foreign Legionnaires a sack of money to shoot her; and, only a couple days beforehand, the planting of a 17-kg bomb at the ANC's office in Brussels by two more of our agents.

Generally speaking, each overt would have a red and a blue plan. The red plan concerned the objectives of the CCB, while the blue represented the cover behind which he operated. For this the regime provided capital for him to set up in business, while bank-rolling the cash flow to ensure his continued success. No region had a single office and so it was difficult for any opposition's respective counter-espionage team to keep tracks on them.

The purpose of all this was to keep the SADF as remotely involved and unaccountable as possible. The overts were, of course, one safe step away, while the coverts were two. If a covert got grabbed, the overts would simply step back and leave him to rot – an unfair but necessary tactic and a risk that the coverts were paid for. But that said, in practice things were altogether different. It wasn't long before unintended consequences, such as financial mismanagement and personal abuse, led the CCB to become not only a rogue element within the South African security apparatus but a criminal one too, involved in drug trafficking, arms dealing, diamond smuggling, extortion, fraud and so on. Since many of the coverts were recruited from society's less virtuous sectors, these people were by principle suspicious and, to the detriment of many an overt, far from stupid. In the end many of the coverts became far closer than anyone had anticipated, leaving men on the street with both a direct line to the most secretive of all the state organs and the possession of information that many would kill for.

By late 1986, then, I was posted back to Rome as part of CCB Section 5 Europe but soon found myself being shifted to Britain. I'd later learn that the then UK head had planned to kidnap the entire ANC leadership during a meeting in London but the operation was thwarted, leaving two Norwegian ex-mercenaries and a British national in custody. It was a daft idea from the outset – killing was one thing but kidnap needs an objective, namely money or an action. We never wanted money and, as for the other, they got it the wrong bloody way round. You see, you can kidnap a national or a minion of a group and demand a response from the leadership but you can't kidnap the leadership and demand a response from the people. Enough said.

Throughout this time my head was constantly spinning. I tried to numb my demons but, like I've said, drugs and drink were never an option as all they did was cement my already entrenched mindset.

Britain by then was a constraining place. And the workload seemed to have become more demanding, never-ending and pointless. We were not a survey group and in no way were we primarily businessmen, especially ones to compete, albeit unfairly, in the epicentre that was London. We were soldiers with suits on but now had our hands bound by Pretoria, in favour of small, meaningless actions like the ones above and the sporadic killings of some overseas activists. I, meanwhile, saw the clock ticking and the pressure mount. I'd been here before, at the beginning of the decade, and knew that wars were never half-hearted; they were all or nothing, until one side succumbed. I became disillusioned and angry with the system I was sworn to uphold, as for every target I suggested the response was negative.

Then, in February 1988, I was informed that the Scottish Trades Union Congress (STUC) was handing out literature promoting a rally in Glasgow to follow the Wembley concert on 11 June to mark Nelson Mandela's birthday. Then, after several more targets for assassination were rejected in late March, I chose to circumvent my command structure and, on returning to Pretoria, went straight to B.M.

Now B.M. was no alarmist but, like me, he was feeling the pinch of a government policy that was dragging its feet. He moaned about how we'd got bogged down in a web of our own bullshit, such as how Sergeant Major Joseph Klue was identified by Godfrey Motsepe in Brussels as the man who shot him and how Dirk K. Stoffberg, a man crucial to our front companies, had been ousted. The boys were preoccupied with covering up tracks, instead of getting things done. We weren't criminals, for fuck's sake – well, not in the real sense – so what was the problem? World opinion? I left the meeting that day with an affirmation from the ageing B.M. that I should do what I could to get the ball rolling.

After the early days with Sacriponte I'd come to learn certain things: that large changes don't come about through small events and that, even if they did, like my Viagra analogy, they were ready to move in any case. Back in London it took me little time to see what I should be doing. In Bologna an attempt had been made to bomb the population into submission, so I would bomb the ANC sympathisers into capitulation. You see, in any group – soldiers, businessmen, the general population – there's only that few per cent who really give a fuck and are able to make a difference. The rest are swayed – like sheep, if you like – to form a collective in which they're told what to think and how to feel it. And that's what's called a popular front. But they're not really involved or motivated in any deep or meaningful way. I mean not one of those bastards who stood shouting 'Free Nelson Mandela' had the slightest care for or notion of what they were asking for.

People just want something to believe in, a quest to give their otherwise boring existences some meaning. I know about that. And in the West we're the worst. We are, at times, nothing more than a bunch of ignorant do-gooding bastards who bounce from one cause to another, at the behest of whoever's mailshot, news report or marketing campaign is bigger, brighter or jazzier than the next. Nobody knew of the butchering that South Africa would endure when the nationalists took over and nobody wanted to know, so long as they could go home after some light entertainment, demonise us racists and pat each other on the back for a job well done: 'We're one step closer to that utopian earth.'

But what had they done? In fact they had shown a terrorist group that by murdering their way through a civilian population, the West, those who hold themselves to a higher moral standard that the rest, are with them. Well fuck that! For every action there's a reaction and if they wanted to join the struggle, then money paid for a ticket was money given for a bullet.

I weighed up the pros and cons of hitting Wembley, the ANC offices or the terrorist leaders when they were on their walkabouts, just like Section 6 had done during those previous years in Stockholm. But no. The areas were too large, the crowds too vast and their movements uncertain. And so back to the STUC and Glasgow. It could be possible to make a mark, a stand, if you like, right there. The IRA was at the height of its mainland campaign and so counter-terrorism procedures were tight. But Scotland had never been touched; nor was it ever likely to be. I mean, sure, one military barracks or another would add an extra yard of welding on top of their already three-yard-high fencing but, beyond that, Scotland was a wide-open door.

I'd already arranged with B.M. that when the time came, I'd signal and he'd send me a body to help carry it out. I could have recruited through the usual outer-circle means but, while a kick-in or whacking is one thing, it takes a special kind of villain to produce what I was aiming for. By mid-April, then, 'A.H.' had arrived. Now I knew this guy well. Apart from the fact that he'd served with 32 Battalion – 'The Terrible Ones' – after being disbanded from the Selous Scouts in 1980 and formally brought into the CCB in late 1985, I was the one who'd recruited him in the first place from the UK in late 1977. And while I was tasked to Europe in the Barnacle days, A.H. had served with 5th RECCE in Phalaborwa, helping to beat Frelimo in Mozambique, a prized and personal posting for all ex-Rhodesians. But even then I chose not to reveal our target, only that people would die and if he wasn't prepared for it then he should say so now. He said nothing. Now I'm no fool. In fact I'd requested A.H., even against the better judgement of B.M., simply because what I was proposing needed a type of insanity and a certainty that what you were doing was right. And that feeling of being right could only come with an inherent hatred of humanity and its stupidities. A.H. was just that person. Still, I'd always felt it necessary to not only keep my team in the dark but always insinuate that there was another lot I was handling, preparing for something else – perhaps something worse. We were trained that way and it made sense, as it bought you time if spies were amongst you. Besides, I'd learned my lesson well. I kept the numbers down and the coverts low.

So, sitting tight in my London flat on the corner of Museum and Great Russell Street, WC1 – the same one I'd been given by the Rhodesian government all those years ago – we put together the components of our work. Now the one thing I wasn't was a bomb maker; that's why I'd conscripted A.H. He was an expert. All I had to do was gather the parts (several kilos of Czech Army Semtex, brought in by a serving British NCO and National Front member, who'd in turn bought it from a Loyalist group in Northern Ireland), as well as make the arrangements for the big day out – 'Operation Great Zimbabwe', so termed by B.M., after the ancient African castle ruins that had been the focus of an ideological conflict, given that no Rhodesian believed they could have been built by Africans 1,000 years beforehand. I could. They looked shit!

Anyway, by early May 1988 agents working within the ANC's London office confirmed 12 June in Glasgow as a definite – and had given me a list of pencilled-in speakers. Due onstage in Glasgow Green that day were to be Bernie Grant MP, fresh from his 1987 election victory and a leading member of the Anti-Apartheid Movement's (AAM's) Executive Committee; Janey Buchan MEP; Oliver Tambo, president of the ANC; and others such as Campbell Christie of the STUC, Trevor Huddleston, the AAM's president, and members of the Popular Movement for the Liberation of Angola (MPLA) and SWAPO. Now when I heard that, I felt good, because of all the people I wanted, Tambo was the one I wanted the most. Apart from being the leader of the ANC, we'd just tried to kill him in Harare, at Hero's Acre – a part of the Warren Hills Cemetery set aside to remember the 'heroes of the revolution', otherwise known to the Rhodies as 'gooks and spooks'. But, as ever, the job had been pulled. Although he'd never admit it, B.M. had told me that A.H. had been assigned, with his particular skills, to work for CCB Section 7 on that job. So I figured he'd love another crack at the whip – when I told him about it, that was, but for now he was still in the dark. Beyond that, though, our agents had also given me information suggesting that Pat Lally, the Glasgow City Council leader, was to be hosting a lunch at the City Chambers earlier that day, which no doubt gave us more options.

On 11 April I made my way north in a Mitchell Self Drive, which I'd sourced for the job, and took a look round the Glasgow City Chambers, with a view to detonating a device during or after the lunch. But no sooner had I set foot on the stairway than I decided against it. Access was impossible and every room would no doubt be swept through before dining. It had to be the concert, then, or some time after it.

The next day, after having checked myself into a local guesthouse, I went to take a good look at the Green. Using information from my man at the ANC office in London, I figured out how it would be laid out, where the guests would arrive from and how long they'd be staying there. But even then I made sure that all of this info was part of a larger and complete package, in which these details were just a few of the many. I planned on having three devices, each one packing a punch. When I returned to London and liaised with A.H., I told him that I'd found three mules from the National Front who would carry them in, before slipping back out ten minutes before detonation. As it turned out, though, only two devices would be made – one to be carried by A.H. and one by me, which would then be triggered remotely.

The more time I spent with A.H., however, the more I went off him. In Angola I'd seen him as a tough, sinewy fighter who wore his guts on the outside but remained humble with others. I'd taken a man and projected a character onto him that I felt suited him. But I now found myself to be quietly disappointed. Acting the hard man didn't impress me. Like racism, physical strength and fighting bravado were the lowest common denominators for your average male on the street. Without interests, intelligence or education, what could we expect from them other than a fixation on skin colour or the size of their muscle mass? But every now and then you'd meet the exception. In the old days they were more common, when the fixation on self-image wasn't nearly so strong and kudos came from actions and not from bravado. Today, however, they're a rarity, and though I really felt that A.H. was one of them, he wasn't. It's not that I was continually testing him but, like a man who's looking for a girl, there were small instances when his reaction was not what I was expecting and so that inverse, that deficit, is what started to shape my conception of him. A.H., then, was not a brave man with brains but a hard man who was nice – an easy mistake to make if you've already typecast him to begin with. Now this bothered me. A.H. still had no idea of what we were doing. Yes, people would die and again, from what I'd seen with my own eyes, I knew he was capable – and I don't just mean as a typical soldier is capable. If he had to shoot ten women to get to the rebel, then he'd do it. And he had. But right then and for this job perhaps even that wouldn't be enough. I needed a bad man, a man who'd beat ten women to death with the limbs of their own children and then kill the rebel behind them. Time would tell but for the moment I was stuck.

Finally, on 8 May, I bought a rail ticket for 12 June from Glasgow to Newcastle and then a ferry ticket to Amsterdam for A.H. He would then be guided back to South Africa via a secret route by a CCB overt. On the same day I bought a plane ticket from Edinburgh to Frankfurt, then Frankfurt to Cyprus, while on the 9th I hired a van with false documents under the name of Helmut Bryms and began our meander north – a slow drive to do a bad thing.

We never said much. We'd tried a few times to make light of what we were doing but it all seemed pointless. In the uncomfortable silence I thought back to the Palme affair and soon managed to fill myself with doubt. Once again I was going out on a limb for no other real reason than satiating my own hunger for chaos. I wanted to stop and think for a moment but my body kept us moving. No one had thanked me for what I'd done in Stockholm, not even Sacriponte, who'd lived to be rich for another day. But it never really bothered me. I was just happy to have done it. I knew they were glad that Palme was gone and I could see the definite merits of pleading sheer ignorance. But here I was again, setting myself up for a fall. I might have been an overt but, should I be caught, there would be no place called home.

Hitting the outskirts of Glasgow carries with it a flavour. To some it's the land that time forgot, while to others it's nothing short of its own city state. Either way it's some place. I've fought in the Congo, Angola and Mozambique but would rather opt for a night out in downtown Soweto than a swift half in a local up there. Like all salt-of-the-earth-type places, its people are renowned for their hospitality, but I've always considered that a myth. I could perhaps be proved wrong but that evening I wasn't. Here we were, two of the heaviest hitters Scotland would see, and we nearly got stabbed to death by a group of youths on our way round to the chippie, A.H. almost losing an eye off the wrong end of a 'bottle i ginger'.

The next morning I told A.H. I was off to see team two. We laughed as I left, him still reeling from the night before. A.H., who was London born, was fixated on the fact that only in Glasgow could you get the nation's favourite soft drink by speaking the one word: ginger. 'Like fucking Chinese,' he said to me, nursing his swelling down. I smirked and slung my jacket on, before making for the door. I knew what he meant, though.

Whether it was right or wrong, I decided to head through to Edinburgh for a social. I hadn't seen my old mate Rod McLean in a couple of years and now wondered if I could get to ruin his life for him. Rod looked great. I saw him outside his house, a huge mansion that towered over the rest, like a lord's manor in amongst the peasants. He smiled – well, not quite – but soon seemed happy enough to see me, given that the last time we'd met, we nearly drowned in the North Sea. But anyway, I had a good day and, by five o'clock, I'd convinced him to come back to Africa. I knew that whatever happened on this job – assuming I made it out – my days in Europe were numbered. I mean I could never retire, not of my own accord, anyway, and so knew I'd soon be reposted, probably to Section 2, working down in Mozambique. He'd work for us there.

On the way back, at Hart Hill, I stopped for fuel and checked in with Pretoria. B.M. wasn't about but had left a message that if I called in, I was to get back in touch the next morning at 0900hrs GMT. There was no way we could talk openly on the phone, not on this line anyway, but we'd devised a simple system where he could warn me if any problems came up. If he asked me how the beer was over here, I should abort and return to London with A.H. If he said that the beer in South Africa was better, I should abort and leave the country with A.H. And if he said that he'd decided to give up drinking for good, I was to stop everything and, on my own, get the fuck back to South Africa asap. I went to bed early that night and, like a player before the day of the big game, I welcomed sleep to bring the moment closer.

Early in the morning of the 11th I checked in as told, to find that all was well from his end. I made a few phone calls myself, around the UK, not asking permission or anything but just to see if anyone had anything they wanted to tell me. But nothing. At that I went back to the room and told A.H. to start priming. I won't go into the types of devices that we used; suffice it to say that each holdall was enough to have a blast radius of 60-plus yards, with a definite-kill zone of over 20 – that's accounting for people getting in the way. As far as I was concerned, this was no football match; this was a political event with the direct purpose of destabilising my country. If these people turned up to support the terrorists, they were combatants by proxy and for that were legitimate targets. I'd wait until the next morning to tell A.H. there was no second team, nor a third, though he'd figured that much out. I'd tell him, then, that we'd be taking the holdalls in ourselves, one from each end of the stage. The target, as he'd already guessed, was Glasgow Green, though he could still have thought it was the City Chambers. I then said I was going out for a paper, just to give myself a few minutes alone to check through my numbers. These were still the days before mobile phones were everywhere, so checking in when you were on the road was a cumbersome business.

Every time I left the room, even if it was just for the toilet, I carried my bug-out kit. In it were documents, passports, bank cards and cash. While in other countries we also packed a weapon, in the UK we left that one out. I walked through the fresh afternoon sunlight wearing nothing but a jumper on top. But I soon felt something was wrong. Yes, I was super-sensitive and even an ice-cream van was cause for concern. But I just felt wrong. I walked to the phone box but didn't pick up the receiver. A gang of youths, the same from the first night we'd got there, had decided to have it out with each other, over the road – knives, bottles and all. So I walked further into town, no more than a mile, and called Pretoria again, before, for no other reason than I had a few pence left over in change, I called a contact in Frankfurt. And was surprised to get the flustered response of 'Thank fuck, man. Get the hell out of there. Do it now!' I nearly fell over.

'What?' I said. But I knew better than to ask why. 'Serious?' I asked.

'Serious!' he replied.

And so I did. There are no second chances in this game

and the jail's full of men reflecting on why they took a left when they could have taken a right. I wouldn't be one of them. I knew this was bad because my contact wasn't supposed to know what I was up to – but he did. No more needed saying. So I put the phone down, hailed a taxi and went straight to the airport, while once again under the name of Helmut Bryms, I flew to Frankfurt – and the job was abandoned.

Why? Well, I nearly choked on my Cornflakes when they told me. A.H., my companion through thick and thin in Rhodesia, Angola and the rest was nothing less than an MI6 operative, sent by the sneaky British bastards, all those years before. It took him years to do so but, within that time, he had literally made it to the innermost workings of the SADF's intelligence community – and I had recruited him! Twice!

A.H., then, is a hero. Instead of killing hundreds, he saved them. And as the concert went ahead, people had a good time, patted each other on the back and never quite knew how close they'd come to being maimed and murdered on one hot sunny day in Glasgow.

And how did the man in Frankfurt know? Money as usual. Someone in the ANC's office in London close to the head of Umkhonto weSizwe, the ANC's military wing, had been made an offer too large to refuse and so had volunteered on 10 May that their communications with British Intel had suggested that they were on top of whatever was being schemed up north. It took me a month and a half to realise that A.H. wasn't in jail but living a new life somewhere in Australia – his lasting legacy. My epitaph, meanwhile, would be somewhat different.

XX

SNAKE OIL

Well, South Africa folded and the nationalists took power.
So far the grand experiment is holding out, I think. Crime
is rampant, Aids is rife and while the great civil war was
confined to four short days, segregation by policy has become
segregation by wealth – or lack of. Like the rest of the world
the gulf is huge, and like the ice caps the space in between
expands at a rate that cannot be sustained. I, however, was
tired – not of the lifestyle but of the constant struggle. I came
to see living as nothing more than a motion, like waves on a
beach, which can't be stopped, only channelled for a while.
Nothing means anything and had I not been the bad one,
then somebody else would have taken my place.

I decided, then, to have a working retirement. I moved to
Mozambique, where Rod McLean spent many a year helping
both of us to hold our fingers in the dam but it didn't take
long for it to give. After that I started to live by his ethos:
that it's not important from where it came or why it is, only
that it's there. And by coming to see that, things that were
once so central to me no longer mattered.

Life, then, is not about pacifying your urges. People are the products of trial and error and against the scale of the age of the earth we're only embryos. I hate this world for what it is now, as much as I hated it then for what it had made me. But now, more than that, I hate myself for how I dealt with the cards I was given. When the regime collapsed and they danced in the streets, I saw my youth all over again. I had assumed that life carried no consequences. A'luta, the beast, had got away scot-free, the only impact he had in the world left resonating with his victims. How else could I see it? It seemed black and white with no in betweens. But I was wrong.

I changed from servant to master, carving Mozambique into my own personal chiefdom. And I made millions. Drugs, arms and countless other valuable commodities transited their way through those unguarded shorelines. Cocaine came from South America, heroin from Afghanistan and arms from the Eastern bloc. These new gods had replaced the ideals of old. East and West stopped mattering, and while parts of the world looked to the future, so others clung onto the past, scared of the change.

All through the '90s I was busy at work. The CCB had formed an infrastructure, which outlived the state that created it. And so, bonded in blood, strength and honour, all the skills we'd once learned and used for our country were now used for ourselves. But there comes a time when the game nears an end and the collection of toys, which you can't take with you, pales in significance to what's truly at stake. When the United States Embassy bombs went off in Kenya and Tanzania in 1998, I knew something about it right away – and so grassed up the group behind them. In 1990 we knew Saddam Hussein was attempting to hit soft targets in Zimbabwe but said nothing. Why? Well, because I was under orders but also because what Saddam was doing was different: there was no false god behind it. The world is not a composite of the supernatural but what is real. Flesh, earth, fire and air are all the gods we have or ever need. It is a quirk of the human animal that justification is sought outwith our own reach or senses.

A'luta raped me. Before he left, he forced me down on the floor and raped me until my blood, mixed with his matter, lay in puddles around me, which I can still feel to this day. It is sorrowful then that he hid behind lycanthropy. He was no more a werewolf than I am. He was vermin, though – scum who had the choice to grow legs but stayed in the swamp instead. I wondered then, if God existed, why we couldn't live more than one life, or at least pass down our experiences to our kids in a way they'd fully comprehend. Perhaps then humanity would get it.

I am not reformed and still hold grudges. And should my country be threatened by those that prefer regression to progress, then once again I will stand up and be counted. It is incredible, then, that those who appease rather than act, those who, like the boy in Mexico, say nothing while his girl is nearly raped, are more worried that their words might cause offence than about the danger of not speaking out. Bullshit! Political correctness is a smokescreen. It's simply not right to place all the earth's people on an equal footing. I am not a racist and now hold a respect for human life but, like design, like systems, like anything in this world that adheres to evolution, some things are just plain better. Why can't I say this? Are we so afraid? If so, of what? That we may upset people with the truth? What is respect? Is it respectful to allow me to keep smoking when you know that it's dangerous? Is it respectful to let me swim in the water when you know that there are sharks? What then should you do – not tell me in case it causes offence? No – you should tell me, because, from my life experience, I know how easy it is to die. I may choose to continue, but then at least the choice is mine . . . and you tried. To say nothing, then, to those in the world who prefer faith to reason, snake oil to sense, is to allow them to piss in a soup that we all have to drink from. South Africa, for many years, was not about race but about reason; race just happened to be on the minds of those few hijackers.

It is not genes that scupper indigenous people, it's nurture. I have met black men who would stagger Einstein and Arabs who could design the next space shuttle. They are people, no different, but – and there is a but – they are born into a world where superstition and myth take priority over the tangible and where knowledge and science are abominations to be scorned.

Myth and religion, like anything else, must compete for hearts and minds in the global marketplace. Like viruses they infect, or don't, depending on the susceptibility of the host they're attacking. That's why they find such fertile ground in children and are able to inhibit the progress of ideas, as even the slightest mental leap would highlight the huge illusion that they're always founded on.

I have Aids. I have had it for some time now but have never let it change my mindset and make me a victim of it in the way that some might as I've always seen it within the context of the everyday struggle of existence. That was until . . . well, I saw it all by chance. I heard her first – her crying, a noise that when I closed my eyes I recognised in an instant. It was just like my mother's solemn lament, a cry of acceptance and sadness beyond anything else. And so I looked up. I was at a clinic in Rome, to get a load of Aids medication. She had it too and was dying, but she had a boy, a young boy, who reminded me of myself. He was around three or four at a push. His mum was white, while his father must have been black. But he looked so fresh, so full of life and, without markings or influence, he lived within a blissful ignorance that only the young can know. But as I focused in, I realised the truth. He was so young and yet so old. He was dying – he had Aids too. I suppose life truly is suffering and luck, or lack of, is random. I fell in love with that woman, though I never knew her name. I fell in love with the boy in a way that I once loved myself, before the 'struggle' began. For the first time since being a child, then, I felt emotion – if not in the heart, then for sure in my mind. It was then, at that moment, in that room, that an unknown woman with a story I would never know became my life without her ever realising it.

The next day I went to the clinic and found she was an in-patient there. I didn't have to be there every day myself but she did – while part of the office dispensed, the other part counselled. I would sit and watch, and through her became the boy that I was before I chose to be somebody else. And I got it – truly this time I did. What the hell is all the money in the world worth if you're dying? What is all the ideology if there are no people to own it and live by it?

The world is what it has always been, a garden that we walk in, but it is we who give a plot to the story, not the other way round. And the story is simple: that the sun will rise in the morning while the moon will come at night. Everything else is a projection of ours, spewed onto a perfect canvas, which then consumes us. Wake up, world! I am evil. I am the Devil. I am the aspect of life that is opposed to all that is good. But I'm only the expression of what has gone before me. I was taught to hate, to kill, to rape and to take. I was taught to feel bad, feel guilty and hold a contempt for myself. But why? There's no original sin; there's not even a true origin, given we're one step removed from those before us.

If I'd never known the consequences of my actions, then at that moment, in that clinic I did. Her in there with her sad tears, her little boy in his blissful ignorance, and us, waiting on the advancement of knowledge to sustain us. We cannot surrender to those who want to regress our lives into darkness – they are blind and are the product of an infected world. There is no God and so no method to reach him. We are it and that is that. Evil is not a place, a state, a person, but an action. Evil is done, not made. I know this from experience and for that I'll now make my amends. Chaos was my name . . . though I'm still living in the darkness.

AFTERWORD

The murder of Olof Palme has never been solved. Athol Visser's version of events joins the competing theories surrounding both the identity of the murderer(s) and the motives for the killing. As this book offers only Athol Visser's point of view, a man whose perceptions and morals are obviously questionable, its portrayal of the Swedish prime minister's assassination should be taken as just that, another point of view in what continues to be an unsolved crime.

MAINSTREAM PUBLISHING